POSTMODERNISM IN PIECES

POSTMODERNISM IN PIECES

Materializing the Social in U.S. Fiction

Matthew Mullins

OXFORD

UNIVERSITY PRESS

Oxford University Press is a department of the University of Oxford. It furthers the University's objective of excellence in research, scholarship, and education by publishing worldwide. Oxford is a registered trade mark of Oxford University Press in the UK and certain other countries.

Published in the United States of America by Oxford University Press
198 Madison Avenue, New York, NY 10016, United States of America.

© Oxford University Press 2016

First issued as an Oxford University Press paperback, 2019

All rights reserved. No part of this publication may be reproduced, stored in a retrieval system, or transmitted, in any form or by any means, without the prior permission in writing of Oxford University Press, or as expressly permitted by law, by license, or under terms agreed with the appropriate reproduction rights organization. Inquiries concerning reproduction outside the scope of the above should be sent to the Rights Department, Oxford University Press, at the address above.

You must not circulate this work in any other form
and you must impose this same condition on any acquirer.

Library of Congress Cataloging-in-Publication Data
Names: Mullins, Matthew, author.
Title: Postmodernism in pieces : materializing the social in U.S. fiction / Matthew Mullins.
Description: New York : Oxford University Press, [2016] |
Includes bibliographical references.
Identifiers: LCCN 2015043797 (print) | LCCN 2016000380 (ebook) |
ISBN 9780190459505 (cloth) | ISBN 9780190067823 (paper) |
ISBN 9780190459512 (updf)
Subjects: LCSH: Postmodernism (Literature)—United States |
American fiction—History and criticism. | Social change in literature.
Classification: LCC PS374.P64 M85 2016 (print) | LCC PS374.P64 (ebook) |
DDC 813/.5409113—dc23
LC record available at http://lccn.loc.gov/2015043797

For Jenny

CONTENTS

Acknowledgments ix

Introduction: The State of Things in Postmodernism 1

1. Reconstructing Social Construction 36

2. Flattening Nature and Culture 65

3. Rewriting Language 103

4. Collapsing Otherness 137

Afterism: The Promise of Postmodernism 170

Notes 187
Bibliography 213
Index 227

ACKNOWLEDGMENTS

I had the great fortune of working with too many smart and generous people to name over the years in which this book took shape. At the University of North Carolina at Greensboro, Christian Moraru, Mark Rifkin, and Stephen R. Yarbrough were instrumental in the genesis and development of what would eventually become *Postmodernism in Pieces*, and have been generous with their guidance and support ever since. Jennifer Feather and Risa Applegarth helped me figure out how to join my conversation, and Nancy Myers and Alyson Everhart made the whole Greensboro journey possible. I would never have made it to Greensboro without the opportunities and direction afforded me by John Morillo, Deborah Hooker, Mike Grimwood, Sheila Smith McKoy, and Tom Lisk at North Carolina State University. I owe Tom a special debt of gratitude for over a decade of questions, encouragement, and friendship. We all need someone to encourage us to "do more," and Tom has been that person for me. Thanks, Tom.

Conversations with Scott Gibson, Craig Morehead, Aaron Chandler, Rose Brister, Zack Laminack, Dan Burns, Sandy Hartwiger, and Belinda Walzer helped me pause and recalibrate at key moments in the writing process. I am also grateful to Josh Toth, Adam Kelly, Mary Holland, and Lee Konstantinou for reading, hearing, and/or discussing various parts of this project via email and at conferences. The peer reviewers for

ACKNOWLEDGMENTS

Oxford provided vital feedback that strengthened the finished product. And I am especially thankful to Brendan O'Neill and Stephen Bradley at Oxford University Press, phenomenal and gracious editors who have made this process a joy.

I want to thank the administration and trustees of Southeastern Baptist Theological Seminary for a generous faculty development fund that enabled me to work through aspects of my argument at a number of conferences. Thanks are also due to the editors of *Arizona Quarterly* and *Critique: Studies in Contemporary Fiction*. Portions of Chapter 1 first appeared as "Material Foundations: Retheorizing Native Writing and Social Construction in Leslie Marmon Silko's *Ceremony*" in *Arizona Quarterly* 70, no. 3 (2014); the revised version is printed by permission of the Regents of The University of Arizona. Portions of Chapter 4 first appeared as "Objects & Outliers: Narrative Community in Don DeLillo's *Underworld*" in *Critique: Studies in Contemporary Fiction* 51, no. 3 (2010); the revised version is printed by permission of Taylor & Francis Ltd.

Finally, I want to acknowledge the love and support of my family: Shirley Head, Robert L. Mullins Sr., Mom and Dad, Pam and John, Irene Kopens, Vince and Sandy, and most of all Jenny, Jai, and Jada. What would any of it matter?

POSTMODERNISM IN PIECES

Introduction

The State of Things in Postmodernism

To read literary and cultural criticism of the last two decades and more is to realize that if you've just arrived at postmodernism's funeral, then you are exceedingly late. Entire books and issues of journals have been devoted to the death of postmodernism, as well as to what it might mean for literature and culture to be "after" or "beyond" it.[1] If dwelling on the past is not your thing, this conversation offers plenty of candidates seeking to become the next big *ism*, such as "metamodernism," "cosmodernism," "digimodernism," and "post-postmodernism," to name a few.[2] What seems inescapable either way is the notion that postmodernism has finally run out of steam. "Let's just say," Linda Hutcheon admits, "it's over."[3] This "death knell," as Josh Toth characterizes Hutcheon's pronouncement, is just one contributor to what Jeremy Green calls the "portentous clatter of death notices" recently issued to postmodernism.[4] But why the death knells and notices? Perhaps because postmodernism has come to be defined by the very phenomena it set out to demystify: language, whiteness, masculinity, heteronormativity, middle-class status, the academy.[5] In *Signs and Cities: Black Literary Postmodernism*, Madhu Dubey offers a practical justification for retaining "postmodernism" as an aesthetic and historic marker, but adds that "to some critics, the very category of postmodernism has been so insidiously racialized—assuming a white Western subject as its normative center—that it bears little relevance for African-Americans and other 'others' of the modern West."[6] Andrew

Hoberek extends this proposition to the realm of class, arguing that the postmodern aesthetic "reflects a white-collar middle-class subject position."[7] Perhaps addressing the end of postmodernism, then, is the only way to engage its legacy without being identified as someone who remains ignorant of its intellectual impasses, or lacks a clear sense of the present. After all, "discussing postmodernity and postmodernism," Marianne DeKoven points out, "can mark one as failing to follow current trends in literary and cultural studies rather than as attempting to understand recent and current cultural history."[8]

And yet, as evidenced by work from critics who retain postmodernism as a framework—such as Dubey, W. Lawrence Hogue, and Amy Hungerford—the life and death of this concept are more indeterminate than they appear.[9] In fact, as Adam Kelly suggests, the drive to identify and name something beyond the postmodern has actually served to validate "postmodernism as a useful historical and aesthetic category: the story being told requires, in the main, that there be a relatively clear postmodern model in fiction which later writers can internalize and react to."[10] In the dialectical spirit of the literary history of the United States, the emergence of a new *ism* necessarily tends to concretize the prevailing *ism* of the day. So, at least on this front, postmodernism's legacy comes into clearer focus, even if it has indeed run out of steam. Although he is among those who argue for such a demise, Toth maintains "that the death of postmodernism (like all deaths) can also be viewed as a passing, a giving over of a certain inheritance, that this death (like all deaths) is also a living on, a passing on."[11] Even in death, postmodernism haunts literary production. Mary Holland takes a different approach, objecting to Toth's and others' death notices and going so far as to insist "that we are seeing not the end of postmodernism, but its belated success."[12] Toth and Holland disagree as to the vitality of the postmodern aesthetic, to be sure, but they both make a case for the persistent presence of postmodernism in contemporary literature and literary studies. Whether alive and well or a lingering specter, what is/was the work of postmodernism? To reimagine aesthetic form? To subvert dominant narratives about social categories? To destabilize assumptions about how language, communication, and thinking operate? To redefine notions of truth?

INTRODUCTION

This book tells a different story of postmodernism in light of what I loosely call the neomaterialisms of our current critical climate, including posthumanism, thing theory, Actor-Network-Theory, and object-oriented philosophy. This story features everyday objects and their quotidian interactions with human subjects as the key players in postmodern fiction and the unlikely shapers of our most foundational assumptions about the relations we call social. Postmodernism, I argue, is a resolutely materialist aesthetic. Although it has traditionally been characterized as a subversive enterprise committed to the demystification and deconstruction of social categories such as race, gender, class, and nation that produce culture, what makes literature postmodern is its preoccupation with the material things and interactions that constitute those seemingly ready-made social categories. The great insight of postmodernism, then, is not that our social categories are somehow artificial or inauthentic, but that they are continuously the products of material processes. Notions such as artificiality or authenticity have no place in the postmodern conversation because they rely on a mode of comparison that is anathema to the postmodern project.

Michel Foucault illuminates this disjunction with lucid definitions of measurement and order in *The Order of Things*. "Measurement," Foucault explains, "presupposes that [. . .] one considers the whole first and then divides it up into parts. [. . .] Order, on the other hand, is established without reference to an exterior unit [. . .] one cannot know the order of things 'in their isolated nature,' but by discovering that which is the simplest, then that which is next simplest, one can progress inevitably to the most complex things of all."[13] Postmodernism is concerned with order—an order that is always in process and which relies on the ontological continuity of things and people. So before the lid is slammed shut on postmodernism as we know it, I would like to reconsider its orthodoxies and make the case that the postmodernism being eulogized is not the postmodernism I know.

Any study of postmodernism must confront its competing definitions. Fredric Jameson's classic formulation of postmodernism as the fundamentally nostalgic and politically impotent "cultural dominant" of late capitalism has proven formative both as an assertion in its own right and as a foil for critics like Hutcheon who claim that postmodernism is "resolutely historical" and "inescapably political."[14] According to Amy Elias, "much of the scholarship about postmodernism published between 1985 and 2000 falls within the range of these two positions."[15] Another defining disagreement "divides writers into those who are committed to mimesis and the representation of 'real' people with 'real' problems and those who are not," as Daniel Grausam explains.[16] "While 'postmodernism' initially gained prominence as a characterization of stylistic innovations in the work of U.S. fiction writers of the 1960s and 1970s," Adam Kelly recounts, "its breadth of cultural reference would later extend almost unstoppably."[17] These paradigmatic conflicts are intimately bound up with one another, and point toward a recognizable aesthetic practice and historical moment in which fiction can be read as interested in its own capacity to represent the relations we variously call social or political, and which form the narrative we call history. Although critics may disagree as to the success or failure of this enterprise, or even as to whether or not it should be called postmodernism, it seems reasonable to assume that when I say "postmodernism" I can trust my reader will understand I am talking about both a literary aesthetic and an historical period characterized by certain orthodoxies that have surfaced in literary criticism of the last fifty years. Thus, I have devoted each chapter of this study to the re-examination of a single orthodoxy of postmodernism across a range of fiction. These orthodoxies are social construction, the ontological dominant, the problem of language, and otherness.

This revisionist approach places my analysis in conversation with a number of recent reconsiderations of late twentieth-century US literature, including formative work by Amy Hungerford and Mark McGurl, among others. Building on, yet departing from, John McClure's *Partial Faiths: Postsecular Fiction in the Age of Pynchon and Morrison*,[18] Hungerford's *Postmodern Belief: American Literature and Religion since 1960* offers a compelling rereading of postmodernism by "attending to religion" to "argue that sincerity overshadows irony as a literary mode when the ambiguities of language are imagined as being religiously empowered."[19] Both McClure and Hungerford chart new territory for scholars which finds postmodern fiction exploring concepts such as faith and belief that were thought to have been rendered obsolete by a prevailing secularism. McGurl's *The Program Era: Postwar Fiction and the Rise of Creative Writing* redefines postmodernism altogether, even doing away with the term itself and replacing it with "technomodernism." For McGurl, technomodernism is one dimension of a three-dimensional model of US fiction since World War II that takes shape in conjunction with the formalization of creative writing in university MFA programs. As for technomodernism, it "is best understood as a tweaking of the term 'postmodernism' in that it emphasizes the all-important engagement of postmodern literature with information technology."[20] He goes on to parse the other two dimensions of the postmodern paradigm as "high cultural pluralism" and "lower-middle-class modernism." My methodology aligns more closely with Hungerford's, as I do not abandon the language of postmodernism, arguing instead that a materialist reading of postmodern fiction results in a productive redefinition of postmodernism. My conclusion, however, resonates with McGurl's in that I ultimately formulate an alternative explanation for why fiction of the last fifty years has taken the direction it has.

If I am asking us to recalibrate our understanding of postmodern fiction from the ground up, why retain postmodernism as a framework at all? Why not simply dispense with this clunky term and its attendant problems and blaze an entirely new materialist trail? There are three primary reasons for keeping this fraught marker. First, postmodernism is an established, accepted, anthologized signpost, or, as Dubey has put it more bluntly, "regardless of whether the term has any decidable referent, it has become a cultural fact."[21] Second, postmodernism serves as a useful umbrella under which literary and cultural critics have gathered a distinctive set of orthodoxies, each of which takes on new life when reconsidered in a different light. Take the idea of social construction, for instance. Social construction has nearly become synonymous with the concept of postmodernism to the point that Michael Bérubé exclaims with some resignation that "it's hard to determine the relevant facts and features of pomo when so much of pomo has questioned how 'facticity' is constructed."[22] I maintain postmodernism as a useful framework because, when read from a materialist perspective, its preoccupation with this idea of constructedness enables us to ask an important question that has heretofore gone unasked: constructed out of what? If our identities, our histories, our social categories, and our knowledge of past and present are all constructed, then what are the materials out of which they have been and are being constructed? Third, holding on to postmodernism for a little longer may very well help us resist the periodizing impulse that often reduces history to a dialectic series of the births and deaths of *isms* and insulates the study of literature from the rest of the world.

With this third reason in mind, maintaining yet redefining the postmodern foreshadows one practical payoff of this project: its rethinking of literary history in the United States in terms of a canonized series of *isms*, including but not limited to romanticism, realism, naturalism, modernism, and postmodernism. There is no hidden power behind these *isms*, only groups of people and works of art who see in themselves something similar to or different from what they perceive in others— usually others from an earlier point in time, though not always, as Ezra Pound's many contemporaneous *isms* attest. For most critics, what is unique about postmodernism in this lineage is that its prefix, *post-*, suggests that its suffix, *-ism*, belongs primarily to the "modern" found at the heart of the word. As Brian McHale explains, "postmodernism is not post modern, whatever that might mean, but post moder*nism*; it does not come *after the present* (a solecism), but after the *modernist movement*."[23] However, whereas McHale argues that the *ism* does "double duty" by also announcing a unique "poetics," I would like to offer what may seem a hairsplitting redirection. Rather than merely representing, announcing, or naming a new *ism*, postmodernism's postness signifies the abandonment of *isms*. That is, postmodernism is not an *ism* at all, but a state or sense of being after *isms*, even a perpetual afterism. I will return to this claim at the end of this introduction and in the various chapters that follow, but will treat it most directly in the conclusion. Such a conclusion is only possible, however, if we are willing to rethink the death of postmodernism by altering our understanding of its life.

Perhaps no one would have been happier to sit graveside at postmodernism's funeral than Irving Howe. His essay, "Mass Society and Post-Modern Fiction," published in the summer 1959 issue of *Partisan Review*, marks a seismic shift in American literature and culture. In fact, the table of contents for that issue can be read as a microcosm of the changes taking place at the time, with Howe's essay situated between a piece by modernist stalwart Robert Penn Warren and poems by John Ashbery and Charles Olson, writers often recognized as progenitors of American postmodernism. In this early attempt to make sense of a new phenomenon in American fiction, Howe suggests that, like the modernist authors who set out to challenge the traditional values of eighteenth- and nineteenth-century literature, these "post-modern" writers work against social conventions in modernist novels. Howe says these emerging writers "recognize that the once familiar social categories and place-marks have now become as uncertain and elusive as the moral imperatives of the nineteenth century seemed to the novelists of fifty years ago."[24] His point in calling attention to a modernist framework of "familiar social categories" is to introduce a new and unfamiliar "mass society" emerging in the late 1950s and early 1960s, a society that cannot be understood purely in terms of preexisting social markers such as class, nation, and religion. For Howe, what drives the emergence of literary postmodernism is the need to challenge these existing social narratives, and so he concludes that this new "post-modern" novel "seems to lend itself irrevocably to the spirit of criticism."[25]

Early essays like Howe's set the tone for a discourse of postmodernism devoted to ceaseless demystification, which has tended to culminate in misguided theories more or less indebted to John Barth's classic essay "The Literature of Exhaustion" (1967). These theories go something like this: in its irrevocably critical spirit, postmodern fiction is forced to work within the confines of that which it intends to subvert, rendering this subversion complicit with, even accomplice to, its target, thus exhausting the literary enterprise. Barth himself points out in the later companion piece, "The Literature of Replenishment" (1980), that "a great many people [...] mistook me to mean that literature, at least fiction, is *kaput*; that it has all been done already; that there is nothing left for contemporary writers but to parody and travesty our great predecessors in our exhausted medium—exactly what some critics deplore as postmodernism."[26] He goes on to point out that he was not even using the term "postmodernism" in 1967, and that, as his later title suggests, he considers the postmodern aesthetic just as replenishing as it is exhausting. Ihab Hassan's argument for the literature of exhaustion as a literature of silence has been similarly appropriated as a doomsday prophecy for literature, even when Hassan makes clear that silence is "more metaphor than concept" and a metaphor for "language that expresses, with harsh and subtle cadences, the stress in art, culture, and consciousness."[27] But in returning to Barth in particular for direction in defining whatever postmodernism is/was, we have looked back to the wrong essays. Because what makes postmodernism different in the larger scheme of literary history in the United States is not necessarily its self-reflexivity, its experimentation, or what Hutcheon calls its politically minded "complicitous critique." Instead, the defining feature of postmodernism is what I would call its materialism, or what Barth calls, in his 1988 essay "Postmodernism Revisited," his own predisposition toward the particular over the general.

With the possible exception of Mary McCarthy, there are no modernist stalwarts in the Fall 1988 issue of *The Review of Contemporary Fiction*, where Barth's essay can be found in a table of contents that includes pieces by Gilbert Sorrentino and a young David Foster Wallace, alongside an article on Richard Brautigan. Although there is some retreading of the ideas and sentiments found in "The Literature of Exhaustion" and "The Literature of Replenishment," "Postmodernism Revisited" is significant because it emphasizes what are, from my perspective, two of the most important features of postmodernism. First, it makes a case for postmodernism's privileging of the particular, or the material, over the general, or the ideal. Second, it points toward the trouble with the *ism*-driven structure of literary history. The first feature prefigures the thrust of this entire study; the second, as I have said, I will extend as a payoff of a postmodern materialism in my conclusion. Barth opens the essay by claiming that he cannot help but feel more disposed to an Aristotelian view of reality over a Platonic view: "Fred and Shirley and Mike and Irma seem intuitively realer to me than does the category *human beings*" just as "the writings of Gabriel García Márquez and Italo Calvino and Salman Rushdie and Thomas Pynchon—even the writings of John Barth—have ontological primacy, to my way of thinking, over the category *Postmodern fiction*."[28] In Raphael's well-known Italian Renaissance masterpiece, *The School of Athens*, Plato and Aristotle are figured side by side amidst a sea of philosophers, mathematicians, and

INTRODUCTION

historians. Plato's right hand points upward to the ideal forms that transcend the physical world, while Aristotle's right hand is extended in front of him, palm facing down to the particular, the immanent, the material. Barth's sense of the particular, I argue, can be mapped throughout the roiling mess that is the postmodern canon and read as a common trait among writers from roughly the 1960s through the early twenty-first century. And although the genealogy of Greek philosophy reifies postmodernism's place in the white, male, Western dialectic of history, postmodern fiction's brand of materialism also marks a rupture in this seemingly homogeneous narrative.

But how is postmodernism's materialism or preoccupation with the particular any different from that of, say, realism or modernism? After all, wasn't it the modernist writer William Carlos Williams who exclaimed that the poet should find "no ideas but in things"?[29] Didn't William Dean Howells define his realist aesthetic as "nothing more and nothing less than the truthful treatment of material"?[30] In short, yes, these writers were deeply concerned with the relationship between thoughts and objects, humans and things, art and everyday life. But I would argue that these earlier aesthetic modes rely on a certain interdependence of humans and nonhumans that does not plague postmodern fiction. That is, these *isms* tend to value material things to the extent that they convey, manifest, and embody ideas to human subjects. In the worlds of postmodern fiction, conversely, things do not exist primarily for humans. Bill Brown's methodology in his pathbreaking study *A Sense of Things: The Object Matter of American Literature* illustrates just how fundamentally the modernist and realist theories of things rely on human reception. Beginning with a meditation on Williams's famous injunction, Brown recounts how he embarked on his investigation into the "object matter" of American literature by turning to texts that "ask why and how we use objects to make meaning, to make or re-make ourselves, to organize our anxieties and affections, to sublimate our fears and shape our fantasies. They are texts that describe and enact an imaginative possession of things that amounts to the labor of infusing manufactured objects with a metaphysical dimension."[31] The objects Brown traces through the realist/naturalist works of Mark Twain, Frank Norris, Sarah Orne Jewett, and Henry James are most illuminating when they shed light on a darkened corner of human experience. Thus, the significance of objects is entangled with, even subordinate to, human being.

Brown's descriptions of his primary texts should come as no surprise given that Howells's "truthful treatment of material" is, in fact, rooted in an aesthetic philosophy in which nonhumans exist for humans and not for their own sake. Just before his famous definition of realism in chapter 15 of *Criticism and Fiction*, Howells reproduces a lengthy quotation from the work of Armando Palacio Valdes in which the Spanish novelist and critic uses the very phrase that William Carlos Williams would popularize in the twentieth century:

> That which in life left us indifferent, or repelled us, in art delights us. Why? Simply because the artist has made us see the idea that resides in it. Let not the novelists, then, endeavor to add anything to reality, to turn it and twist it, to restrict it. Since nature has endowed them with this precious gift of discovering *ideas in things*, their work will be beautiful if they paint these as they appear. But if the reality does not impress them, in vain will they strive to make their work impress others.[32]

Novelists are endowed by nature with an uncanny ability to lift the veil from the faces of things to reveal the ideas waiting there to be uncovered. Howells thus builds a case for Jane Austen as the most "artistic of the English novelists" because she, above Charles Dickens, George Eliot, and all others, tells the truth about things. Howells's declaration about realism, however, can be read as a direct descendant of Eliot's, as two of her most well-known aesthetic statements characterize art as "a humble and faithful study of nature" and "the faithful representing of commonplace things."[33] Like Valdes and Howells, Eliot's fealty to nature and the commonplace is dependent on "men who see beauty in these commonplace things, and delight in showing how kindly the light of heaven falls on them."[34] In each of these cases the nature of things depends on human reception.

Williams's "no ideas but in things" ultimately offers little variation from the realist theories of Valdes and Howells or the slightly more romantic realism of Eliot, but begins to move toward the radicalized sense of things that evolves in postmodern fiction. In his analysis of Williams, Brown explains that what drove the doctor/poet was modernism's need for a new idiom that would "recognize things as the necessary condition for ideas."[35] This figuration of things and ideas poses a challenge to the hierarchy of human and nonhuman beings by rendering both not only interdependent on one another for human understanding but also codependent for their mutual existence. Or, as Brown credits his poetry workshop leader, "the modernist's point, as Ken tried to emphasize, wasn't that things should replace ideas, but that ideas and things should somehow merge." The road to postmodernism is paved in Brown's next sentence: "This was Williams's anti-Emersonian effort to achieve what is, after all, an Emersonian effect: overcoming the subject/object opposition, and contesting the ontological distinction between thoughts and things."[36] The successful dissolution of this binary for Emerson, and for the modernists as well, would indeed frustrate the ontological distinction between thoughts and things, but it would do so by pulling the latter into the sphere of the former. That is, things become valuable for the ways in which they are not so different from thoughts, and nonhumans are valued for their human qualities. The postmodern aesthetic is resolutely materialist, in contrast, because its ontology is radically "flat"—to borrow a term from the object-oriented philosophers—refusing to privilege human being over nonhuman being at the level of ontology.

In the Western tradition, materialism has typically denoted two schools of thought: classical antiquity's "ontological question about the basic stuff of the universe and how it is organized" and the European Enlightenment's "experimental method of the new physics and its refusal of non-material explanations of physical processes."[37] In the twentieth century, Marx's influence on literary theory led to the evolution of historical and cultural materialisms that—while insightful and indispensable—shifted materialist inquiry from the material domain of "basic stuff" to the so-called forces of economic and social production as the building blocks for the structures of society.[38] While certain writers and texts in the postwar era have been tagged with the postmodern label, discussion of materialism in this literature has focused on demystifying the social forces such as race, class, and nation that supposedly produce culture, rather than on the material constitution of those social forces themselves.[39] Thus, in re-examining the critical orthodoxies of postmodernism in light of the "basic stuff" that provides "material explanations" for the social, *Postmodernism in Pieces* makes a case for postmodern fiction's commitment to the significance of mundane things in the formation of these so-called social forces, not because of what they can tell us about humans but because of what they can tell us about the networks of relation themselves. In this light, postmodernism becomes an integral proving ground for the emergence of the various neomaterialisms that are currently driving critical approaches in philosophy, sociology, anthropology, and science studies, as well as in literary criticism.

The significance of historical and cultural materialisms cannot be overlooked, however, in considering the emergence of these neomaterialisms. In the 1960s and 1970s anthropologists such as Clifford Geertz, philosophers like Richard Bernstein, and cultural critics like Raymond Williams challenged the dominant understanding of culture as something wholly separate from human nature. Geertz famously insisted that "there is no such thing as human nature independent of culture."[40] This claim is fundamental to neomaterialism, showing up in the work of nearly all the theorists I engage in the following pages. Renato Rosaldo recounts that "the political turbulence of the late 1960s and early 1970s began a process of unraveling and reworking that continues into the present." Rosaldo's own field of anthropology experienced nothing short of a revolution: "the transformation of anthropology showed that the received notion of culture as unchanging and homogeneous was not only mistaken but irrelevant (to use a key word of the time). Marxist and other discussion groups sprang up. Questions of political consciousness and ideology came to the foreground."[41] The broad influence of Marxism is irrefutable. In his introduction to *Marxism and Literature*, Williams narrates the emergence of the New Left alongside unprecedented access to "older work, notably that of the Frankfurt School [. . .] and especially the work of Walter Benjamin; the extraordinarily original work of Antonio Gramsci; and, as a decisive element of the new sense of the tradition, newly translated work of Marx."[42] In literary studies, these developments would produce New Historicism and Cultural

Materialism, the latter of which especially sets the stage for a neomaterialist approach to literature. Neomaterialist approaches diverge from these important critical movements, however, in their insistence on the primacy of objects. Brown's "thing theory" has been perhaps the most influential current of neomaterialism for literary studies, but his 2001 special issue of *Critical Inquiry* demonstrates that this wave, like the one before it, has been interdisciplinary from the start. Not only does Brown locate the foundation for his theory in writers from various fields, such as Arjun Appadurai, Susan Stewart, and Nicholas Thomas, but he also includes scholars from across the academy in the special issue, including physicist Sidney Nagel, art historian Christina Kiaer, and anthropologist Michael Taussig. In the introductory essay, Brown channels Appadurai's work in *The Social Life of Things* to point out that turning our attention to things "depends on a certain 'methodological fetishism' that refuses to begin with a formal 'truth' that cannot, despite its truth, 'illuminate the concrete, historical circulation of things.'"[43] In other words, a theory of things begins with the challenge of thinking *from* them rather than thinking *about* them in the context of familiar philosophical, social, or historical frameworks. This shift in emphasis further clarifies the distinction between neomaterialist approaches and New Historicism and Cultural Materialism, in which Graham Harman sees "few traces of nonhuman entities amidst all this discussion of mutually conditioning forces. What we find instead is a historicism of the human subject as shaped by various disciplinary practices."[44] In fact, such practices are only ever the products of the more quotidian circulations of things. Bruno Latour articulates this inversion in *Reassembling the Social: An Introduction to Actor-Network-Theory*: "'social' is not some glue that could fix everything including what the other glues cannot fix; it is *what* is glued together by many *other* types of connectors."[45] The primacy of things as connectors drives *Postmodernism in Pieces*, and renders Latour's work indispensable to the particular brand of materialism that I develop through a rereading of US fiction of the last half century.

Latour's version of Actor-Network-Theory requires a constant reversal of our thinking; it is always cogent and commonsensical on the page, but difficult to keep straight when we encounter the infamous "social"

INTRODUCTION

as an explanation for all kinds of problems in everyday life, from de facto segregation in US public schools to the availability of flu shots. The weight of *Reassembling the Social* rests on a subtle yet significant distinction between two basic approaches to the relations we call social. The first approach he calls the "sociology of the social," and the second he calls the "sociology of associations." Under the sociology of the social, society or the social order is a "domain of reality" distinct from "other domains such as economics, geography, biology, psychology, law, science, and politics." This approach imagines the social as a phenomenon, a force, a substance that can be used to explain other phenomena, and it has dominated sociology for the last century, becoming "common sense not only for social scientists, but also for ordinary actors via newspapers, college education, party politics, bar conversations, love stories, fashion magazines, etc." Under the sociology of associations, on the other hand, there exists no "social force," no substance that we might identify as social. Instead, the social is a network assembled of and by material actors, both human and nonhuman, hence Actor-Network-Theory. Here's how Latour articulates the distinction in terms of academic inquiry:

> whereas sociologists (or socio-economists, socio-linguists, social psychologists, etc.) take social aggregates as the given that could shed some light on residual aspects of economics, linguistics, psychology, management, and so on, these other scholars, on the contrary, consider social aggregates as what should be explained by the specific *associations* provided by economics, linguistics, psychology, law, management, etc.[46]

This distinction leads Latour to value material objects, or what he calls "nonhuman actors," equally with human actors in an effort to account "for how society is held together, instead of using society to explain something else,"[47] and also to privilege the idea of "worknets" as an optimal model for thinking about the social where "it's the work and the movement, and the flow, and the changes that should be stressed."[48] What happens when we stop treating the social as a preexisting substance whose presence can help us account for the way things are, and start investigating the material interactions and relations of human and nonhuman actors who exist on the same ontological playing field?

For some philosophers on the vanguard of rethinking things, such questions may not go far enough. Taking an even more radical approach than theorists generally associated with Actor-Network-Theory, Speculative Realists such as Quentin Meillassoux, Graham Harman, Iain Hamilton Grant, and Ray Brassier have challenged the assumed centrality of human perception. Object-oriented philosophers like Harman, Timothy Morton, and Ian Bogost have pioneered an ontology that "puts things at the center of being."[49] In *Guerrilla Metaphysics*, Harman outlines his object-oriented philosophy, which "holds that the relation of humans to pollen, oxygen, eagles, or windmills is no different in kind from the interaction of these objects with each other."[50] This radically flat ontology is situated in response to what Meillassoux calls the default "correlationism" that has dominated modern philosophy since Kant, and which assumes the impossibility of considering "the realms of subjectivity and objectivity independently of one another."[51] Bogost traces the shape and history of correlationism succinctly in *Alien Phenomenology, Or What It's Like to Be a Thing*:

> Being, this position holds, exists only for subjects. In George Berkeley's subjective idealism, objects are just bundles of sense data in the minds of those who perceive them. In G. W. F. Hegel's absolute idealism, the world is best characterized by the way it appears to the self-conscious mind. For Martin Heidegger, objects *are* outside human consciousness, but their *being* exists only in human understanding. For Jacques Derrida, things are never fully present to us, but only differ and defer their access to individuals in particular contexts, interminably.[52]

Bogost harbors no warmth or nostalgia for this legacy, characterizing it as "the tradition of human access that seeps from the rot of Kant." Like Latour, Speculative Realists and object-oriented philosophers are interested in flattening ontology, that is, they want to erase distinctions between things in terms of their fundamental being. More often than not, this erasure focuses on decentering human existence as somehow superior to nonhuman existence: "we can no longer claim that our existence is special *as existence*."[53] Levi Bryant translates Harman's object-oriented philosophy into an object-oriented ontology, or what Bogost calls "Triple-O" for short.[54] Bogost's objection to Actor-Network-Theory is that although all things exist equally for Latour, "entities are de-emphasized in favor of their couplings and decouplings" and thus "interactions sit outside rather than within the being of a thing."[55] In other words, Latour is still more interested in relation than in things-in-themselves, but a theory of things-in-themselves is necessary for a right understanding of relations.

Bogost finds similar points of disagreement with the posthumanist crowd. Despite Cary Wolfe's assertion that posthumanism recontextualizes human perception "in terms of the entire sensorium of other living beings and their own autopoetic ways of 'bringing forth a world,'" its implicit impulse to extend and further human existence in particular renders posthumanism "not posthuman enough" for Bogost.[56] The spirit of object-oriented ontology is vital to this book because it has the capacity to destabilize our default assumptions about the existence of nonhuman actors. However, because this is a literary study interested in how representations of material circumstances create common experiences among diverse readers, I draw most from Latour's Actor-Network-Theory *because* of its investment in relation as fundamental to thinking about things in themselves. That is, my own questions are less directly aligned with Speculative Realists like Meillassoux or object-oriented philosophers like Harman, and more precisely consonant with new materialists like Latour or Jane Bennett.[57] I do not mean to conflate Speculative Realism, new materialism, object-oriented philosophy, object-oriented ontology, Actor-Network-Theory, and posthumanism. Each of these theories has come to represent a distinctive emphasis among groups of scholars which often overlap but just as often disagree over specific questions, especially about how to conceive of the relationships between human and nonhuman actors. What all seem to share in common, Steven Shaviro observes, is that they "seek to elaborate new ways of grasping the world, outside of anthropocentric paradigms and grounded in a firm commitment to realism."[58] My own analysis builds on this common motivation and expands on insights from across the spectrum of what I have been loosely calling "neomaterialisms," but also adamantly insists on the significance of history.[59] The Triple-O gang provides a frame for pushing our thinking about things in postmodern American fiction into a new ontological space that just might be radical enough for Latour's Actor-Network-Theory to change the way we think about the historical formation of the networks, or "worknets," that we call social. In other words, I want to suggest that postmodern fiction builds Latourian "worknets" on top of an object-oriented "flat ontology" to represent social categories as the material outcomes of the interactions of things and people, rather than as a priori categories into which various things and people can be said to fit.

The metaphor of constructing, building, or making is central for Latour and crucial to my own methodology, which attempts, as Latour would say, to avoid confusing what I "should explain with the explanation."[60] Rather than construing postmodernism as an aesthetic enterprise committed to the demystification and deconstruction of givens such as race, class, gender, or nation, I read these categories as the phenomena for which postmodern fiction can offer material explanations. The resulting analysis leads to a redefinition of postmodernism in general—and postmodern fiction in particular—as a neomaterialist aesthetic committed to revealing that our relations are not social, whatever that might mean, but processual, in progress. However, I am not prepared to jettison the crucial lineage of postmodern theory handed down from pivotal thinkers including Jean Baudrillard, Jean-François Lyotard, and Ihab Hassan, Fredric Jameson, Andreas Huyssen, and Linda Hutcheon. For each of these theorists, what makes literature postmodern is its promise or failure to critique existing social narratives and structures. But when we re-examine the social as a "worknet" composed of and by various human and nonhuman actors, what becomes apparent is that the critical, deconstructive power of postmodern fiction is actually the product of its constructive capacity. Thus, I am not denying the demystifying powers of postmodernism; I am merely asking us to reconsider such orthodoxies in light of the material construction of the social fundamental to the postmodern project and evidenced especially in fiction. In this way I hope to avoid the more atomist view of materialism decried by Harman and to develop a materialist reading in

INTRODUCTION

which, as Alexander R. Galloway puts it, "everything should be rooted in material life and history, not in abstraction, logical necessity, universality, essence, pure form, spirit, or idea."[61]

So what do I mean when I say things, objects, actors? Are these terms interchangeable? John Frow's references to classical antiquity and the European Enlightenment noted earlier suggest what James Knapp and Jeffrey Pence state explicitly in their special issue of *Poetics Today* entitled "Between Thing and Theory": "the 'thing itself' is among the most seductive and elusive notions in the history of Western metaphysics."[62] Even if we were to confine ourselves to studies of the "thing itself" in the twentieth century alone, we would be forced to grapple with treatises ranging from Bertrand Russell's chapters on the existence and nature of matter in *The Problems of Philosophy* (1912) to Martin Heidegger's 1950 lecture on "Das Ding," eventually translated and published as "The Thing" in *Poetry, Language, Thought* (1971), to Donald Winnicott's psychoanalytic theory of "transitional objects" in *Playing and Reality* (1971).[63] The complex history of thinking about things can be paralyzing, and one central challenge is nomenclature. When I reference things, objects, stuff, or the materiality of everyday life, what I generally mean are the glass bottles, balls of twine, socks, baseballs, toy drums, cigarette butts, target arrows, and rings that populate the worlds of the fictional narratives under investigation. I am most interested in what a character in Walter Abish's novel *How German Is It* calls the "*thingliness* intrinsic to all things,"[64] and in what this "thingliness" can tell us about the relations between things. For the sake of my prose (and my readers) I have chosen not to settle on one word for these "things" and then stick with that word throughout. Such an approach would inevitably drive us all mad. However, ignoring the rich scholarship on the differences between things, objects, actors, and nonhumans would be equally unacceptable. Therefore, though I will often use the terms "object," "thing," and "actor" interchangeably, I want to address one of the most pertinent distinctions briefly now, as it will help to illuminate my interest in the "thingliness" of things.

If things are going to play important roles in shaping the social, then we must be willing to recognize in them some form of agency, resistance, or singularity. Philosophical discussions of the agency of objects tend to differentiate between those mired in human determination and those that retain some independence from human meaning. The former are typically classified as "objects" and the latter as "things." Heidegger develops one of the most helpful juxtapositions of thing and object in his meditation on a clay jug. In its ability to stand on its own, the jug is characterized, for Heidegger, by "the self-supporting independence of something independent" and thus it "differs from an object." He goes on to explain that "when we take the jug as a made vessel, then surely we are apprehending it—so it seems—as a thing and never as a mere object."[65] Brown carries this philosophical discussion into the realm of literary theory, not through a jug, but through a window in A. S. Byatt's novel *The Biographer's Tale*. Brown concentrates on a dirty window that causes one of Byatt's characters to look at the glass instead of looking through it. "We begin to confront the thingness of objects," Brown says, "when they stop working for us: when the drill breaks, when the car stalls, when the windows get filthy, when their flow within the circuits of production and distribution, consumption and exhibition, has been arrested, however momentarily."[66] The agency of objects makes them things in the philosophical tradition of materialism, but the difference between object and thing has historically been one of human perception. In the pages of this study, where human perception will not be the deciding factor in the agency of nonhumans, I will employ various terms as designators of material stuff.

Admittedly, I am tracing this material stuff across the pages of literary texts and not across the parking lot behind my building. That is, I am asking us to consider the agency of things in the forms of squiggly marks on compressed tree pulp, not by gathering and engaging them with our hands. The problem, endemic to all literary studies, is the gap between the world in which authors, readers, and their sunglasses live and the world in which narrators, characters, and their sunglasses live. The problem is representation. In his classic work, *Mimesis: The Representation of Reality in Western Literature*, Erich Auerbach grounds literary representation of reality in the Western tradition in two basic styles: one that privileges uniform and thorough description, clear meaning, and the foregrounding of all events, and another that illuminates some events and characters more than others, makes abrupt shifts in time and place, and leaves meanings obscure.[67] Regardless of which representational model a given text embodies, challenges, or extends, the question at issue for any study of objects as represented in literature is this: Are we talking about things, or are we talking about language? For Roland Barthes, to talk about the reality of objects as they appear in literature is to talk about a real-world effect produced by the fictional world. In an essay concerned with the "insignificant gestures, transitory attitudes, insignificant objects, redundant words" of Flaubert and Michelet, Barthes argues that "Flaubert's barometer, Michelet's little door finally say nothing but this: *we are real*; it is the category of 'the real' (and not its contingent contents) which is then signified; in other words, the very absence of the signified, to the advantage of the referent alone, becomes the very signifier of realism: the *reality effect* is produced." Barthes insists that the concerted effort of modern realist writers "to make notation the pure encounter of an object and its expression" is not mere mimesis, but an active verisimilitude that renders literary discourse a formative player in the fashioning of lived experience.[68] The effects generated by language and those generated by objects are not as dissimilar as they might seem.

To begin answering the question of whether we are talking about things or talking about language, then, we must be willing to rethink discourse, language, words as entirely separate from things. Although Brown differentiates his own work from that of literary critics interested in "discourse" or "the 'social text'" by championing an attention to "the objects that are materialized from and in the physical world that is, or had been, at hand,"[69] a theory of things in fiction need not be developed in opposition to a theory of discourse. Brown ultimately nuances this position in a note to his introduction by referencing René Girard's lament that "it has now become more or less axiomatic that 'words' and 'things' must go their separate ways, or at least that they cannot 'imitate' each other."[70] Girard goes on in the first essay of *To Double Business Bound* to explain how the distance between reality and fiction created by the mirror of mimesis is not an empty space, but one occupied by desire. In fact, in his reading of Dante's adulterous lovers, Girard reveals that for Paolo and Francesca it is the written account of Lancelot and Guinevere that ultimately catalyzes their own physical love and seals their fate: "It is the book itself, Francesca maintains, that plays the role of the diabolical go-between, the pander, in her life. The young woman curses the romance and its author." Lest we point out that this example falls flat because Francesca's fall from grace, though enacted by a fictional world, takes places within Dante's fictional hell, Girard further develops his theory of mimetic desire in the case of Don Quixote. "He has his imitators," Girard reminds us, "and the novel of which he is the hero had its plagiarists."[71] Carrying the effects of Cervantes' fictional world into Cervantes' own world, Girard demonstrates that desire is inherently mimetic, that our actions in the real world can be driven by desires ignited in the fictional world. So too do the objects we encounter on the page in their black-and-white forms enliven and recall other experiences we have had with such objects through our other senses. The worlds of text and sense are at least located within the same galaxy.

When I talk about things in the worlds of postmodern fiction, I am ultimately talking about multiple versions of things. To read the word "baseball" in a text is not to touch the object thrown by a major leaguer at Great American Ballpark in Cincinnati to be sure, but to read the word is to be awakened to the memories and experiences that shape your understanding, or lack of understanding, of the word. In his explication of Sir Philip Sidney's late sixteenth-century theme of "the fictional world as heterocosm, a universe apart," McHale argues that "in effect, the only ontological difference that the heterocosm approach admits is the opposition between fictional and real. This does not mean, however, that *no* relationship exists between the fictional heterocosm and the real world."[72] McHale's point is to emphasize ontological disruption as a unique and defining trait of postmodern fiction, and while I agree with his point and will return to it in a later chapter, for now what is important to note is that the world of language is not an alternate universe from the universe of things. When I analyze passages from literary texts, focusing on representations of everyday objects, I am examining versions of these things that create effects in readers. These effects are the products of diverse causes, ranging from firsthand experiences with physical forms of the objects in question to images of such objects as they appear on television and in film to memories derived from stories told by family and friends. While this range suggests a variability as infinite and individualized as the experiences of readers who have read Don DeLillo's

Underworld or Toni Morrison's *Jazz*, the finite nature of the objects themselves ultimately imposes a limited spectrum of possibilities.

Each of the following chapters is organized in part by the orthodoxies of postmodernism, but all the analyses begin with things. Structuring my readings around these nonhuman actors, I trace their circulations throughout and across narratives to see what kinds of networks they participate in constructing, rather than beginning with the larger networks as irreducible explanations for the order of things in the worlds of the texts. This approach allows me to avoid the problematic "what-can-postmodernism-tell-us-about-race" or "what-can-gender-tell-us-about-postmodernism" methodologies that presume the nature of the very social categories they are intended to explain. Each venture into the world of a given text focuses on a specific object or set of objects and works from these things to discern how relations are being made. What becomes apparent as this methodology is employed across the corpus of postmodern fiction is that the social categories we tend to imagine as static explanations for other phenomena are, in fact, processual products themselves. Paradoxically, then, fluidity is the constant. This focus on process is a cornerstone of neomaterialist thought across disciplines. Rosaldo's assessment of the advent of processual analysis in anthropology is instructive. Prior to the rise of processual analysis, anthropology was dominated by the "lone ethnographer" who "aspired to the holistic representation of other cultures" and "portrayed other forms of life as totalities. [. . .] in this tradition, culture and society determined individual personalities and consciousness; they enjoyed the objective status of systems. Not unlike grammar, they stood on their own, independent from the individuals who followed their rules."[73] Processual analysis shook these foundational views and contributed to the aforementioned anthropological revolution that began with figures like Geertz in the 1960s. "Processual analysis," Rosaldo explains, "resists frameworks that claim a monopoly on truth. It emphasizes that culture requires study from a number of perspectives, and that these perspectives cannot necessarily be added together into a unified summation."[74] Culture, like language, literature, and ideology, as Williams maintains in *Marxism and Literature*, is not a static concept to be explained or achieved, but a dynamic, constitutive, material process.[75]

INTRODUCTION

Because preoccupation with process is pervasive throughout so much of the fiction published in the second half of the last century, I have chosen to focus on a handful of texts that I submit are representative both historically and aesthetically. From the experimental and metafictional writings of the 1960s and 1970s, to the denaturalizations of race, gender, class, and nation that saturate the 1970s and 1980s, to the historiographic metafiction popularized in the 1980s and 1990s, and on into the twenty-first century, this book calls on a cross section of novels and stories to demonstrate the prominence of material things in the landscape of postmodern fiction. I have excluded some canonical postmodern writers such as Thomas Pynchon, Kathy Acker, and Ishmael Reed, who might also fit especially well with my methodology, and focused on writers from the 1990s and 2000s, as opposed to what some might consider the more typically postmodern decades of the 1960s–1980s. My rationale is twofold. First and most simply, so much good work in postmodern literary studies has examined these canonical writers that I believe my analysis will be easy to map onto their writings, and so I focus on writers and connections that have been less exhaustively explored in this conversation. Second and more integral to my project, I have chosen to examine primary texts and connections between texts that will challenge the framework of postmodernism as a literary period in the *ism*-driven tradition of romanticism, realism, naturalism, and modernism. If the postmodern aesthetic is resolutely materialist and fundamentally processual, as I suggest, then it may spell the end of this particular brand of periodization. I have thus chosen to read and relate writers whose lives, works, and influence might challenge our received understandings of postmodernism as a period.

This approach figures the texts themselves as active agents, Latourian actors that shape culture. They are certainly not produced in a vacuum, and so it follows that if the material conditions that produce the texts affect their production, then the texts themselves may also affect the material conditions in which they are produced. Nowhere is this principle clearer than in DeKoven's preface to *Utopia Limited: The Sixties and the Emergence of the Postmodern*, where she tells the story of her evolving

INTRODUCTION

view of postmodernism over the course of many years spent teaching its texts and contexts:

> My view of postmodernism underwent a long evolution, from an initial embrace of it as a continuation of the earlier twentieth-century and sixties avant-gardes, to a rejection of some of its most vocal proponents' simplistic, monolithic, reductive repudiation and often demonization of modernism, to a wary respect for some of its formulations, to my current sense of it as a complex, multivalent, non-self-consistent "cultural dominant."[76]

Her long-term engagement with the literary and theoretical texts themselves shaped her understanding, and not only that, but they seem to have shaped the culture as well. "The social-political-cultural-psychic context for those values and commitments," she explains, "the lifeworld or structure of feeling within which they now found their home—had changed materially: we had entered postmodernity."[77] DeKoven goes on, like Rosaldo, Raymond Williams, and others, to narrate the political turbulence of the day: the New Left, Woodstock, Vietnam. Rosaldo emphasizes that "[t]each-ins, sit-ins, demonstrations, and strikes set the political tone for this period on American college and university campuses."[78] His work on anthropologist Néstor García Canclini can help us theorize the material impact of texts as actors in this political environment: "García Canclini sees the artist as one link in a syntagmatic chain that extends from the creations of the artist's studio to the marketplace of private galleries."[79] When juxtaposed with "paradigmatic," the term "syntagmatic" signifies in important ways for this study. Each writer, each work of literature, does not merely fill some gap in a paradigm. We are as far away from T. S. Eliot's "Tradition and the Individual Talent" as we can possibly get. Rather, each writer and each text are consequential actors in a sequence whose existence resonates with other actors and whose circulation, or lack thereof, affects the sequence. Every actor is marked by its various associations and interactions.

The texts I examine here actively intervene in the culture that produces them by offering a vision of that culture as a material process. If postmodernity can be understood, as DeKoven suggests, "as both the 'cultural logic of late capitalism' (Fredric Jameson's crucial theorization) and also as the engine of egalitarian populism and of the politics of subjectivity," and if that understanding can be achieved "by means of textual analysis,"[80] then the texts themselves must play significant parts in the formation of the postmodern. If this is the case, then postmodernism cannot be treated exclusively as a conceptual paradigm because it cannot be used to explain the texts. Rather, postmodernism is what must be explained by the texts. The texts are formative, or constitutive, of the very concept we have typically used to explain them. The first-generation, neomaterialist anthropologists have it right: we should think syntagmatically, not paradigmatically. "If the only constant at the dawn of the third millennium is change," observes Rosi Braidotti, "then the challenge lies in thinking about processes, rather than concepts."[81] Texts are material actors, constituents helping to shape the feminist, New Left, civil rights, Black Power, and antiwar movements, not mere byproducts of these abstract forces. "Aesthetic events," Timothy Morton argues, "are not limited to interactions between humans or between humans and painted canvases or between humans and sentences in dramas. [. . .] When you make or study art you are not exploring some kind of candy on the surface of a machine. You are making or studying causality. *The aesthetic dimension is the causal dimension.*"[82]

But isn't it conventional wisdom that postmodernism is essentially abstract, theory driven, perhaps even anti-materialist? Is postmodernism not the *ism* in which the cultural logic of late capitalism drives the society of the spectacle and holds us hostage to the precession of simulacra?[83] For some critics the recent neomaterialist revival is a great awakening of sorts for a culture mired in postmodern abstraction. In *A Sense of Things*, Brown offers a strong rationale for troubling the boundaries of Marxist materialism in particular when he describes the "gambit" of his work as the trade-off of "sacrific[ing] the clarity of thinking about things as objects of consumption, on the one hand, in order to see how, on the other, our relation to things cannot be explained by the cultural logic of capitalism." But he also points out that a key factor prompting his study is the question of "why literary critics, historians, and anthropologists might have turned their attention to things in the midst of the 'abstraction [that] increasingly determines our lives'—an updated, intensified version of the abstraction said, by Simmel and others, to characterize modernity."[84] Having just spoken of Henry James's representation of material objects in *The American Scene* as prefiguring the "postmodern fate of the object," and "the artistic reproduction of 'objects as they're felt, not as they are,'" it should come as no surprise that Brown believes his poetry group struggled to think about things because they "had begun to inhabit a postmodernity that had too little sense of things."[85] Brown's implicit, and at times explicit, characterization of a fundamentally abstract postmodernism—cultural instead of material—is far from shocking given the legacy of key postmodern theorists who assert that postmodernism renders all experience cultural.[86] Whereas critics like Linda Hutcheon have offered the counterargument that the very work of postmodern theory and fiction is to reveal that everything has always been cultural,[87] I reread postmodern fiction to examine how postmodernism construes culture itself as a product of material arrangements.

Although this materialist methodology does not originate with my inquiry into the everyday worlds of postmodern fiction, *Postmodernism in Pieces* extends the neomaterialist conversation in literary criticism in two substantial ways. First, as I have explained, a materialist reading of postmodern fiction can revise our understanding of postmodernism in general by revealing that the postmodern aesthetic is just as constructive as it is deconstructive, that it is resolutely materialist and not abstract or purely theoretical play. Second, an attention to what Brown calls "the object matter of American literature" has not yet been focused on literature of the late twentieth- and early twenty-first centuries. Trendsetting studies by Brown, Susan Stewart, Lori Merish, and Barbara Johnson have concentrated on earlier texts. Stewart's *On Longing* is one of the first forays into a literary version of neomaterialism.[88] Examining the relation between materiality and meaning, she turns to a variety of literary works but rarely ventures into the postwar era except in the realm of theory. "Providing a prehistory of consumer subjectivity and agency" and "the discursive processes through which commodities first became identified as privileged vehicles of subjective expression and civic identification," Lori Merish's *Sentimental Materialism* offers illuminating treatments of a variety of "domestic artifacts" from the late eighteenth through the mid-nineteenth centuries.[89] Brown's *A Sense of Things* enacts his "thing theory" in the worlds of late nineteenth- and early twentieth-century writers, including Twain, James, and Jewett. In the philosophy-driven *Persons and Things*, Barbara Johnson considers the roles of things in the world of literary modernism with her treatment of the "self-consciously *unpoetic*" objects in Marianne Moore's poetry.[90] I owe a great debt to each of these critics, and have been able to extend this analytical framework into the postwar era because the theoretical foundation for thinking about things in US literature is so sound.

To understand the literature of the last half-century as resolutely materialist is to reconsider not only the nature of postmodernism, but also the predominant structure of US literary history that could produce such a cumbersome *ism* in the first place. Tracing its history in the *Oxford English Dictionary*, the evolution of the suffix -*ism* has led to its current denotation of "a form of doctrine, theory, or practice having, or claiming to have, a distinctive character or relation." But if fiction of the last fifty years reveals that all our doctrines, theories, and practices are the constant products of ongoing material processes that are notable because of their capacity for change, then the distinctiveness that stands as the key feature of any *ism* is a subordinate characteristic of postmodernism at best. At the same time, postmodernism does not signify the end of history, as some have maintained, or any other apocalyptic reckoning of art, economy, or politics. Ironically echoing Virginia Woolf, Samuel Cohen says of the terrorist attacks of 9/11 that "on or about September 11, 2001, human character did not change,"[91] and so I would say about the emergence of the postmodern. Postmodernism's relation to previous *isms* is less like a schism and more like the open space a schism contains, more like the hollow space of Heidegger's jug. Postmodernism is a revelation that the seemingly irreducible categories that govern our existence—categories such as race, class, and nation—are and have always been processual. Postmodernism is less a self-contained, distinctive aesthetic/historical marker and more a signifier of what has always been the case. For fiction to be *post*modern is for it to be after modern ways of thinking about literature, after demystification, after suspicion, after *isms*.

Far from gesturing toward something specific or recognizable like post-postmodernism, metamodernism, or digimodernism, I mean to suggest that the critical discourse of postmodernism renders such conversations, including those about postmodernism itself, obsolete—hopefully, even this one. As Barth remarks in "Postmodernism Revisited," "terms like Romanticism, Modernism, Late-Modernism, and Postmodernism are more or less useful and necessary fictions: roughly approximate maps, more likely to lead us to something like a destination if we don't confuse them with what they're meant to be maps *of*."[92] There is a resonance here between Barth's maps and Latour's Actor-Network-Theory in that both are wary of confusing what should be explained with the explanation. Thus, in my own narrative of postmodern fiction I want to echo McGurl's admission that his construction of a new narrative of literary production following World War II "will not come to the resounding conclusion of a post-program era but will trail off into an uncertain future."[93] But I want to expand such a confession by suggesting that this uncertainty is largely the product of postmodernism itself. McGurl reinforces Barth's injunction not to confuse literary maps with the terrains they are intended to illustrate by quoting from Adorno and Horkheimer, who argue that "classification is a condition of knowledge, not knowledge itself, and knowledge in turn dissolves classification."[94] Postmodernism, in my view, dissolves the old maps of US literary history, and further suggests that they have always been in a state of dissolution, even from their very inceptions. The knowledge through which the postmodern aesthetic accomplishes this dissolution is the materialist mindset that sets limits on all knowledge and existence at the edges of what is materially possible. In other words, postmodernism does not reveal that we have just begun to construct the social, to experience constant flux, to get lost in the meanings of words, or to define ourselves in terms of otherness. Postmodernism's materialist aesthetic reveals that these things have always been the case.

What we talk about when we talk about postmodernism is a respite from the many narrow and stultifying *isms* that we have invented and have relied on to provide a way of classifying aesthetic features and so-called social structures that cannot be fixed in time or space by words, things, or people because they are in fact constituted by those entities. If it *is* anything, postmodernism is seeing these relations in their most material and fundamental states of flux. By showcasing the simplest actors in the construction of social networks, postmodern fiction calls our attention away from ourselves, away from our own preoccupations, and toward the material world that all humans and nonhumans constitute and share in common. Such a shift in focalization necessitates a movement away from human essence as the centerpiece of relationality and precludes an overly reductive comparison of measurement that more often than not results in the exclusion, alienation, and/or marginalization of people and things based on perceived differences in being. This postmodern order of things is, as Foucault would say, "established without reference to an exterior unit . . . but by discovering that which is the simplest, then that which is next simplest" until we eventually reach "the most complex things of all."[95] Postmodernism shows that we are not the point. The singular individual, even the human community, is but a small beacon thrown from a boat moving through uncharted waters. Who or what is the point, then? The point is the very notion and experience of relating, belonging. In its revelation of the order of things, postmodern fiction is also a gathering, an assembling of human and nonhuman actors.

This theory of postmodern fiction runs counter to predominant theories of literary history in general, and of postmodernism in particular. Regardless of whether postmodernism is viewed as a mere intensification of modernism, a historically recurring literary phenomenon, or some kind of clean break with all that comes before, most critics would agree that it is a critical project and not an exercise in belonging. As Rita Felski explains in her recent work on the hermeneutics of suspicion, postmodern fiction is typically seen as so fundamentally critical that the burden of suspicious interpretation is shifted from the critic to the literary text "because it is already doing the work of suspicion for us, because it is engaged in the negative work of subverting the self-evident, challenging the commonplace, relentlessly questioning idées fixes and idées recus."[96] But when I turn the pages of postmodern fiction, what I find are hosts of things, people, words that need to be gathered together. I find I am offered the opportunity to build something, and I would argue that this is the task of the literary critic who takes postwar US fiction as her object of study. This turn from Howe's "spirit of criticism" that has haunted postmodern fiction and criticism since 1959 resonates with Latour's explanation for why critique has "run out of steam": "We explain the objects we don't approve of by treating them as fetishes; we account for behaviors we don't like by discipline whose makeup we don't examine; and we concentrate our passionate interest on only those things that are for us worthwhile matters of concern."[97] Debunking is not the sole enterprise of literary criticism, and neither is it the sole enterprise of postmodern fiction. Latour pleads with his readers that "the critic is not the one who debunks, but the one who assembles. The critic is not the one who lifts the rugs from under the feet of the naïve believers, but the one who offers the participants arenas in which to gather."[98] If the critic has typically allowed postmodern fiction to shoulder the weight of suspicion, as Felski points out, then perhaps we might also allow postmodern fiction to do the work of assembling, gathering, constructing.

If this study is successful, it should rewrite postmodernism out of the dialectic of US literary history as an antithesis, or even a synthesis, of realism and modernism. And yet, I hope this move will not be read as ahistorical. I am not advocating for a view of postmodernism divorced from history, but for a view of postmodernism as something other than a historical construct of the same genus as romanticism, realism, and modernism. Given all the talk about postmodernism's death, this re-examination is appropriately uncanny, suggesting as it does that the postmodernism we all know and love—or hate, or feel indifferent toward—has lived a secret life all these years. In the inductive spirit of neomaterialism, this conclusion is finally the product of re-examining the orthodoxies of postmodernism, and these re-examinations are, themselves, products of analyses that begin with things. Chapter 1, "Reconstructing Social Construction," redefines social construction. In an effort to avoid problematic essentialisms, literary theories of postmodernism have mistakenly appropriated the phrase "socially constructed" to signify that our social categories are without essence, and the critical discourse has virtually equated this lack of essence with artificiality. This chapter asks, if an identity or social category is constructed, then constructed out of what? The answer is that the social is constructed out of things, people, stuff. Perhaps all reductionist arguments in favor or critical of the postmodern project can be traced back to a fundamental misunderstanding of social construction. A case in point would be the fault line that runs through postmodernism, separating what have been variously characterized as two distinct stages, phases, or generations of postmodern writers. In many studies published over the last decade or so, a number of influential critics, including Amy J. Elias, W. Lawrence Hogue, Wendy Steiner, Timothy Parrish, Amy Hungerford, and Jeremy Green have pointed out that this fault line troublingly tends to demarcate one group of writers as postmodern that is predominantly white, male, and concerned with aesthetic experimentation, and another group as postmodern that is predominantly nonwhite, nonmale, and concerned with politics of race, gender, class, and nation. This division raises important questions, such as why—when so many women and writers of color have experimented with aesthetic form—have white male writers dominated the academy's discussion of literary postmodernism? How has postmodernism—an enterprise fundamentally committed to heterogeneity—led to an unmarked centering of whiteness and maleness, rendering gender the property of women and race a marker of people of color? The answer lies in diverging views of social construction.

I solve the social construction problem by dispelling the tension between constructivism and essentialism. In a US context, the predominantly white male writers of postmodernism's so-called aesthetic stage do not have the same anxieties about their individual and collective identities being constructed as do the writers of the so-called political stage, primarily because social construction's critique of essentialism does not endanger their well-established authority to speak. But what if constructed and essential are not incongruous? I work through this theoretical tangle by turning to the particularly troublesome relationship between postmodernism and Native writing, looking specifically at balls of thread, calendars, and Coke bottles in the work of Leslie Marmon Silko as a means of redefining social construction. My analysis of these everyday objects in Silko's *Ceremony* (1977) recalibrates the concept of social construction and develops a materialist theory of identity that allows for adaptation, change, and survival, without sacrificing what Craig Womack calls "social reference," or the customs, lands, and values that point to a distinctive Native American literary tradition.

Chapter 2, "Flattening Nature and Culture," explores the foundations of a revised social construction by decentering human characters as the catalysts for the formation of social networks. In one of the most

INTRODUCTION

formative studies of postmodern fiction, Brian McHale argues that the dominant marker of postmodernism is its preoccupation with ontology. What makes fiction postmodern, in my view, is not only its preoccupation with the ontological realm, as McHale suggests, but also its tendency to flatten its ontological worlds through an emphasis on the agency and significance of everyday objects. In other words, ontology is not only dominant in postmodern fiction, but also flat. If postmodern fiction's ontological dominant is essentially a flat ontology, then in the worlds of these texts everyday things play roles that are as important as those of the most significant human characters. I open the chapter with an analysis of the infamous "Sokal Hoax" in which a physicist and two cultural studies scholars engaged in a heated debate over the value of postmodern literary theory. Ultimately, both sides fall into the same trap of making an ontological distinction between nature/objects and culture/humans that is not borne out in the fiction typically characterized as postmodern.

In examining how attending to everyday things can dissolve the nature/culture binary in postmodern fiction, I start with a close reading of a ring in Jonathan Safran Foer's *Everything Is Illuminated* (2002) before moving on to examine the roles of two other rings—in Toni Morrison's *Jazz* (1992) and Jonathan Lethem's *The Fortress of Solitude* (2003), respectively. The result is a radical decentering of humans as the loci of social networks. This decentering of humans facilitates a rethinking of larger collectives as lowest common denominators of relation that can organize our understanding of individuals and can be swept away with a generalizing whisk of the hand as "social" explanations. The chapter establishes the flattened ontology of postmodern fiction by leveling the playing field between humans and nonhumans in Foer's work, and then illustrates the process by which seemingly unfamiliar persons and things are assembled through the jazz-like structure that drives Morrison's novel. Finally, it compares and contrasts the possibilities and consequences of a flattened ontology with an ontology that remains dependent on familiar social categories in Lethem's fictional world.

Chapter 3, "Rewriting Language," recasts language, the long-standing centerpiece of postmodern metafiction and postmodern literary theory,

INTRODUCTION

as a material phenomenon by cultivating a non-linguistic-centered reading of postmodern fiction. The literature most often identified as postmodern has taken on many names over the last half century, including metafiction, surfiction, the literature of exhaustion, and the literature of silence. These monikers all point in some way to the prominent trend of making writing the subject of postmodern narrative. This chapter begins with a brief historicization of the coincidence of postmodern fiction and the theoretical waves of poststructuralism and the "linguistic turn." Each of these modes of thought imagines not only writing but society at large as semiotic systems in which individual elements derive their identities or meanings from their places within the system. The critical consensus locates language play at the heart of the postmodern aesthetic, but having established the material domain as the foundation for postmodernism, I turn back to a few texts that overtly call our attention to linguistic play and reread them from a materialist vantage to see what a non-linguistic-centered analysis can reveal about postmodern fiction.

When we are willing to expand our approach to postmodern fiction beyond the linguistic realm to include the material objects of everyday life, what becomes clear is that all actors, including language itself, function as what Latour calls "mediators" instead of as "intermediaries," meaning that all actors do more than simply transport; they transform meaning. John Barth's classic work of metafiction *Lost in the Funhouse* (1968) has been a staple in discussions of postmodernism's linguistic wheel-spinning over the course of the last four decades. My materialist reading focuses on the ever-increasing presence of objects in the Ambrose cycle of stories, culminating in Barth's emphasis on a "name-coin" in the collection's title story. In a novella, entitled "Westward the Course of Empire Takes Its Way," David Foster Wallace rewrites "Lost in the Funhouse" in his 1989 collection *Girl with Curious Hair*. Reading these two versions of Ambrose's story side by side reveals a material dimension to postmodern fiction echoed in the recalcitrance of an electric stove in "Here and There," an earlier story in Wallace's collection. "Here and There," like *Lost in the Funhouse* and "Westward," withholds closure and features human and nonhuman actors working in cooperation and opposition to demonstrate the flux of our in-process existence. The interaction of objects in each of these stories reveals not a preoccupation with language as some abstract phenomenon, but a fascination with the material. Barth accentuates this significance by using material objects to reimagine his protagonist's family unit, while Wallace revises romantic love. In both cases, connections between characters that seem to hinge on language play are finally explained by the more mundane things that constitute those relations, and are then rearranged to bring the characters to moments of personal revelation. Language in postmodern fiction is another coin or stove.

Chapter 4, "Collapsing Otherness," turns to nonhuman actors that populate Don DeLillo's *Underworld* (1997) and Julia Alvarez's *How the García Girls Lost Their Accents* (1991) to ask what we might learn by moving away from otherness as foundational to the construction of social networks. Otherness has been misunderstood as foundational when it is actually only definable in the context of the inclination of actors toward one another. Leslie Fiedler helped make "otherness" the cornerstone of postmodernism in his oft-cited 1965 essay "The New Mutants." Although Fiedler focuses especially on the ways in which WASP males buck the Enlightenment narrative of their sex, his idea of differentiation from tradition through "otherness" works its way into the larger discourse of postmodernism until it becomes a defining trait in postmodern theories of sociality. Otherness has been understood incompletely in postmodernism's attempts to redress the hegemonic social imaginary of Enlightenment modernity. The objects in DeLillo's and Alvarez's novels show how postmodern fiction is marked by an intrinsic interest not solely in otherness but in "inclination," or what philosopher Jean-Luc Nancy calls the *clinamen* of fundamentally relational beings.

DeLillo and Alvarez do not merely enact Nancy's idea of *clinamen*, but take it in a new direction by asking us to include nonhuman actors in the realm of beings that incline toward one another. The obsession with otherness that has dominated the critical discourse of postmodernism arises out of a legitimate need to engage with the ethical implications of the differences we encounter when actors are exposed to one another. In the process, the inclination that precedes otherness has been pushed to the side and, more often than not, has been ignored altogether. *Underworld* follows the trajectory of a famous baseball across nearly half a century as it circulates through the lives of numerous characters, drawing actors together. The novel ultimately demonstrates that community is developed out of common interactions, and not in the contrast between "societies." Alvarez's *How the García Girls Lost Their Accents* features a series of objects—culminating with a toy drum brought from the United States to the Dominican Republic—that can help us reconcile Nancy's theory of inclination with Latour's theory of the social as always constituted by work. When we foreground the treatment of everyday objects in postmodern fiction, these texts uncover an inclination of various actors that ultimately *produces* the otherness that has been understood as foundational.

In the conclusion, "Afterism: The Promise of Postmodernism," I explore the implications of a redefined postmodernism for literary history. In this framework, postmodernism becomes a recognition of the boundlessness that actors require to move about and form relations without the restrictions imposed on them by an insistence on preexistent doctrines, theories, or practices. Rather than marking an end of history, or even just literary history, this theory of postmodernism-as-recognition reorients literary studies by moving away from periodizing *isms* and thematic social categories alike. Each narrative under investigation features everyday things as vital actors in the formation of networks that do not conform to the well-established parameters of familiar social categories. However, none of these networks dismisses the effects of nationality, race, gender, class. A materialist reading does not neutralize the consequences of placing our faith in such categories, much less the material conditions that have produced them and been produced by them. Rather, it redresses those effects by offering characters who have been marginalized by them the opportunity not only to work within, but also to revolutionize, systems of power since such systems do not exist apart from their material making. This reality, postmodern fiction suggests, has always been the case, but many have not been in a position to see. As I reassemble postmodernism piece by piece, my hope is that an alternative theory will begin to materialize before our eyes, a theory that is grounded, not on lifting the rug from beneath our feet, but on the rug itself as one of a myriad of actors that might help explain the order of things.

Chapter 1

Reconstructing Social Construction

A fault line runs through postmodernism, separating what have been variously characterized as two distinct stages, phases, or generations of postmodern writers. In her influential study *Sublime Desire: History and Post-1960s Fiction*, Amy J. Elias distinguishes between these two "stages of development" by describing the first as "a late-modernist, metafictional phase predominating in the 1960s and 1970s," and the second as "an antimodernist phase of cultural critique predominating in the 1980s and 1990s, centering on politics of race, class, gender, and nationhood."[1] W. Lawrence Hogue also identifies two modes of postmodern fiction, framing them as distinct reactions to modernism/modernity: "If the postmodern writer chooses the abstract, rationalist paradigm of modernity, he is likely to get caught up in using postmodern techniques to attack instrumental reason and other Enlightenment ideas [...] If he chooses the world-system paradigm in addition to using postmodern techniques to attack reason, he will offer a planetary alternative to five hundred years of Eurocentric hegemony."[2] Hogue's postmodern writer is faced with a choice between Elias's metafictional and social stages, but Hogue takes the difference one step further by connecting the first mode with Eurocentricity and the second with a more global outlook. Wendy Steiner reveals the logical result of this bifurcation in her contribution to *The Cambridge History of American Literature* in which she challenges a troublesome generalization that had become commonplace by the turn of the millennium, namely, that the first and aesthetically experimental stage is predominantly the territory of white male writers, while the second, politically minded and more aesthetically realist, stage is typically the purview of women writers and writers of color.[3] Although it might be more accurate and productive to theorize these stages as parallel streams rather than linear phases, the division they gesture toward has gained serious traction.

Having developed some critical and historical distance from the second half of the twentieth century, literary scholars now interested in thinking about postmodernism in the past tense have been faced with the task of evaluating this divide. Building on Steiner's work, Amy Hungerford points out that "at worst, that opposition suggested a hierarchy of value in which the writing of mainly white male authors such as Thomas Pynchon, John Barth, William Gaddis, and Don DeLillo was deemed 'literary' whereas the work of writers such as Toni Morrison, Philip Roth, Louise Erdrich, Leslie Marmon Silko, Alice Walker, and Joan Didion was thought to be mainly concerned with the sociological aspects of fiction."[4] Both Steiner in 1999 and Jeremy Green in 2005 complicate this binary by pointing out the myriad exceptions that all but outnumber the rule, but each critic comes to a different conclusion. Steiner insists that "the absolute boundary between the two visions— between 'high' postmodernism and women's, ethnic, or minority art— is a fiction maintained by a mind-set lodged in modernism."[5] She thus saddles literary and cultural critics—she names Jerome Klinkowitz as a prime example—with having created this distinction, and basically collapses all truly postmodern writers into the second, politically minded stage.[6] Green, in direct response to Steiner, maintains the value of aesthetic experimentalism, and takes Steiner to task for what he sees as her minimalizing of formal innovation. Pointing out the "antirealism" of nonwhite and nonmale writers such as "Ishmael Reed, Toni Morrison, Maxine Hong Kingston, Clarence Major, Nathaniel Mackey, Theresa Hak Kyung Cha, Jessica Hagedorn, and Cynthia Kadohata," Green posits the inverse of Steiner's argument by making the case that all postmodern writers, at least to some extent, share the legacy of the first, aesthetically experimental stage.[7]

Although separating the postmodern stages along racialized and gendered lines is surely an oversimplification, there are also clear and substantive reasons for why these generalizations have surfaced over the last few decades. As Timothy Parrish argues in *From the Civil War to the Apocalypse: Postmodern History and American Fiction*, there is an important battle raging within post-1960s fiction "to claim authority over the present, which means, for the combatants, the truth of the past. From this perspective, *history, rather than identity*, is the common ground of postmodern writers."[8] Parrish goes on to point out that the postmodern texts at the center of his analysis envision narrative as truth and "should be distinguished from the 'aesthetic' postmodernism associated with Barth, Donald Barthelme, Robert Coover, William Gaddis, or William Gass."[9] Parrish's list of white male writers reinforces the perception that there remains a racialized and gendered divide in the battle over the orthodoxies of postmodernism. My goal here is not to undo or disprove this bifurcation, as Steiner and Green set out to do in their respective ways. Neither do I want to rationalize it, as does Mark McGurl in his powerful study *The Program Era*, in which he offers "high cultural pluralism" as a way to account for figures such as Philip Roth who "would join the modernist literary sophistication of his higher educational training with the ethnic experiential specificity of his upbringing."[10] Instead, I want to grapple with how and why this fault line has emerged. Why—when so many women and writers of color have experimented with aesthetic form—have white male writers dominated the academy's discussion of literary postmodernism? How has postmodernism—an aesthetic, historic, and philosophical enterprise fundamentally committed to heterogeneity—led to an unmarked centering of whiteness and maleness, rendering gender the property of women and race a marker of people of color?

The answers to these questions, I argue, can be traced back to the concept of social construction. In a US context, the predominantly white male writers of postmodernism's aesthetic stage do not have the same anxieties about their individual and collective identities being constructed, as do the writers of the so-called political stage, primarily because the challenge to essentialism posed by social construction does not endanger their well-established authority to speak. "As with modern American literature," Hogue explains,

> most mainstream postmodern American fiction, even as it challenges and undermines conventions and expectations in the

modern novel, tends to redact Eurocentric (male) subjectivity as privileged and fixed and to victimize/fetishize/underrepresent the Other—people of color in the periphery, Woman, the poor of the center, the dominated classes of the marginalized, the global periphery, the American Indian, the African American, or African American cultural forms.[11]

In her landmark essay "Postmodern Blackness," bell hooks articulates this disjunction: "the unwillingness to critique essentialism on the part of many African-Americans is rooted in the fear that it will cause folks to lose sight of the specific history and experience of African-Americans and the unique sensibilities and culture that arise from that experience."[12] Craig Womack clarifies the broader difficulty for literary and cultural studies:

> the rise of minority-area studies within the university has occurred simultaneously with the burgeoning radical skepticism that questions the very legitimacy of the kind of racial identity categories that minority studies has often embraced, many theorists problematizing long-held notions of any kind of collective identity, emphasizing their constructedness and the fluidity between inside and outside boundaries and deemphasizing any kind of essential, inherent, or universal basis for such identities.[13]

Thus, social construction has served as a kind of continental divide separating writers into the two different streams of postmodernism, based in part on its commitment to demonstrating that social categories are constructed rather than essential, fluid rather than inherent. But what if constructed and essential are not incongruous? Postmodern fiction posits no such incongruity. As a case in point, I want to turn now to the particularly troublesome relationship between postmodernism and Native writing, looking specifically at the work of Leslie Marmon Silko, as a means of redefining social construction as a key orthodoxy of literary postmodernism and contending that the tension between construction and essentialism can be resolved by examining the everyday things that organize the lives of characters in Silko's fiction.

WHAT IF CONSTRUCTED DOES NOT MEAN ARTIFICIAL?

Silko's 1977 novel *Ceremony* tells the story of Tayo, a young, mixed-race Laguna whose service in the US Army during World War II has left him physically and emotionally damaged. Tayo struggles to readjust to life on the Laguna Pueblo reservation without his cousin Rocky, who died by his side as a fellow prisoner of the Japanese. The army doctors and the traditional Laguna medicine men have been equally unsuccessful in helping Tayo, and so he is taken to a Navajo medicine man named Betonie who performs a healing ceremony that Tayo must complete himself. Betonie's ceremony is unique because it utilizes traditional stories and cures as well as contemporary objects such as calendars and Coke bottles. Like Tayo, the Laguna Pueblo reservation in New Mexico is suffering as drought drains the life of the land and its people. With Rocky gone, and his uncle Josiah having passed away while the boys were at war, Tayo sets out to find the lost cattle that Josiah had been breeding to survive the harsh conditions of the American Southwest. In the process he encounters a woman named Ts'eh, who helps him find his cattle and reconnect with the land. The healing ceremony is only completed after Tayo has restored the cattle. All the while he has struggled to manage his relationship with a group of fellow Native army buddies who like to drink and fight. Tayo finally resists the urge to murder one especially vile ex-soldier who tortures Tayo's friend. These narrative threads converge as Tayo realizes that the seemingly concrete divisions that typically demarcate individuals and groups are actually part and parcel of a much larger fluid and irreducible order of things.

Ceremony has garnered a staggering amount of critical attention from both Native and non-Native critics, ranging from Charles Larson's early treatment in *American Indian Fiction*, to Paula Gunn Allen's "recover[y] of the feminine" in *The Sacred Hoop* to Rick Mott's recent discussion of digitizing the text for twenty-first-century students. At its best, this body of criticism attends to the novel's and its characters' "ability to interpret the patterns within changing cultural and historical contexts," as Chadwick Allen has observed.[14] But this conversation has also turned to typically postmodern conventions, such as hybridity, indeterminacy, and social construction, to discuss the novel in terms of "the postmodern reality of hybridized traditions, mixed races, and crossed borders," with critics claiming that "*Ceremony* is neither entirely Indian-based nor completely western but a hybrid of both."[15] Such theorizations of the relationship between the novel and postmodernism have been troubling for two reasons. First, they tend to reduce Native peoples, both individually and collectively, to the lowest common denominators of binary social categories by approaching these categories as if they were substantive things holding definable groups together. Second, they often disconnect Native peoples from important historical, cultural, and geographical markers by emphasizing the constructed nature of Native identity. These two effects, among others, have created tension between Native writing and the discourse of postmodern critical theory, offering a prime example of how and why postmodernism has come to name "both the stylistically innovative writing from the 1960s to the 1990s, such as that by Pynchon or Barth, and the literature of the period as a whole."[16] Silko's *Ceremony* has been categorized under each and both categories at various points since its initial publication in 1977, but its resistance to such facile categorization raises more questions about the two streams of postmodernism than it resolves, especially in relation to the postmodern orthodoxy of social construction.

The problem of theorizing Native writing and social construction has innumerable subtleties, but two basic dimensions. The first dimension is that social construction is desirable for some Native writers and critics of Native writing because it carves out a space for "tribal memories and the coherence of heard stories."[17] Gerald Vizenor defines this process as the "survivance" and triumph of "postindian" warriors over what he calls manifest manners: "Manifest manners are the simulations of dominance; the notions and misnomers that are read as the authentic and sustained as representations of Native American Indians. The postindian warriors are new indications of a narrative recreation, the simulations that overcome the manifest manners of dominance."[18] Elsewhere, Vizenor calls on Brian McHale's articulation of postmodernism as a mode that creates new insights and coherence by generating more and more discourse, and argues that "Native American Indian literatures are tribal discourse, more discourse. The oral and written narratives are language games, comic discourse rather than mere responses to colonialist demands or social science theories."[19] Thus, for Vizenor the social construction of Native identity is useful because it multiplies the meaning of "Indian," allowing for infinite "recreations," and thereby making it difficult to define Native Americans in static terms.[20] Critics such as Kimberly Blaeser rely on Vizenor's work insofar as it "check[s] the process of literary annihilation and free[s] Native American identity from the grasp of literary colonialism."[21] Others, like Womack, acknowledge the value of Vizenor's contribution on this front but raise the second dimension of the social construction problem by questioning whether or not there should be unlimited free rein in defining "Indian."

Noting Vizenor's theoretical faith in poststructuralism and postmodernism, as well as Blaeser's study of Vizenor, Womack asks, "Do we want to remove 'Indian' so far from its social reference that definitions are no longer possible?"[22] Jace Weaver offers what could be read as a direct answer to this question in his contribution to *American Indian Literary Nationalism* when he argues that "despite postmodern claims of fragmented, fractionated, and multiple identities, Native identity is not freewheeling and infinitely refracted. One cannot, for instance, dream oneself Indian while possessing no Native ancestry. Not even the most louche critic would contend so."[23] Both Womack and Weaver object to the tendency of postmodernism in general, and social construction in particular, to disconnect Native peoples from the formative values, geographical spaces, family histories, and land rights that constitute the very identities they are writing, historicizing, preserving, and strengthening. One central concern is that Native writing gets subsumed by Western traditions: "Hybridity, postmodernism, and postcolonality," Weaver claims, "are the twenty-first century 'smelting pot' in which diverse metals become alloyed into one."[24] Womack and Weaver are certainly not alone or unjustified in their objections, and neither is this concern exclusive to Native writing or writers. Paula Moya, for instance, asserts that under the postmodern critique of identity "social and cultural identities, it is argued, are similarly fictitious because the selves they claim to designate cannot be pinned down, fixed, or definitively identified. Moreover, identities are not simply fictitious; they are dangerously mystifying. They are mystifying precisely because they treat fictions as facts and cover over the fissures, contradictions, and differences internal to the social construct we call a 'self.'"[25] Once again, it is the notion of social construction that incites a controversy over identity insofar as "constructed" seems to be a synonym for fictitious and artificial, or at least antithetical to any form of essence. But is this view of construction accurate? In short, the answer is no. To argue that something is socially constructed should not be understood as a case against its essence because the so-called social forces doing the constructing are themselves the constant products of material interactions.

The idea of construction is nothing new to discussions of identity in postmodernism or Native writing, but the term typically employed, "socially constructed," has most often been used to designate the revelatory effects of deconstruction. That is, when a given identity is *decon*structed, we see that it was always socially *con*structed. On the surface, it seems obviously inconsistent to claim that a paradigm devoted to tearing down—deconstruction—should also be defined by its commitment to building up—social construction. This disconnect arises from a fundamental misunderstanding of social construction. Standing on the shoulders of early postmodern intellectuals such as Susan Sontag and Leslie Fiedler, most literary theorists have contended that what postmodernism teaches us is that our social categories have been manufactured, as opposed to arising naturally. Linda Hutcheon's fabulous denaturalization of dominant narratives in *The Politics of Postmodernism* is a case in point, as is Satya P. Mohanty's more recent argument that "postmodernists in particular insist that identities are fabricated and constructed rather than self-evidently deduced from experience, since—they claim—experience cannot be a source of objective knowledge."[26] Whether intended or not, such theories have equated "constructed" with "artificial." Bruno Latour explains this misunderstanding by recalling his deflation upon learning how colleagues in the social and natural sciences reacted to his theory of the assembly of social networks: "To say that something was 'constructed' in their minds meant that something was not true. They seemed to operate with the strange idea that you had to submit to this rather unlikely choice: *either* something was real and not constructed, *or* it was constructed and artificial, contrived and invented, made up and false."[27] Similarly, in an effort to avoid problematic essentialisms, literary theories of postmodernism have appropriated the phrase "socially constructed" as a means of signifying that our social categories are without essence, and the critical discourse has virtually equated this lack of essence with artificiality.[28] The bifurcation of postmodernism into two stages is, in part, the result of this multidimensional irony. If the concept of social construction simply reveals that our social categories and narratives are all equally artificial, then everything we know about the social is equally false, or, what amounts to the same thing, equally true. However, if "constructed" is not a synonym for artificial, nor antithetical to essence, then perhaps the fiction that has typically been construed as postmodern due to its commitment to social construction can, in fact, tell us something valuable about the everyday experiences, objects, and persons that constitute the individual and collective associations that we call "social."

In discussions of the relationship between Native writing and social construction, the conflation of constructed with artificial is commonplace among Native and non-Native critics alike. Womack uses the term to discuss the plight of "minority scholars [who] discover that the very notion that they constitute a 'they,' a distinct group with the ability to distinguish itself from other groups and claim a right to speak on its own behalf, is a constructed notion that 'only' exists inside their heads."[29] Anything constructed seems not to exist in the material world, but only in the theoretical realm. Robert Dale Parker explains the title of his book, *The Invention of Native American Literature*, by clarifying, "I use the word *invention* to suggest an air of the provisional, of ongoing process and construction, as opposed to a natural, inevitable effusion of Indian identity."[30] Construction is defined in contradistinction to what is "natural." I do not blame Womack, Parker, or any other individual critic for what seems to me an equivocation; we are all laboring under a mistake that has surely become a part of the fabric of literary studies. But what if "constructed" does not mean "artificial"? What if a constructed identity is literally one built out of material circumstances, assembled from the various things, people, and places of everyday life? What if a constructed identity is essential, natural? How might literary postmodernism be revised in light of Native writing? How might Native American criticism benefit from a theory of identity that allows for adaptation, change, and survival, but does not sacrifice Womack's "social reference" or the customs, lands, and values that point to a unique and vibrant Native American literary tradition? The answer, I believe, is that recalibrating our understanding of "constructed" can address both dimensions of the social construction problem by precluding static and reductive discourses about Native writing—or any individual or collective discourse—and by recognizing a national Native American literature, or, as Weaver would say, by letting "a thousand separatisms bloom."[31]

CONSTRUCTED OUT OF WHAT?

Perhaps the most straightforward way to demonstrate that constructed does not mean artificial is to answer the question: What is the stuff, the literal materials, out of which the social is constructed in the worlds of literary texts? Works of narrative fiction turn to everyday objects as well as human subjects, or what narrative theorist David Herman calls "actants," and the stories located in these actants, as materials out of which the social is constructed.[32] I want to move from a merely intellectual social construction to a material construction of the social out of actants. Latour has pointed out that the traditional understanding of society as made up of enduring social ties "begs the question of how and through which means this increase in durability has been practically achieved," and he adds that "to jump from the recognition of interactions to the existence of a social force is, once again, an inference that does not follow from the premise."[33] Latour also uses the term "actant," and defines it along with the term "actor" in *Politics of Nature* as "a term from semiotics covering both humans and nonhumans; an actor is any entity that modifies another entity in a trial."[34] In *Reassembling the Social*, Latour asks that we think of both human subjects and material objects as "actors, or more precisely, *participants* in the course of action waiting to be given a figuration."[35] As I will demonstrate in the analysis of Foer, Morrison, and Lethem in the next chapter, social construction overtly invites us to consider both objects and subjects as significant actors in the formation of the various networks of relation that we identify as social. Specifically, social networks are built, at least in part, out of things, stuff ranging from calendars, to carburetors, to cashews. The recent interest in such everyday objects, as evidenced by the popularity of neomaterialism, has fostered consideration of the roles these inanimate objects play in the organization of the lives of animate subjects, but following Latour and Womack, the distinction between subject and object breaks down even further.

The significance of both human and nonhuman actors is as important to Womack as it is to Latour: "If all language is socially mediated, as some would claim, some native thinkers might respond, 'Yes, but it is also mediated by others besides humans.'"[36] I am not simply arguing that we should think of all Native writing as necessarily invested in social construction, let alone postmodernism. Instead, what I am suggesting is that there is a significant resonance between a theory of social construction that accounts for the material and the interest of many Native writers and critics in resisting the impulse to "privilege subject positions, that is, human perceptions."[37] The relevance of materiality to both approaches leads to a recognition of the agency and significance of nonhuman actors in the determination of human experience, which often manifests itself in the absence of facile distinctions between "manmade" and "natural" things. As the narrator of Linda Hogan's novel *Power* (1998) says of her aunt's house, "The house is sinking back into the earth and Ama would let it. It is the natural thing."[38] I do not merely mean to graft Silko or *Ceremony* onto the postmodern critical tradition, or to suggest either as a textbook example of social construction, but rather to consider how this novel constructs various identities out of material circumstances, and, in the process, redefines our understanding of what it means to say that something is socially constructed.

The paradox that Silko uncovers at various points in her work is that the constructed identity gets represented as artificial, while the resulting social categories produced are branded as natural. She highlights this irony in an essay first published in *The Nation* in 1994, in which she recalls various run-ins she has had with local, state, and federal officials when driving through states or crossing state lines in the United States. Once, while being detained, she remembers realizing that the officers were profiling her and other travelers based in part on the various material aspects of their appearances: "White people who appear to be clergy, those who wear ethnic clothing or jewelry and women with very long or very short hair (they could be nuns) are also frequently detained; white men with beards or men with long hair are likely to be detained, too."[39] However, while it is things, the material stuff such as clothing and jewelry, that mark these various drivers and passengers as either "religious" or "ethnic," their social status is ultimately reduced only to the larger categories of race, religion, and gender. What is missing from this profiling tactic is the realization that the categories the officers believe will aid them in their job are actually products of the various material actors they almost unconsciously seek out. The officers' techniques seem to indicate that the particular relationship a person has with her material surroundings determines her social identity, but their actions scream out that the larger and more familiar social category is what matters. Silko's novel accentuates this disjunction by resisting the reductive categorization of its mixed-blood protagonist Tayo as perpetually stuck between worlds of race and nation. As a whole, *Ceremony* reveals whiteness, Nativeness, and Americanness as in-process, but very real, markers of individual and collective identity as Tayo builds his identity out of the various materials he encounters throughout the novel. But it is important to note that Tayo's construction of the social is also represented as an expansion of the ongoing construction of identities that has been in process for generations. The novel's redefinition of social construction through materiality thus allows for the adaptation that Vizenor and Blaeser imagine as ideal, while also taking into account the essential features that Womack and Weaver argue are critical for theorizing Native writing.

BUILDING MATERIALS

Nonhuman actors play an important role in determining Tayo's social station from a very young age. Born to a prodigal Native mother and an unknown white father, Tayo is raised alongside his cousin Rocky by his Auntie and her husband Robert, his uncle Josiah, and his grandmother. Rocky is bound for success, but Tayo seems doomed to the low position in the family that his mother occupied before him. When Tayo comes into the household for good, Auntie maintains a distance between the two boys using the most mundane of everyday objects: "When she was alone with the boys, she kept Rocky close to her; while she kneaded bread, she gave Rocky little pieces of dough to play with; while she darned socks, she gave him scraps of cloth and a needle and thread to play with. She was careful that Rocky did not share these things with Tayo, that they kept a distance between themselves and him."[40] Rocky is supplied with the necessary materials out of which to build imaginary worlds and games, while Tayo is denied these things and is forced to think about his empty-handedness. A new materialist theory of things is useful here because it can help us attend to the agency of the objects in the novel, to ask questions such as "How do objects mediate relations between subjects, and how do subjects mediate the relation between objects? How are things and thingness used to think about the self?"[41] Such questions provoke us to consider what Bill Brown calls the "object matter" of literature.

Silko's "object matter" reveals a distance between Tayo and Rocky that we might normally identify as a social distance predicated on the racial and familial differences between the two boys. But to explain this separation in "social" terms is to risk missing and misunderstanding its more material nature and to hazard relying on each character's racial identity as a ready-made, and therefore familiar, explanation. As the boys grow older, Rocky is given other advantages intended to help him construct a life of success that is virtually conflated with non-Nativeness by the authority figures in his life, from his white teachers to his own mother. Rocky becomes an A-student and star athlete whose teachers tell him, "'Nothing can stop you now except one thing: don't let the people at home hold you back.' Rocky understood what he had to do to win in the white outside world" (51). These things and attitudes—good grades, athletic prowess, perhaps a letterman jacket—are the materials out of which whiteness is constructed. White authority figures supply Rocky with these materials and encourage him to build what they can only perceive as a white identity in opposition to a static and limited nativeness. In such moments, the novel reveals that whiteness is not given, normative, or unconstructed, despite its hegemonic status in US culture. When presented with the opportunity to volunteer to fight in World War II, Rocky jumps at the chance. Auntie actually wants her son to go to war, but she explains to Grandma that Tayo should not be allowed to go: "Rocky is different [. . .] but this one, he's supposed to stay here" (73). From childhood to young adulthood, Tayo and Rocky are distinguished by the things and opportunities available to them, from which they construct their respective places in the larger social world; for many of the characters, however, this construction process is overshadowed by its own products: the "white outside world" of America set aside for Rocky, and the Native "here" where Tayo belongs. Like Auntie, the boys long for white and Native to operate as totalizing logics, a priori categories, when, in fact, white and Native are being shaped by grades, pieces of dough, and military service applications.

Not all Silko's characters are blind to the material construction of larger social categories such as white, Native, American, and Mexican that present themselves as irreducible. Paula Gunn Allen identifies two sets of characters in *Ceremony*, and argues that "those in the first category belong to the earth spirit and live in harmony with her, even though this attunement may lead to tragedy. Those in the second are not of the earth but of human mechanism; they live to destroy that spirit, to enclose and enwrap it in their machinations, condemning all to a living death."[42] Extending Allen's assertion, I would like to alter the distinction by claiming that those in the first category are conscious of the fluidity of interactions between actors that constitute the social, while those in the second category are blind to the material and rely on the larger and more facile categories that are said to comprise the social.[43] Rocky's academic, athletic, and patriotic attempts to conform to the "white outside world" and become "American" are indicative of the quest for an Americanness that does not exist in the sense that he imagines because that marker is always changing. His desperation and confusion in the face of the in-process matrix of social relations is contrasted by the Navajo medicine man Betonie's embrace of the materiality of everyday objects in the healing ceremony he performs to help Tayo overcome the sickness he brought back from the war.

Although Tayo's sickness manifests itself physically through nausea, alcohol addiction, and vomiting, the Laguna elders and army doctors alike seem to agree that the source is psychological. The army doctors are unable to help Tayo overcome what they diagnose as the symptoms of "battle fatigue" (31), but Silko does not merely contrast "white medicine" with "Indian medicine," even if some characters in the novel do make such a distinction. Auntie reminds her mother, who is worried about Tayo and wants to call a medicine man, "You know what the Army doctor said: 'No Indian medicine.' Old Ku'oosh will bring his bag of weeds and dust. The doctor won't like it" (34). But Old Grandma insists, and Ku'oosh is called. He comes with blue cornmeal and stalks of Indian tea; the ceremony, however, is ineffective. The army doctors and Ku'oosh prove unsuccessful in their attempts to heal Tayo because their approaches misapprehend the cause of his illness. The army doctors blame the war and then liquor (53); Ku'oosh gestures toward "an absent white father" and the differences between Native and white warfare (35–36). Ku'oosh does briefly put his finger on the root of the sickness when he tells Tayo that "this world is fragile," and uses a word to express "fragile" that is "filled with the intricacies of a continuing process, and with a strength inherent in spider webs woven across paths through sand hills where early in the morning the sun becomes entangled in each filament of web" (35). But his remedy consists only of stagnant, traditional things such as the blue cornmeal and the tea stalks. The narrowness of the army doctors' and Ku'oosh's treatments cannot account for the "continuing process," or fundamental flux, of the disease. Tayo's sickness is, in fact, the product of something much larger that, in his own words, has "been going on for a long time" (53). Thus, the appropriate treatment must also be growing, changing, and dynamic.

    The cause of Tayo's disease seems to be that his participation in the war has somehow disconnected him from his "true" identity. For the army doctors, this means that his affinity and empathy for his cousin and even for the dead Japanese have severed Tayo from his American individualized selfhood (125). For Ku'oosh, this means that he has somehow become detached from his Lagunaness in "the white people's war" (36). Both treatments accordingly set out to force Tayo back into these respective social positions, and both treatments imagine these categories as static. Their methods depend on an understanding of the social as a set of stable categories into which Tayo must merely be reinserted in order to feel better. But what if Americanness and Lagunaness are not preexisting categories? What if these categories are instead in-process constructions? At the same time, how can "Laguna Pueblo" or any such category be anything other than an established collection of traditions and rituals passed down from generation to generation? Silko's Navajo medicine man Betonie intimates that a better question would be, how can any such category remain the same after being passed down from generation to generation?

The fluidity of tradition is materialized in the objects that comprise the healing ceremony Betonie designs for Tayo. After arriving at Betonie's home, a hogan built into the side of a hill overlooking the Gallup ceremonial grounds, Tayo looks around the place and is overwhelmed by the confused and chaotic collection that occupies the dwelling. He sees herbs, roots, hides, boxes bound in brass, newspapers, cardboard, clothing, rags, twigs, telephone books, Coke bottles, pouches and bags, hammered silver buttons, gourd rattles, deer-hoof clackers, calendars. Betonie's collection of ceremonial objects does not respect the boundaries of either the medical practices of the army doctors or the traditions of Ku'oosh. Nowhere is this observation clearer than in the calendars that Tayo notices and that give Betonie "some place to start" the ceremony. These Santa Fe Railroad calendars feature scenes with "Navajos herding sheep, deer dancers at Cochiti, and little Pueblo children chasing burros" (121). This commercialization of Native life is probably not what Tayo had expected to find in the home of a Navajo medicine man. But he soon remembers his uncle collecting the same calendars and thinks to himself, "On the reservation these calendars were more common than Coca-Cola calendars. There was no reason to be startled. This old man had only done the same thing" (121). When he tells Betonie that he recognizes two of the calendars, Betonie begins the healing ceremony by explaining, "All these things have stories alive in them" (121). Thus, the ceremony begins with Tayo's memories of a commodification of Native life on the pages of a calendar published by a railroad company notorious for its exploitation of Native land and peoples.

The calendars might be seen by white consumers as representative of an authentically Native way of life, while Native peoples might view them as misrepresentations designed to perpetuate romanticized visions of Native life in the minds of non-Natives. Betonie recognizes them for what they are, for better or worse: material objects that form Native identity in the eyes of both Native and non-Native peoples.[44] What is important about Betonie's characterization of the calendars is the fact that they "have stories alive in them" (121). The living, breathing nature of the stories indicates that the army doctors misunderstand the ideal of American individualism and that Ku'oosh misunderstands Laguna Pueblo identity to some extent because they do not account for the indefiniteness of these modes of being. Betonie contrasts his own healing ceremony with those of other Native healers such as Ku'oosh:

> "The people nowadays have an idea about the ceremonies. They think the ceremonies must be performed exactly as they have always been done, maybe because one slip-up or mistake and the whole ceremony must be stopped and the sand painting destroyed. That much is true. They think that if a singer tampers with any part of the ritual, great harm can be done, great power unleashed." He was quiet for a while, looking up at the sky through the smoke hole. "That much can be true also. But long ago when the people were given these ceremonies, the changing began, if only in the aging of the yellow gourd rattle or the shrinking of the skin around the eagle's claw, if only in the different voices from generation to generation, singing the chants. You see, in many ways, the ceremonies have always been changing." (126)

The calendars speak to changes in perceptions of Nativeness itself by gathering images of Navajos, Cochitis, and Pueblos together in the pages of a single object. That is, for unversed consumers, these distinct peoples might mistakenly be viewed as identical, or perhaps for the Santa Fe Railroad Company, modern-day Natives are nothing more than the nostalgic representatives of a "museumified" way of life who may increase ticket sales or commercial purchase. Still others might view the calendars ironically as signs critiquing westward expansion via the railroads. The calendars are both illustrative and formative of concepts of Nativeness and of Anglo presence in North America.

Nativeness, like whiteness, is not constructed in any artificial or purely theoretical sense. Laguna Pueblo identity has a material foundation; it is constructed, in part, *out of* these calendars. Brown's "thing theory" is illuminating here, as he enacts Betonie's notion that things "have stories alive in them" by pointing out that thinking from things can initiate "new thoughts about how inanimate objects constitute human subjects, how they move them, how they threaten them, how they facilitate or threaten their relation to other subjects."[45] The calendars help move our reading of Tayo's character away from a desire to pin down his identity, and toward a method for tracing the many material things, connections, and relations that shape his existence. If Tayo's identity is constructed, but constructed *out of* his material circumstances, then it is not so far removed from any reference "that definitions are no longer possible," as Womack rightly worries. Instead, Laguna Pueblo has very clear and substantial references in the material world, but is also irreducible to some static or reductive definition because that material world is constantly adapting. This year's calendars will be replaced by next year's; the design of Coca Cola's bottles will change over time, as will the very materials out of which the bottles are made, but these alterations do not render the objects themselves any less real, nor do they sacrifice their essence. Tayo's identity is essential, but that essentiality is constructed out of the material world of which he himself is a part.

Betonie's ceremony is not designed to help Tayo reconnect with his unchanging Laguna Pueblo self or to serve as a critique of the troubling and naturalized narratives of the wandering, disappearing, and drunken Indian that wind their way through popular lore as well as US Indian policy. Instead, the ceremony provides Tayo with the necessary materials that enable him to contribute to the ongoing construction of Laguna Pueblo identity. "Isolated from the world, in the army hospital," Susan L. Dunston points out, "Tayo is 'white smoke,' fading 'into the white world of their bed sheets and walls'; he is 'invisible' and silent. Neither accurately observed nor actively observing, he is dead to the world and it is dead to him."[46] In stark contrast to the diagnostic methodologies of the army doctors and of Ku'oosh, Betonie's approach avoids the oversimplified categories that are treated as irreducible in favor of focusing on the more elemental components of those categories.

When Tayo wonders if his problems might stem from the fact that his mother was Laguna and his father white, Betonie responds, "'nothing is that simple [. . .] you don't write off all the white people, just like you don't trust all the Indians'" (128). The problem is the "witchery" that seeks to divide the otherwise complete world into tidy compartments. Silko presents the story of the witchery in verse rather than prose, and we are not entirely sure who sings, speaks, or chants it, insinuating that its rightful position lies outside the narrative proper. The story goes that white people are the products of a contest among a diverse collection of Native witch people to see who could produce the most impressive powers. Finally, one witch bests all the others by telling a story about a *"white skin people who see no life / when they look / they see only objects. / The world is a dead thing for them / the trees and rivers are not alive / the mountains and stones are not alive. / The deer and bear are objects / They see no life"* (135). The witchery always seeks to create opposition, to set up binaries, for instance, between whites who "see only objects," and Natives who ostensibly see something more.

But the witchery itself is also diverse. Some of the witches at the great contest untie "skin bundles of disgusting objects: / dark flints, cinders from burned hogans where the dead lay" (134). These witches use their materials to assemble charms and powers. But the witch whose story speaks white people into being does not gather its charm out of material objects at all. It "just [tells] them to listen" (135). After the prize is won, the other witches ask the speaker to take back what it has said, but it responds *"It's already turned loose. / It's already coming. / It can't be called back"* (138). This most sinister witchery presents itself not as a material construct but as an inevitable statement of what is the case. The great myth of whiteness is that it is somehow unconstructed, and here we witness the origins of that myth. The "white skin people" of the witch's story see no connection between themselves and the world around them. They seem to exist, somehow, apart. It's not that they actually are unconnected from that world, but rather that they "see no life." They do not understand themselves as beholden to and made out of the world. This witchery is the most evil spell of all because of its comprehensiveness. Those who "see only objects" imagine a relation between themselves and those objects that cannot be anything but hierarchical. They can only imagine the world as it exists for them.

Silko ultimately refutes the idea of any unconstructed power, perspective, or category when she reveals that even the witchery is constituted of material objects. Near the end of the novel, some of Tayo's war buddies and fellow Indians who have grown to despise him kidnap his friend Harley in an attempt to draw Tayo out of hiding so they can kill him. The men are drunk, and Tayo has a screwdriver with which he could easily attack and kill them, saving his friend: "This was the time. But his fingers were numb, and he fumbled with the screwdriver as he tried to rub warmth back into his hands. [. . .] He moved back into the boulders. It had been a close call. The witchery had almost ended the story according to its plan; Tayo had almost jammed the screwdriver into Emo's skull the way the witchery had wanted" (253). The witchery is not a self-sustaining power, but rather a narrative that is made out of material components and those who fear it.

The witchery needs the screwdriver in Tayo's hand to perpetuate its work and to make Tayo into "another victim, a drunk Indian war veteran settling an old feud" (253). Thus, the most deadly kind of witchery is that which claims to have no material basis for its power to establish entire groups. The witchery that creates white people is merely spoken, not assembled from material things. This witchery, which presents itself as a force that exists independent of any more fundamental constituencies, recalls Latour's "sociology of the social" because it casts such social narratives as the "drunken Indian" and the "white outside world" as substantive phenomena that can be used to account for other phenomena, and ignores the fact that such "forces" are actually constituted by more quotidian things and interactions. Silko demonstrates the material possibilities for resisting and remaking the witchery by having Tayo move back into the boulders and pocket the screwdriver. In that moment, rather than giving in to the perceived power of the witchery, Tayo reveals that this power is not some ethereal force, but rather the product of the interaction of the actors involved in the conflict. His recurring battle with the stereotype of the drunken Indian throughout the novel is finally won here, as Silko demonstrates that such identities are the products of associations among human and nonhuman actors and that they can be assembled and reassembled according to a character's engagement with her or his material surroundings.

The point here is that whiteness and Nativeness themselves are processes. Both are constructed out of available materials. Neither is coterminous with the existence of the world. Neither is a preexisting phenomenon that describes the lives of those who seem to fit within its parameters, even when other networks of actors do their best to make it appear so. Critics have dealt with the survival, fluidity, change, and endurance of Native identity and culture in *Ceremony*,[47] and whiteness has also been revealed as processual;[48] however, a materialist attention to the things that constitute a significant portion of such markers reveals that race, culture, and nation are much too large to serve as bases for understanding individual and collective identity. Everyday, nonhuman actors disrupt our understanding of the social by shifting the starting point entirely from some category to the material interactions between calendars, screwdrivers, Coke bottles, and people that are the figurae of those larger categories. These objects provide a prism through which to view the novel's larger reconstruction of Tayo's identity because their historical and cultural significance, as well as their capacity for being rearranged, enacts a remaking of the two categories that seem to exert the most pressure on him: white and Laguna Pueblo.

"IT IS THE PEOPLE WHO BELONG TO THE MOUNTAIN"

What should be clear by now is that Tayo cannot simply be stranded "between these two worlds" of whiteness and Nativeness because they do not exist in that static, totalizing sense. As with Spurgeon's analysis in *Exploding the Western*, many postmodern readings of *Ceremony* tend to reify familiar social categories by misunderstanding Paula Gunn Allen's basic ideas about harmony versus human mechanism in Native writing. In his book on Romantic theory and postmodernism, Lou Freitas Caton calls on Allen's *The Sacred Hoop* as a foil against which to argue that novels like *Ceremony* can be most productively read in terms of the trope of polarity. Caton turns to Allen as a critical opponent because she suggests that Tayo's sickness arises from a non-Native view of the world that results in a "separation from the ancient unity of person, ceremony, and land."[49] Caton's basic disagreement with Allen arises from a dispute over the idea that Native cultures understand the world in holistic, organic terms while Western cultures understand the world in separatist, fragmented terms. Caton wants to find a similarity between these two views by arguing for a Western vision of unity in disunity. But the problem with his reliance on the binary of dualism and organicism is that such an approach misreads Allen's embrace of wholeness and resistance to dualism. Allen's and other critics' rejections of this brand of polarity do not arise out of some naïve ignorance of the fact that "cultural difference needs to be arbitrated within a field of commonality in order to exist as a coherent, albeit diverse, collection of works," as Caton argues.[50] Instead, this juxtaposition of wholeness to dualism stems from a legitimate concern over how such views of the world tend to reduce opposing cultures to their lowest common denominators to identify both difference and similarity. Allen does not buy into critical approaches like Caton's because such positions necessarily define Native peoples in static terms. The view of the world Allen identifies in *Ceremony* is both constructed in the material sense and also holistic, much like the webs woven by Thought-Woman, the spider, throughout the novel.

Thus, to suggest, as Caton does, that "Tayo's recovery hinges on replacing constructed beliefs with organic beliefs; he becomes healthy because he grows to feel an inherent relationship between all life forms" is to misread Betonie's healing ceremony.[51] To pitch constructed beliefs against organic beliefs is to misunderstand construction, and also to conflate constructed with whiteness and organic with Nativeness. Silko's representations of Native cultures do not contrast "constructed" and "organic." What the materiality of the ceremony reveals instead is that whiteness and Laguna Puebloness are both processes that are constantly affected and altered by the actors out of which they are made, and that, in turn, the resultant networks also change the actors themselves and their subsequent influence on other networks. Following the healing ceremony, Silko makes this materialist process clear in her depiction of a folding steel chair kept in the meetinghouse on Tayo's reservation. Tayo appears before a council of elders to update them on his health, and, as he enters the kiva, "The old men nodded at a folding steel chair with ST. JOSEPH MISSION stenciled in white paint on the back. He sat down, wondering how far the chair had gone from the parish hall before it came to the kiva" (256). The chair was once presumably one among many folding steel chairs from the St. Joseph Mission, but it now props Tayo up in front of the Laguna elders who occupy the room alongside "boxes and trunks with tarps pulled over them to protect them from uninitiated eyes" (256). Although the St. Joseph Mission has spray-painted its name on the chair, even this designation cannot contain the object. Tayo wonders about the chair's trajectory, imagining the path it has taken to Laguna "from the parish hall." The chair seems endowed with some agency as it makes its way from the St. Joseph's Mission to the kiva at Laguna through a journey Tayo cannot fathom, and yet here it is, providing him with a seat as he tells the story of his healing ceremony.

What we do not discover is how far the chair might possibly go beyond the kiva. The chair as actor certainly plays an important part in Tayo's ceremony as it supports him during the final stages, but considering how far the object has come, it seems fair to point out that its story is also in process. Who knows where the chair might end up next, or how it might affect some other situation? As Womack explains, "The objects of my perceptions, nonetheless, have their own stories, not just the ones I impose on them."[52] Betonie says something similar at the beginning of the ceremony when discouraging Tayo from blaming his illness on white people: "'Look,' Betonie said, pointing east to Mount Taylor towering dark blue with the last twilight. 'They only fool themselves when they think it is theirs. The deeds and papers don't mean anything. It is the people who belong to the mountain'" (128). Much like the caretakers at St. Joseph's sought to claim the chair by branding it with the name of the mission, the philosophy of private property has led those who pushed across North America to title the land to themselves by recording their names on pieces of paper. In both cases, the relationship between material object and human subject is more complicated than anyone anticipates because the things have "stories alive in them," as Betonie says. The nonhuman actors have agency in the lives of human actors. Nowhere is this insight more important than in the moment when a group of cowboys hired to protect private land happen upon

Tayo searching for his uncle's stolen cattle. They apprehend him, but the mountain provides a mountain lion, and the men are more interested in tracking the rare animal, so they abandon Tayo.

In this scene, both whiteness and Nativeness are cast as products of these characters' respective relationships with the material world: "the destroyers had tricked the white people as completely as they had fooled the Indians, [. . .] But the effects were hidden, evident only in the sterility of their art, which continued to feed off the vitality of other cultures, and in the dissolution of their consciousness into dead objects: the plastic and neon, the concrete and steel" (204). The cowboys think of the mountain itself—"these goddamn Indians got to learn whose property this is!"—and the lion—"greasers and Indians— we can run them down anytime. But it's been a couple of years since anybody up here got a mountain lion"—in different terms, and this is what separates them from Tayo (202). The primacy of this relationship to the material is crystalized through Silko's characterization of Emo, another Indian veteran, who attempts to kill Tayo. Emo's relation to the material world resembles the cowboys' much more than it resembles Tayo's. Whenever the Indian veterans gather to drink at a local bar, Emo always eventually breaks out his prize trophy from the war: a Bull Durham tobacco pouch filled with human teeth. One night Emo pours the teeth out onto the table and pushes "them into circles and rows like unstrung beads; he scoop[s] them into his hand and [shakes] them like dice" (60). The teeth are described as Emo's souvenirs, and we are told that they come from the corpse of a Japanese soldier. Much like the cowboys, Emo wants to arrest these objects in time and space. He maintains them as a physical connection to the war that, for a moment, allowed him, a Native person, to be American in the eyes of those who consider themselves to be American.

Whiteness and Nativeness are thus not fictitious or stable categories into which individual human actors can be neatly situated. Instead, whiteness and Nativeness are literal, material processes. Emo clings to the teeth because they remind him of how white people in the army thought of him: "he was the best, they told him; some men didn't like to feel the quiver of the man they were killing; some men got sick when they smelled the blood. But he was the best; he was one of them. The best. United States Army" (62). If whiteness and Nativeness were a priori markers, then Emo's bag of human teeth would operate differently because Emo is a Native person. In other words, the novel as a whole is working toward the in-process nature of Native identity, and Silko accomplishes this representation, in part, by aligning a Native character more closely with white people than with his "fellow" Natives in terms of his relationship to the material. Laguna Puebloness is not only a matter of blood or skin, as we know Emo looks down on Tayo for being "part white," a "half-breed" (57). Emo is ostensibly not of mixed-blood, yet it is clear by the novel's end that Tayo is a more ideal representative of Laguna Pueblo than Emo, who participates in two killings and is finally banished from the reservation by the same elders who bear witness to Tayo's healing after the ceremony. "White," "Native," "American," and "Laguna," are, in fact, the products of material circumstances and the interactions of human and nonhuman actors, including, but not limited to, parentage and birth. Emo does not somehow become less Laguna Pueblo, but he can be read as a character who both undermines and distorts the construction of whiteness and Laguna Pueblo through his engagement with the material domain of the novel. Emo relies on his ancestry to establish him as Native, but conforms his desires to those of the people he imagines as "real" Americans. In doing so, he contributes to the construction of whiteness and to the conflation of whiteness and Americanness. At the novel's end we find Tayo more closely aligned with the elders at Laguna, and Emo with the soldiers who lusted after death and counted bloodshed as an indicator of Americanness during the war.

This distinction relies on a willingness to change our perception of the relationship between human and nonhuman actors and of the concept of construction. Returning to Betonie's claim that it is not the mountain that belongs to the people, but "the people who belong to the mountain," *Ceremony* reveals that human actors are not merely producers, consumers, and users of nonhuman actors, but that we "belong" to the same network. Without this reconstructive agency, the social cannot truly be remade because the variables of the equation (static categories such as white, Laguna, American) always remain the same, even when rearranged into different configurations. When the variables always remain the same, then no matter how they are organized, the equation will always only produce some combination of those variables. What makes social construction significant is its commitment to revealing both how those variables themselves are products of more quotidian material interactions and how there is not such a large gap between the significance of human subjects and material objects as actors in the formation of individual and collective in-process identities, a flattening of ontology that I explore in the next chapter.

MATERIAL EFFECTS AND CAUSES

Social construction is not at odds with either fluidity or essence; it simply foregrounds the actors that reveal both as material processes. To say that an identity, for instance, is constructed is to acknowledge that it is *in medias res*, or to point out that it is "processual," to borrow a term from Weaver.[53] What *Ceremony*'s interest in scraps of cloth, calendars, steel chairs, and screwdrivers reveals is that Laguna Pueblo, American, Navajo, and white are in-process assemblages, not paint-by-number groupings or artificial-theoretical concepts. The formal structure of the novel itself reflects this commitment to process, as even its conclusion is a beginning. The books opens with a poem and then the word "Sunrise," which is suspended alone on the second page. While we might expect the novel to end with "sunset," it ends instead with, "Sunrise, / accept this offering, / Sunrise" (262). Rather than reducing this aesthetically experimental feature to the context of first-stage postmodernism or the novel's political preoccupation with identity to second-stage postmodernism, I find it more productive to consider how Silko's novel actually prompts a revision of such orthodoxies of postmodernism through its materialization of social construction. Acknowledging *Ceremony*'s material construction of identities is not simply to incorporate either the writer or her work into the critical tradition of postmodern American writing, but to consider how Silko's contribution to a Native American literature might compel us to reimagine central conventions of American literary discourse in general and postmodernism in particular.

Perhaps the most immediate payoff of rethinking social construction in this way, then, comes in the form of a revised approach for understanding the two so-called stages of postmodernism. Rather than collapsing the two stages of postmodernism, as Steiner and Green do in their respective ways, we must come to terms with the material causes and effects of this split and understand the split itself as both cause and effect. McGurl makes the most productive move in this direction when he identifies the creative writing program as a material context for the production of "high cultural pluralism," but this theory is finally a more sophisticated attempt to write the divergent stages out of literary history. In contrast, retheorizing social construction as a resolutely material phenomenon helps us see how the two generations of postmodernism are themselves products of material processes. In this case, the figures and practices of literary criticism separated the recognizable group of postmodern writers into two distinct camps based, in part, on their own conceptions of how everyday objects organize the lives of human subjects. If this claim seems a stretch, then consider the critical genealogy of postmodernism. From Irving Howe to Andreas Huyssen to Linda Hutcheon, theorists have characterized postmodernism in terms of its antimodern aesthetic and political response to the mass-produced cultural artifacts of a consumer society, and what are these artifacts ultimately but the Barbie dolls, records, reprints, and refrigerator magnets of everyday life? "The diversity of mass culture," Huyssen points out as early as the mid-1980s, "was now recognized and analyzed by critics who increasingly began to work themselves out from under the modernist dogma that all mass culture is monolithic Kitsch." And here, without the aesthetic/political coding that we see in Elias, Hogue, Steiner, and other twenty-first-century critics, Huyssen notes,

> It was especially the art, writing, film-making and criticism of women and minority artists with their recuperation of buried and mutilated traditions, their emphasis on exploring forms of gender- and race-based subjectivity in aesthetic productions and experiences, and their refusal to be limited to standard canonizations, which added a whole new dimension to the critique of high modernism and to the emergence of alternative forms of culture.[54]

Huyssen provides a model of postmodernism that does not rely on the standard two-phase structure. He reads these women writers and writers of color as fundamentally invested in rewriting "mutilated traditions" and transgressing "standard canonizations." In other words, before the two-phase structure was popularized, critics like Huyssen saw so-called political writers of the second phase doing the experimental rewriting of history commonly associated with the first phase. The camps, stages, or phases of postmodernism are not a priori categories into which writers should be funneled, nor are they merely artificial or fictitious collectives. They have become commonplace, for better or worse, because of differences in the ways critics and writers have understood and shaped postmodernism itself—at least in part in its relationship to the actual things that give rise to concepts like mass production and commodification.

There is no need to undo the divide (is such a project possible?), but neither must we simply accept it as somehow unproblematic. The point is that it has been materially constructed over time, and our challenge is to come to terms with this process so as not to misunderstand the deep disparities in experience and voice it represents. To say that the stages of postmodernism are social constructs, then, is not to say that they are somehow inorganic or inauthentic, any more than it is to say that *Ceremony*'s construction of whiteness or Nativeness is artificial. Social constructs are made out of things, and the work of the critic of postmodern literature and culture is to understand these things and their associations. As an orthodoxy of postmodernism, social construction is resolutely material and fundamentally processual. It precludes postmodernism from being a periodizing or aesthetic marker that can be easily divided along gendered or racialized lines, and instead emphasizes such social markers as effects of material circumstances without dismissing their ability to serve as causes to other effects. Thus, for Native writers and critics like Gerald Vizenor or Kimberly Blaeser, concerned with the reduction of "Indian" to a static and stereotypical avatar, a materialized theory of social construction can illuminate the ways in which Nativeness is adapting to, changing, shaping, and being shaped by material contexts over time. Likewise, for those like Craig Womack or Jace Weaver, who are wary of disconnecting "Indian" from its material references, this view of social construction allows for how the fluidity of Nativeness is always an adaptation or change in association with concrete, everyday material domains.

This redefinition of social construction walks a fine line, balancing between the need to account for the processual nature of the collectives we typically call social, while also validating and explaining the material effects that categories like race and nation produce in the everyday lives of characters in books and people in the world. After all, predominant representations of race in the United States, for instance, certainly affect the experiences of its occupants in very material ways on a daily basis. However, to treat race as a settled rubric whose various subcategories are reliable in helping us organize our relations to the world and each other can paper over the ways in which race is constantly under construction. As critical race theorists have shown specifically in the dynamic of white and non-white relations, "In one era, a group of color may be depicted as happy-go-lucky, simpleminded, and content to serve white folks. A little later, when conditions change, that very same group may appear in cartoons, movies, and other cultural scripts as menacing, brutish, and out of control, requiring close monitoring and repression."[55] Such problematic and shifting understandings of race are grounded, I would argue, in the concept of otherness, which privileges difference as the defining trait of identity and has been sanctioned as a postmodern orthodoxy. I will return to otherness in Chapter 4, but first I need to reexamine the nature of and relationship between the very actors out of which the social is constructed in literature: the subjects and objects that populate the worlds of fiction. The critical discourse of postmodernism has upheld a long tradition of opposing subject and object, culture and nature, which a materialist view of social construction asks us to reconsider. In the next chapter, I explore this most fundamental of binaries in postmodern fiction to demonstrate how a materialist reading offers a much flatter view of postmodern ontology.

Chapter 2

Flattening Nature and Culture

"There *is* a real world; its properties are *not* merely social constructions; facts and evidence *do* matter. What sane person would contend otherwise?"[1] Physicist Alan Sokal's non-question may seem like a non-starter, but as the wave of postmodernism crashed in the mid-1990s his voice represented the frustrations of many intellectuals across the ideological spectrum. Sokal's infamous contribution to a special "Science Wars" issue of *Social Text* in 1996 gave voice to these frustrations and set off a firestorm in the academic community. Andrew Ross, one of the journal's editors, explains in his introduction to the special issue that cultural studies' interest in the hard sciences is essentially an interest in "the rise of a privatized knowledge society" that "creates a hierarchy of technical expertise and, in particular, releases scientists from public accountability on the grounds that their critics 'just don't know enough.' "[2] The editors were especially concerned with the language of objectivity and authority associated with the sciences in light of their ties to governments, corporations, and political organizations: "If scientific knowledge is not beholden to market forces," Ross asks, "why is it that geologists know more about oil-bearing strata than other strata, or that virologists know more about viruses that attack tobacco than about other strains?"[3] Sokal, on the other hand, perceived those in cultural studies as proponents of a facile relativism that denies the existence of an "external reality." The physicist wanted to see if "a leading North American journal of cultural studies [would] publish an article liberally salted with nonsense if *(a)* it sounded good and *(b)* it flattered the editors' ideological preconceptions."[4] So he composed such an article and sent it to the editors as a general submission. Ross eventually included Sokal's "Transgressing the Boundaries: Toward a Transformative Hermeneutics of Quantum Gravity" in the "Science Wars" issue. When his work was accepted, it seems Sokal's worst fears—and greatest hopes—were confirmed. The hoax was revealed in an essay Sokal published in the May–June 1996 installment of *Lingua Franca* in which he provides numerous examples of factual inaccuracies, ludicrous claims, and unsupported conclusions from his own article, and characterizes the *Social Text* crowd and their ilk as examples of "the intellectual arrogance of Theory—postmodernist *literary* theory, that is—carried to its logical extreme."[5] *Lingua Franca* then invited a response to Sokal from Ross and fellow *Social Text* editor Bruce Robbins, followed by yet another answer from Sokal, and finally a host of comments from academics in a variety of disciplines. In his initial confession, Sokal explains that the root of his anger is buried in the Left's abandonment of two centuries of scientific progressivism: "we have believed that rational thought and fearless analysis of objective reality (both natural and social) are incisive tools for combating the mystifications promoted by the powerful." He views Robbins and Ross as representatives of an epistemic relativism that "betrays this worthy heritage and undermines the already fragile prospects for progressive social critique."[6] Robbins and Ross respond by clarifying their intentions toward the hard sciences: "Why does science matter so much to us? Because its power, as a civil religion, as a social and political authority, affects our daily lives and the parlous condition of the natural world more than does any other domain of knowledge."[7] These two camps represent what Ian Bogost and Levi Bryant recognize as the two dominant ways of thinking about the world today: scientific naturalism and social constructivism.[8] The first holds that matter constitutes and can explain everything. The second looks to human perception as the primary explanation for everything. While the "Sokal hoax" and other high-theory happenings may have mercifully disappeared in the critical rearview mirror, this two-sided battle, as represented in the Sokal/Ross volley, continues to confuse the legacy of postmodernism by maintaining a problematic opposition between nature and culture.

What is most interesting about these hostile positions is that their bulwarks are built on philosophical common ground. Tracing the history of the scientific naturalism/social constructivism conflict, Bogost points out that its roots are sunk deep in the Western tradition, the first side beginning with Democritus and Epicurus, the second side running coterminous with the humanistic tradition itself. "That the two sides have so long argued about how to approach worldly knowledge," Bogost marvels, "has only shrouded the real problem. To wit: both perspectives embody the correlationist conceit."[9] That is, both understand nonhuman entities' existence primarily in terms of human beings; nature exists for culture. In the case of the Sokal hoax, both Sokal and the *Social Text* editors seem committed to a basic division between the human relations they think of as social and the nonhuman world they imagine as natural. Sokal's correlationism shows up in his characterization of "objective reality" as having "both natural and social" dimensions. Ross and Robbins's correlationism is evident in their distinction between the human phenomenon of science as a "social and political authority" that affects the "condition of the natural world." The crux of the exchange between the two camps concerns the nature of the relationship between these two worlds. Sokal accuses Ross and Robbins of disregarding the natural world in favor of dwelling on the social as a filter for knowledge, while Ross and Robbins launch a counteroffensive against scientists like Sokal for failing to see that their scientific certainty about the natural world is always situated within a cultural context. In the heat of battle, both camps draw a line between what Levi Bryant calls "the world of nature and the world of the subject and culture."[10]

Are humans not a part of nature? If I jump into a lake created by the Army Corps of Engineers, will I get any less wet than if I jump into a lake formed by the slow movement of a glacier over the course of millennia? If marine biologists sink a ship to create an artificial reef, is there a statute of limitations on the reef's artificiality? Do the sea creatures who live in that reef live in an artificial world? What about the hunter-gatherers of Papua New Guinea? Do they live in a world less contrived than the inhabitants of Manhattan? What world is this, after all, and what is the place of humans in this world? Such ontological questions about the relationship between nature and culture are nothing new to literary studies of postmodernism. Brian McHale provides what has been perhaps the most productive framework for thinking through such questions in his theory of the "ontological dominant" of postmodern fiction. McHale draws the concept of the dominant from the work of the Russian Formalists Jurij Tynjanov and Roman Jakobson, the latter of which defines it as "the focusing component of a work of art" that "rules, determines, and transforms the remaining components."[11] As an alternative to theories of postmodern literature built on catalogs of aesthetic features and/or ideological commitments, the dominant "can both elicit the systems underlying these heterogeneous catalogs, and begin to account for historical change." For McHale, then, the focusing component of postmodern fiction is "the ontology of the literary text itself or the ontology of the world which it projects."[12] Unlike modernist fiction, which he asserts is preoccupied with epistemological questions, postmodern fiction is predominantly concerned with ontological questions. In short, the theory of the dominant allows McHale to distinguish postmodern fiction from modernist fiction without forcing him to argue that postmodernism abandons the aesthetic practices of modernism or that it develops entirely new features. Instead, the concept of the dominant facilitates the larger historical claim that there has simply been a recognizable shift in which aesthetic practices and features are most important, and that the shift can be productively called "postmodernism."

In the trenches of writing, reading, and analyzing literary texts, McHale refers to postmodern fiction's ontological dominant as an "ontological perspectivism" through which some literary texts disrupt, or come between, "the text-continuum (the language and style of the text) and the reader's reconstruction of its world." The nature/culture binary is a blind spot in this ontological perspectivism, a lacuna somewhere between "the *process* of construction and its *product*, the thing constructed."[13] What occupies this blind spot are the *materials*, both nonhuman and human, out of which the *product* is produced through the construction *process*. But the significance of these materials has been overlooked as the result of theoretical approaches that continue to make unchallenged distinctions between culture and nature and that privilege the human over the nonhuman. Literary fiction of the last half century can be read as shying away from this bifurcation. What makes fiction postmodern in my view is not only its preoccupation with the ontological realm, as McHale suggests, but also its tendency to flatten its ontological worlds through an emphasis on the agency and significance of everyday objects. In other words, ontology is not only dominant in postmodern fiction but also flat. If postmodern fiction's ontological dominant is essentially a flat ontology, then in the worlds of these texts, everyday things play roles that are equally important as those of the most significant human characters.

I have covered the basics of flat ontology in the Introduction, but to reframe it in the context of the ontological dominant, I would simply say that a flat ontology is one that makes no distinction between things that exist in terms of their existence. "In short," Bogost explains, *"all things equally exist, yet they do not exist equally."*[14] That is to say, of course a ring is not the same thing as a person or a pencil, and none of these entities must necessarily be valued equally, but in terms of their basic being they occupy the same ontological plane. This flattened ontology dissolves the natural/social binary that has plagued the discourse of postmodernism in a simple but fundamental way by abandoning the ontologically distinctive domains of the subject and the object in favor of what Bryant calls "a single plane of being populated by a variety of different types of objects including humans and societies." Bryant refers to the gatherings of humans and nonhumans alike as "collectives," where "society and nature do not form two separate and entirely distinct domains that must never cross. Rather, collectives involving humans are always entangled with all sorts of nonhumans without which such collectives could not exist."[15] Bryant's notion of the collective proves helpful in the ontological worlds of postmodern fiction because it provides a framework for recognizing and considering the roles that nonhumans play in the formation of those networks of relation that we humans typically call "social." Although Bryant, Bogost, and many of the object-oriented philosophers are especially interested in the possibilities of collectives that have absolutely nothing to do with humans, my focus here is on the kinds of collectives that do involve humans, specifically those that have typically been figured as preexisting, static social categories such as race, class, nation, gender, and so on. But the possibility of collectives that do not include humans is vital to this study because the kind of truly flat ontology that imagines humans and nonhumans as ontological equals can only be possible if we are willing to accept the prospect of networks in which humans do not play a significant role.

To develop a flat ontological perspectivism in postmodern fiction, I want to begin with a brief analysis of a ring in Jonathan Safran Foer's *Everything Is Illuminated* (2002) before moving on to examine the roles of significant objects in Toni Morrison's *Jazz* (1992) and Jonathan Lethem's *The Fortress of Solitude* (2003). As it happens, the significant object in each of these novels is also a ring, and there is a fortuitous symmetry in tracing a singular kind of thing across multiple texts to see what kinds of arrangements are possible. Foer's flattened ontology immediately pulls us out of the abstractions that accompany philosophy and theory, rendering the agency of a nonhuman actor palpable. The purpose of this first textual reading is to draw my theory of postmodern fiction's flattened ontological dominant from the world of a novel to allow the various human and nonhuman actors to define their collective(s) in relation to one another. The result is a radical decentering of humans as the loci of social networks. This decentering of humans lays the groundwork for rethinking the nature of the larger collectives that are typically acknowledged with a generalizing whisk of the hand as "social" explanations. The purposes of this chapter are (1) to establish the flattened ontology of postmodern fiction by leveling the playing field between humans and nonhumans in Foer's work; (2) to illustrate the process by which seemingly unfamiliar persons and things are assembled through the metaphor of jazz that drives the narrative structure of Morrison's novel; and (3) to compare and contrast the possibilities and consequences of a flattened ontology with an ontology that remains dependent on familiar social categories in Lethem's fictional world. The result is a new approach to postmodern fiction, one not dependent on the nature/culture binary and thus able to, as Latour would say, reassemble the social.

DO THINGS ALWAYS EXIST FOR HUMANS?

Everything Is Illuminated tells the story of a young man named Jonathan Safran Foer, who travels from the United States to Ukraine in search of the small shtetl from which his grandfather escaped during the cancerous expansion of Hitler's Third Reich. The journey is narrated through three main components: a book being written by Jonathan's young

Ukrainian tour guide, Alex Perchov; letters from Alex to Jonathan; and fantastical sections devoted to a history of the shtetl itself, written by Jonathan. These narratives finally collide late in the novel as Jonathan, Alex, and Alex's grandfather discover the place where the shtetl formerly stood. All that remains is a single house occupied by a single old woman they believe to be the young girl named Augustine from a photo Jonathan was given by his grandmother. The house is filled with things, Alex tells us in his unique brand of English:

> There were many boxes, which were overflowing with items. These had writing on their sides. A white cloth was overwhelming from the box marked WEDDINGS AND OTHER CELEBRATIONS. The box marked PRIVATES: JOURNALS/ DIARIES/SKETCHBOOKS/UNDERWEAR was so overfilled that it appeared prepared to rupture. There was another box, marked SILVER/PERFUME/PINWHEELS, and one marked WATCHES/WINTER, and one marked HYGIENE/SPOOLS/ CANDLES and one marked FIGURINES/SPECTACLES.[16]

At first the many things in the jam-packed house seem obvious symbolic representations of the destroyed shtetl, and yet as some of the contents of these boxes are unpacked and the stories of the items are told, the relationship between things and persons takes an unexpected turn.

Among the many "queer things like combs, rings, and flowers," the woman pulls a wedding ring from a box labeled "REMAINS." She recalls that her friend had buried the ring inside a jar and told her "just in case." She then insists that Jonathan take with him a box labeled "IN CASE." Jonathan says to her, through Alex, that he cannot possibly take the box, and the following exchange ensues between the woman, Alex (the narrator), and Jonathan (the hero) which bears reproducing at length here:

> "I did not understand why Rivka hid her wedding ring in the jar, and why she said to me, Just in case. Just in case and then what? What?" "Just in case she was killed," I said. "Yes, and then what? Why should the ring be any different?" "I do not know," I said. "Ask him," she said. "She wants to know why her friend saved her

wedding ring when she thought that she would be killed." "So there would be proof that she existed," the hero said. "What?" "Evidence. Documentation. Testimony." I told this to Augustine. "But a ring is not needed for this. People can remember without the ring. And when those people forget, or die, then no one will know about the ring." I told this to the hero. "But the ring could be a reminder," he said. "Every time you see it, you think of her." I told Augustine what the hero said. "No," she said. "I think it was in case of this. In case someone should come searching one day." I could not perceive if she was speaking to me or to the hero. "So that we would have something to find," I said. "No," she said. "The ring does not exist for you. You exist for the ring. The ring is not in case of you. You are in case of the ring."¹⁷

The ring does not exist to be found by Jonathan and Alex. They can only comprehend the object in relation to their quest, but its existence and significance cannot be explained in terms of their search for the shtetl. Here Foer explores our tendency to appropriate the nonhuman for human purposes. The ring resists any such attempts as evidenced by the fact that it refuses to fit on Jonathan's finger:

> She attempted to put it on the hero's finger, but it did not harmonize, so she attempted to put it on his most petite finger, but it still did not harmonize. "She had small hands," the hero said. "She had small hands," I told Augustine. "Yes," she said, "so small." She again attempted to put the ring on the hero's little finger, and she applied very rigidly, and I could perceive that this made the hero with many kinds of pain, although he did not exhibit even one of them. "It will not harmonize," she said, and when she removed the ring I could see that the ring had made a cut around the hero's most petite finger.¹⁸

If the ring's significance was dependent upon its discovery by Jonathan and Alex, then it would certainly have slid easily onto our hero's finger in an Odyssean flash of revelation. But the object resists. It cannot simply be made to fit Jonathan's finger. In fact, it injures him, leaving a cut as evidence of its lack of "harmony" with his skin. The ring is the ultimate *thing* in this moment—its "thingness," in Bill Brown's parlance, made painfully obvious by its refusal to work for the characters in the novel.

I have chosen rings as the focalizing things of this chapter because they are substantively natural and unavoidably social at the same time. They are typically made of metals found in nature, such as gold or silver, and yet these natural materials are fashioned into perfect circles, signifying class status or relationships between humans. Rings refuse the natural/social binary. They exist only a few degrees Fahrenheit from losing their circular forms. Is a melted ring still a ring? We invest them with meaning, but the ring does not necessarily take on these meanings. A wedding ring may be lost and picked up by stranger who sells it for cash. It is then melted down and becomes part of a gold bar or a necklace. Does it still represent love and fidelity? To what extent was the love and fidelity it once represented actually formed by the ring itself? The woman who loses her ring is accused by her partner of not wearing it on purpose. The partner becomes jealous, believes she is cheating. Their love tarnishes. The separation between natural and social is not as neat and clean as Alan Sokal or even the *Social Text* crowd imagines. The social is a constant product of the more quotidian material interactions of persons and things. The ontological dominant of postmodern fiction can be read as a preoccupation with these material interactions. Rather than asking epistemological questions about social arrangements that seem like the irreducible building blocks of our larger societies, postmodern fiction meditates on the flat ontological realm of people and things as the more fundamental constituents of the social.

Foer's particular brand of flat ontology demonstrates the agency of things to create history and memory where there was none. But the ring's resistance to Jonathan's intentions leaves us with the question of *how* nonhuman actors are able to accomplish this work. Through what means can humans exist in case of nonhumans? How can the hero of Foer's novel exist in case of the ring? In Brown's pioneering "Thing Theory" essay he raises questions not only about the nature of things, but also about "the subject-object relation in particular temporal and spatial contexts," questions he rightly thought, back at the turn of the millennium, might "precipitate a new materialism that takes objects for granted in order to grant them their potency—to show how they organize our private and public affection."[19] In the years since, Brown's hunch about a new materialism has proven well founded, even if many of the neomaterialists that populate the pages of this study would say that his vision relies too much on human access. But Brown's emphasis on the agency of nonhumans to organize the lives of humans opens the door for a radically flat ontology, and holds it open for an answer to my own questions about how people can exist in case of things. Brown wonders about how things "organize our private and public affection," and while these affections may have served as markers of *subjectivity* under the nature/social binary, they are also *subject to* the properties and circulation of objects under a flat ontology. Humans and nonhumans alike interact in complex networks of desire. Since we cannot desire something or someone whose existence is entirely unknown to us, then desire must, in some way, always be produced by that which is desired. Once desire is kindled, the actions that are taken to fulfill that desire might be attributed to the desired thing, person, or even effect. This process of desire resembles the heart of any jazz music composition, in which the desire for musical freedom and novelty draws familiar notes and melodies into spontaneously reimagined, even unrepeatable, relationships, and so I turn now to Toni Morrison's novel that bears the title *Jazz* to consider how yet another ring organizes the lives of humans, blurring the lines between nature and culture.

IMPROVISING THE SOCIAL

The late Billy Taylor, iconic musician, educator, and activist, describes jazz music as "spontaneous composition," implying the constant and immediate assembly and reassembly of recognizable components into ever-new configurations. Taylor elaborates in a Kennedy Center lecture, arguing that "most people have a wrong idea of what improvisation is. Improvisation is spontaneous composition, and in order to compose spontaneously you have to have some sense of form. You have to have a sense of content. You have to know the language that you're using."[20] If we take Miles Davis's rendition of "Autumn Leaves" as a case study, then what we find in the typical jazz composition is the performance of a familiar melody by Davis on the trumpet, followed by a series of improvisations of this melody played on other instruments until Davis finally cuts back in, returning to the original melody. Thus, the heart of any jazz number is the spontaneous reassembly of the various components of the familiar melody into new configurations. This understanding of jazz music provides an illuminating rationale for the title and structure Morrison chooses for her 1992 novel *Jazz*, which Marcel Cornis-Pope has described as "interested in re-creating rather than merely representing black experience."[21] Jazz improvisation spontaneously composes—meaning literally that it gathers in the moment—notes that have typically been connected in familiar configurations into arrangements ranging from the eerily similar to the utterly unrecognizable. The mathematically endless possibilities of this form highlight the value of its "in-processness," and uncover its flexibility to account for unexpected changes.

In an interview given the year after *Jazz* was published, Morrison says of the novel that she "put the whole plot on the first page. In fact, in the first edition the plot was on the cover, so that a person in a bookstore could read the cover and know right away what the book was about."[22] In the span of the first five sentences, Morrison's enigmatic narrator does, indeed, give away the book's central conflict as well as its resolution:

> Sth, I know that woman. She used to live with a flock of birds on Lenox Avenue. Know her husband, too. He fell for an eighteen-year-old girl with one of those deepdown, spooky loves that made him so sad and happy he shot her just to keep the feeling going. When the woman, her name is Violet, went to the funeral to see the girl and to cut her dead face they threw her to the floor and out of the church.[23]

This plot is the familiar melody. The early revelation of the narrative's driving events and entities frees Morrison to construct a jazz-inspired meditation on the historical complexities that have set this plot in motion. The novel is resolutely historical and structurally "jazz-like," as Morrison herself has described it,[24] because like any good jazz number it supplies us with the familiar melody up front and then proceeds to improvise on that melody, offering a variety of renditions and perspectives from different instruments and voices before finally returning to the original melody, which we then hear with new ears. *Jazz* begins with the tragic story of Joe Trace, his wife Violet Trace, and Joe's affair with Dorcas Manfred. It then moves on through a series of historical retellings of key moments in these characters' lives, and ends after Dorcas's death with the new trio of Joe Trace, Violet Trace, and Dorcas's friend Felice. However, what is significant about the return to what sounds like the original melody at the end of the novel—in which Felice has replaced Dorcas in the triangular relationship with Joe and Violet—is that the intervening improvisations have had a profound effect on this familiar story; they have, in fact, changed the tune. But what has been overlooked in readings of this complex narrative is the essential role of nonhumans in the success of its composition, and of one object in particular: an opal ring given to Felice by her mother.

This everyday item drives characters in the novel to do unexpected things and bears witness to unspeakable events: it instigates theft, causes a daughter to question her mother, witnesses murder, and draws a young woman to the house of her best friend's killer. Most readings of *Jazz*, however, tend to focus on either the novel's mysterious narrator or its complicated narrative structure. Critics have argued that the narrator could be anything or anyone from a recent immigrant to the city to the city itself to some incarnation of jazz music.[25] Morrison herself, in an interview with *Belle Lettres*, has said "the voice is the voice of a talking book," identifying the book as its own narrator.[26] The narrative structure can be as difficult to follow as an improvisation of a familiar tune.[27] In any jazz composition, it is the familiarity of the original melody that renders the improvisations abstract. In other words, the assemblages that take place in the midst of what Billy Taylor calls "spontaneous composition" only strike us as new, unfamiliar, or difficult to follow because we know the original melody so well. Nancy J. Peterson is helpful here, as she argues that the narrative revisions of Golden Gray's story, one of the novel's many narrative threads, are not examples of the narrator's willingness "to overlook Golden Gray's faults," but of how the "commitment to looking again brings more details into the picture, which pose[s] new contradictions, and thus her former narrative can no longer offer neat evaluations."[28] Peterson's insight is so instructive because it demonstrates that the improvisational narrative structure not only brings us back to the absences and presences of history, but also complicates our understanding of the present.

Past and present must both be composed out of something, however, just as jazz improvisation is composed out of the notes from a familiar melody. After all, to compose is not to create *ex nihilo* but to gather various pieces together. The opal ring is a vital thing in the composition of the novel's present. Morrison uses the ring to join her disparate narratives together and then transition back into the novel's central story. After Dorcas's funeral, her friend Felice goes to the Traces' home in search of the opal ring she had loaned the dead woman. Felice strikes up a friendship with Joe and Violet, and they invite her back for dinner on another occasion. As the novel winds down, Joe, Violet, and Felice are cultivating a friendship that does not seem destined to end in the way we might expect given Joe's track record with Dorcas. In fact, as Peterson has pointed out, "Violet, Joe, and Felice do not reenact the lover's triangle that previously led to tragedy. They instead make possible a future for themselves." Peterson even remarks on the ring, noting that "Felice initially comes to the Traces' apartment to get some help in recovering the opal ring from her mother that she had lent to Dorcas and to tell Joe not to be so broken up about Dorcas."[29] What I want to emphasize here is the centrality of the ring as an actor in remaking the story's central melody. Lest we overlook the significance of the return to the triangular relationship that was laid out at the novel's beginning, Morrison insists in her "Art of Fiction" interview with the *Paris Review* that "the jazz-like structure wasn't a secondary thing for me—it was the raison d'étre of the book."[30] Without Felice's need to search for the ring, she does not ascend the steps of Joe's and Violet's building, she does not inquire after her ring, she is not invited inside, or questioned, or engaged in conversation, or asked to return. The characters do not "make possible a future for themselves," as Peterson has so eloquently observed, without Felice's search for this singular object.

The ring first enters the narrative abruptly and without any contextual explanation when the narration is handed over for a time to Felice.

Felice explains that she grew up in her grandmother's house, as both of her parents worked in the neighboring town of Tuxedo and spent most of their time there and on trains between her grandmother's home and their boss's home: "When they'd come home, they'd kiss me and give me things, like my opal ring" (198). This moment marks the first mention of the ring in the entire novel, and then a few pages later, when recounting the local gossip about Violet Trace, Felice says of the gossips, "They're wrong about her. I went to look for my ring and there is nothing crazy about her at all" (202). Felice's story of the ring unfolds awkwardly, with her first mentioning the thing out of nowhere, implying that it has been lost, and only then diving backward into the object's complicated history. Immediately following her declaration of Violet's sanity, Felice exclaims, "I know my mother stole that ring," and proceeds to recount how the ring came into her possession as a gift from her mother following an embarrassing incident at Tiffany's. Felice and her mother visit the store to pick up a package for her mother's boss, and as they wait they look at a velvet tray filled with rings, trying some of them on. After a moment a man comes over and politely shakes his head. Felice's mother explains, "I'm waiting for a package for Mrs. Nicolson," and the man smiles and responds, "of course. It's just policy. We have to be careful" (202–203). Although Felice cannot say definitively that the ring is stolen, when her mother presents her with an identical piece the next morning, saying her boss had given it to her, Felice voices her suspicions, "Maybe they made lots of them, but I know my mother took it from the velvet tray" (203). Who could blame Felice's mother? She is an honest, hard-working woman doing her best for her children, someone who gives "quarters she finds on the seat to conductors on the trolley," someone "so honest she makes people laugh" (215). The clerk's suspicion seems so damaging and deadly because it is reproduced in Felice, who sees her mother's act as a kind of valor imposed upon her by the degradation of racial prejudice.

The ring might easily be read here as a symbol that enacts a critique of race. However, when we simply bracket and accept "race" as a familiar category, ignoring its constituent materials, we end up with the same old suspicious hermeneutic that reifies race as a static and known quantity in the first place. In other words, if we pay less attention to the ring itself than we do to the human actors and social categories we take for granted in this exchange, such as race, class, and gender, then of course we end up with a critique of race because we treat both whiteness and blackness as recognizable markers whose definitions are clear and undisputed. To read the ring as a mere interruption of the black/white binary is to tacitly accept the parameters of that binary as they have been narrated to us. But when we refuse to bracket social categories, the ring becomes an actor that mediates race. When we focus on the ring itself, rather than on the abstract systems of relation it might critique, we can begin to see how those abstract systems come into being. This reconstructing of the social is immediately obvious once we value the ring equally with the human actors in terms of the novel's narrative progression. What is less obvious, perhaps, is the new way of seeing herself that the ring creates for Felice.

The ring enables Felice to reimagine herself and her own agency as she juxtaposes her mother's reification of racial categories with Violet's aggressive sense of self. The dangers of challenging the ontological foundations of a familiar category such as race should not be overlooked, however. The goal is never to dismiss or ignore race. In fact, just the opposite is the case. The very real effects that such categories have on daily life drive this study, as they often seem incongruent with the perceptions that the categories themselves are the causes of these effects. In his cogent treatise on race and US fiction, Charles Johnson traces the African American literary lineage from the poetry of Phillis Wheatley and the personal narrative of Gustavus Vassa, through William Wells Brown's first novel, to the stories of Charles Chesnutt, the creative explosion of the Harlem Renaissance, and the full force and aftershocks of the Black Arts Movement. He summarizes the effects of this tradition by pointing out that black writers' concern with meaning and life in literature

> has led to the creation of various racial ideologies for the African experience. [...] There is an almost point-by-point correspondence among esthetics, social theory, and the conception of humanity here; but let us come down to cases: the problem with all this is that it is ideology. While ideology may create a fascinating

vision of the universe, and also fascinating literary movements, it closes off the free investigation of phenomena.[31]

With his finger on the pulse of the very problem I examine here, Johnson has called our attention to the circuitous difficulty of starting with race as a frame for understanding the social. I do not ignore the vast and serious implications of this concept in US literary history. Neither do I minimize race itself by asserting that it is "merely" constructed. As we have seen in the previous chapter, "constructed" does not mean artificial or inorganic for postmodern fiction. What I do emphasize are the material associations that constitute race, the most mundane objects and actions that might change a character's course of action. Every actor, human and nonhuman, is important, and when every actor matters, the rearrangement of even the most everyday things can alter the larger collectives we call social.

The ring juxtaposes Felice's mother with Violet by demonstrating that black folks' actions need not always be predicated on the actions of white folks. Although there is some agency in Felice's mother's theft of the ring as she defies the authority of the well-dressed clerk, she also manages to fulfill his every expectation of her as a black woman who is more likely to steal than the "normal" clientele, the white women for whom the rings are left out on the counter. In any analysis that separates object world from subject world, whiteness will remain unexamined; whiteness will equal agency and blackness will equal response because even the theft is a rejoinder, a rebellion, an act of spite, always already presupposing that Felice's mother's actions are unequal and opposite reactions to those of white people. From this perspective, the ring serves as a mere symbol, and this symbol always signifies the possibility of "white people" as a normative measuring stick and "black people" as a homogeneous shortcoming. Morrison throws this presumption into relief by creating the jammed-together term "whitepeople," which maps the tendency in the United States to speak of black people as a uniform group onto white people, but she also actively counters it by having Felice imagine how Violet would react to the scenario in Tiffany's.

Violet would not have stolen the ring, or at least she would not have stolen the ring and then claimed it was the fruit of a white woman's generosity. During Felice's initial visit to the Traces' apartment to look for the ring, Violet invites Felice to return the following Friday for dinner, and Felice agrees, although she does not truly plan to come back. On Thursday, however, she decides to go after recalling the way Violet had talked about the "me" inside herself during her previous visit: "The way she said it. Not like the 'me' was some tough somebody she had put together for a show. But like, like somebody she favored and could count on. A secret somebody you didn't have to feel sorry for or have to fight for" (210). The young woman is drawn to this aspect of Violet's being, especially because of the stark alternative it provides to her mother. Felice contrasts Violet's "secret somebody" with the honest "somebody" who would return lost quarters on the trolley and yet who needed to "steal a ring to get back at whitepeople and then lie and say it was a present from them" (210). Morrison resists the tendency to define blackness in opposition to whiteness and vice versa. Whiteness is not a given. Race, in this moment, is not an irreducible category that can be easily defined through negation, but a product of the ring's circulation among the various characters. This insight does not dismiss race as a concept or as a meaningful organizer of experience. After all, there is no question that Morrison places herself and her work squarely in the lineage of African American literature and history: "a very large part of my own literary heritage is the autobiography. In this country the print origins of black literature (as distinguished from the oral origins) were slave narratives."[32] But in Morrison's fiction this tradition is living, breathing, fluid, marked by its adaptability, strength, endurance, and resistance to stasis. Thus, blackness cannot simply be a response to the call of whiteness as it seems to be in Felice's mother's life. Instead, Violet's existence and identity as a black woman is built inductively from the ground up. The "me" inside her is the ongoing product of her experiences in the world and does not require justification or vindication in light of the experiences of others.

Blackness also cannot simply be a response to the call of whiteness because whiteness, too, is under construction. Despite its cultural status as virtually synonymous with American, David Roediger notes that whiteness has been fluid since the first Congress, who "voted in 1790 to require that a person be 'white' in order to become a naturalized citizen of the U.S. Difficulties arose when "the hopeless imprecision of the term left the courts with impossible problems of interpretation that stretched well into the twentieth century."[33] The definition of whiteness became a legal matter in the nation's early days, and the law's struggle to keep up with the fluidity of whiteness often causes it to obscure just how in-process whiteness is. This problem has been evident since the nineteenth century, when, as Ian Haney López points out, "White as a racial category underwent rapid transformation in the United States." Time and again, he continues, the courts have been "forced to recognize that the common knowledge about who was White had changed since the original restriction had been penned in 1790."[34] It was Morrison who helped turn the critical gaze on whiteness in America's literary imagination in her landmark study *Playing in the Dark*, where she examines how "the process of organizing American coherence through a distancing of Africanism became the operative mode of a new cultural hegemony." This cultural hegemony is largely defined by the conflation of whiteness with Americanness. Thus, whiteness becomes normative in a national context, creating the potential pitfall of a progressive theory of racialization and social construction that might not account for the processual nature of whiteness. "American means white," Morrison explains, "and Africanist people struggle to make the term applicable to themselves with ethnicity and hyphen after hyphen after hyphen."[35] Deferring recourse to racial categories and starting instead with materials like the ring can help us see the ways in which whiteness has also been defined through difference, through centuries of legal definition via negation. Morrison exposes this negation in *Jazz* by sending Felice's mother to Tiffany's on behalf of her boss, Mrs. Nicolson, whose absence from the scene constructs Felice's and her mother's blackness as a peculiar presence and her own whiteness, by contrast, as mere being.

Following the ring's trajectory through the novel takes us from Tiffany's to the Traces' apartment where, on Felice's second visit, we discover that the object was buried with Dorcas. This absence causes the object to operate much like Heidegger's famous jug. Returning for a moment to the distinction between "thing" and "object" discussed in the introduction, philosophers and theorists from Heidegger to Bill Brown have argued that we encounter things as "things" when they offer some form of resistance to human access or assert their autonomy in some way. Objects, on the other hand, are marked by human access. Heidegger argues, "the jug's thingness resides in its being *qua* vessel. We become aware of the vessel's holding nature when we fill the jug. The jug's bottom and sides obviously take on the task of holding. But not so fast! When we fill the jug with wine, do we pour the wine into the sides and bottom?"[36] The sides and bottom, or presence of the jug, or that which is human-made, do not constitute its thingness. The absence is what makes the thing a thing. So too with Morrison's ring. It is the void at a ring's center that makes it a ring, and the absence of the ring upon Felice's return to the Trace apartment illuminates its agency as a thing because even though the object of her quest is missing, Felice is left with the Traces and sets another date to return with records for which Joe promises to buy a Victrola so they can all dance. Joe and Violet's surname cannot be overlooked here as the trace of the previous love triangle between Joe, Violet, and Dorcas is picked up and reimagined in the burgeoning relationship between Joe, Violet, and Felice. Like any good jazz composition, the original melody is being resumed, but the familiar tune has been altered. This time the song will not end in death, as it did with Dorcas, whose name recalls the New Testament disciple whose death in the Acts of the Apostles was marked by extreme mourning. Rather, when Felice leaves the Traces' apartment after her second visit, Joe's parting words reveal a more promising coda as he remarks, "Felice. They named you right. Remember that," referring to "happy" as the meaning of Felice's name (215). Thus, death is literally replaced with happiness.

The ring does not exist in case Felice should come along and find it. If this were the case, then the ring's absence would preclude the narrative's closure; it would prevent the return to an original melody slightly retooled. Her existence in case of the ring alters the way she sees herself. Recall that she initially decides not to go back to the Traces' apartment for dinner. After all, she went looking for the ring, and the ring is not there to validate her search. But she ultimately does return because she realizes that her relations to others and to herself can be reimagined. The ring does not have to signify for her in the way it did, say, for Dorcas. Dorcas originally wanted to borrow Felice's ring to complete her ensemble for a party. She intended to impress and attract Acton, a young man for whom she wished to leave Joe and for whom Joe would finally murder her. Felice explains that desire and jealousy fired Dorcas's pursuit, recalling how the other female partygoers' covetousness excited her. "That's the way all the girls I know think: how to get, then hold on to, a guy and most of that is having friends who want you to have him, and enemies who don't." Felice continues, "I guess that's the way you have to think about it. But what if I don't want to?" (216). Just as the ring has led Felice to reimagine blackness and whiteness, so too its presence and absence reorganizes her understanding of herself as a woman. She can imagine the object as something more than a thing that would "match her bracelet and match the house where the party was" (215). Dorcas had only been willing to subject all persons and things to the seemingly irreducible concepts and categories that "all the girls" imagined. For Felice, the ring becomes something more than an accent in an ensemble. The ring is a presence that defies the parameters of race for her mother, an absence that does not make Violet uncomfortable, and an actor whose exit from the stage clears a space for Felice to fill in the lives of Joe and Violet as they come together to assemble a new network.

But the ring's success in assembling a new social collective among Felice and the Traces has an earlier, more unsuccessful antecedent in the novel. When Joe and Violet originally leave rural Virginia for the City, they ride a segregated train up from the South. While the train is south of the Mason-Dixon line, a "green-as-poison curtain" separates the white and black diners in the dining car. Once the train enters Delaware, the curtain is pulled back and "the whole car could be full of colored people and everybody on a first-come first-serve basis. If only they would" (31). The object separating white from black, a flimsy piece of cloth, has the agency to segregate the car, even after it is whisked away. The curtain signifies in at least two ways here. First, it suggests that the effects of generations of racialization cannot be walked back with the swipe of a curtain. The idea here is that race as a made thing—as a phenomenon constructed out of materials like the curtain—is fluid but unbelievably powerful. Second, the curtain calls attention to the materiality and tenuousness of race. The black attendant walks through, calling the black ticketholders to breakfast, hoping that they will avail themselves of the desegregated table, but "he never got his way, this attendant. He wanted the whole coach to file into the dining car, now that they could" (31). When the narrator says that "[o]nce in a while it happened," that a few African Americans are willing to cross the formerly curtained space and enter the dining car alongside white people, these black folks are all described in terms of material possessions: "Some well-shod woman with two young girls, a preacherly kind of man with a watch chain and a rolled-brim hat might stand up, adjust their clothes and weave through the coaches toward the tables, foamy white with heavy silvery knives and forks" (31). Even in this moment we see how the ability to enter the formerly white dining car is at least marked, if not constituted, by the material circumstances of characters' wardrobes/persons: the nice shoes, the watch chain, the fine hat. And once again, whiteness is exposed as passing itself off as an absence. The dining car remains the territory of white people, both before and after the curtain is swiped away. The attendant need not call the white passengers to the table. They simply go. In the chasm created by the curtain, Morrison insists that the construction of race through difference is not the sole property of people of color. Whiteness, too, is property.

If *Jazz* is literally a jazz composition, then what we know about that musical form suggests that the novel itself might be invested in gathering a variety of events and entities into different configurations in a manner similar to how the opal ring rearranges the lives of characters in the narrative. Earlier I referenced Morrison's description of the book itself as the narrator of *Jazz*. What are we to make of the physical text as a narrator? What are the implications of a thing that speaks to us? Morrison's self-proclaimed talking book marks a single waypoint in a much longer tradition treated at length by Henry Louis Gates Jr. in his seminal study *The Signifying Monkey: A Theory of African-American Literary Criticism*, which provides helpful context for reading *Jazz* in the larger trajectory of African American literature.[37] Psychoanalytic theories of object relations that originate with Sigmund Freud and evolve through the work of Melanie Klein have also been offered explicitly as a lens for reading *Jazz*.[38] However, the weakness of this approach is its dedication to the immaterial space between writer and reader. A materialist reading, on the other hand, emphasizes the significance of the book itself as an actor in erasing the gap, or at least minimizing the distance, between writer, reader, and text—as a useful means of shifting our theory of reading away from a binary between sociality and materiality. Tracking a shift from the nature/culture binary treats the natural and social both as parts and products of one another. As Latour observes, "when any state of affairs is split into one material component to which is added as an appendix a social one, one thing is sure: this is an artificial division imposed by the disciplinary disputes, not by any empirical requirement."[39] By making the book itself the narrator of its own story, Morrison creates a material object that is also a social object, or, in keeping with my argument in this chapter: she flattens the nature/culture binary altogether. Rather than deepening the divide between material and social, this complex narrative voice is a thing we can hold in our hands, look at, listen to, read aloud.

The book itself, like the ring or the green curtain, is a thing that recreates and regathers the narrative threads of history into a fabric of social connectivity as Joe, Violet, and Felice dance together in the unknown future of the narrative, unbeholden to the Joe-Violet-Dorcas triangle that resulted in death and tragedy. Thus, when the novel ends by speaking to us about Joe, Violet, and Felice, we, the readers, are also being gathered into the narrative remaking of a history that includes the fictional world of the novel and the world in which we sit reading it: "But I can't say that aloud; I can't tell anyone that I have been waiting for this all my life and that being chosen to wait is the reason I can. If I were able I'd say it. Say make me, remake me. You are free to do it and I am free to let you because look, look. Look where your hands are. Now" (229). What if we were to view Morrison's novel, not only as a produced object or a self sufficient thing? Instead, what if the book is a thing just like the ring is a thing? In other words, what if we were to stop constantly separating our understanding of the world into the two oversimplified categories of "the world" and "our perception of the world"? Jonathan Lethem's novel *The Fortress of Solitude* addresses such questions by introducing a magical ring into an otherwise realist narrative. Lethem's ring is just as important an actor as the two main characters of the novel, and its possibilities for flattening nature and culture are explored just enough to be tragic for the ways they ultimately go unrealized.

WHEN NATURE/CULTURE OVERSHADOWS THE MATERIAL

The Fortress of Solitude, Lethem's most ambitious and sprawling novel, is divided into two halves by a short middle section of liner notes written by the novel's protagonist, Dylan Ebdus, to commemorate a box set of CDs capturing the life's work of his best friend's father. The first half of the novel, "Underberg," is set in the 1970s and is narrated in a third-person omniscient voice that follows Dylan in his evolving friendship with fellow stickball-playing, graffiti-tagging, comic book–loving, Dean Street hero Mingus Rude. Dylan and Mingus come from two very different families. Dylan's parents, especially his mother, are political progressives who see themselves as helping to integrate a minority community by moving into the Gowanus neighborhood of Brooklyn, and especially Dean Street, which is dominated by African American and Puerto Rican residents. However, Isabel Vendle, the aristocratic matriarch of the neighborhood, envisions the Ebduses as the first white building block in a gentrification project that will convert Gowanus into the swank "Boerum Hill" of her dreams. Mingus's parents have recently divorced, and he has come to Gowanus with his father, Barrett Rude Jr., a former R & B singer and icon with the group The Subtle Distinctions. After a stint in prison, Barrett Rude Sr. also joins the household. Dylan's and Mingus's friendship is worked out in the street games they play with other kids on the block, and solidified on the walls, billboards, and train cars of Brooklyn as they share the graffiti tag "Dose." Mingus constantly vouches for Dylan and lends him the ultimate credibility by allowing him the use of the tag when Dylan fails to come up with an alter ego of his own: "It's a happy solution for both. The black kid gets to see his tag spread farther [. . .] What's in it for the white kid? Well, he's been allowed to merge his identity in this way with the black kid's, to lose his funkymusicwhiteboy geekdom in the illusion that he and his friend Mingus Rude are both Dose, no more and no less."[40] Lethem's experiment with race, gentrification, class, and history through the merging identities of Mingus and Dylan reaches its apotheosis in the small silver ring given to Dylan by a black derelict.

The ring empowers Dylan with the magic of flight, which he then shares with Mingus by sharing the ring, paying his friend back for "Dose" with the superhero figure "Aeroman." In a novel characterized by its "realist commitments,"[41] the presence of the ring disrupts the world of the story for characters and readers alike. However, even the fantastic powers of the ring cannot prevent the erosion of the boys' relationship in the face of the stormy realities of race and class. By the end of "Underberg," Dylan's mother has left, his father continues to work like a monk in the attic, and Dylan has finished his secondary school career at a selective high school without the objections of his mother, who was always so proud to have her son be one of "only three white children in the whole [public] school" (23). On his way to Camden, "the most expensive college in America" (270), Dylan stops by Mingus's house and buys back a bunch of comics from his friend who needs the money to support a drug habit. This moment in the novel marks a clear contrast in the trajectories of the two characters, as Dylan also buys the ring back from Mingus, who ends up shouting his friend out of the house as the youngest Rude intervenes in what becomes a violent exchange between his father and grandfather. Following the liner notes memorializing Barrett Rude Jr.'s time as lead vocalist for The Subtle Distinctions, the novel undergoes a drastic change in voice as the second half, "Prisonaires," is narrated in the first person by Dylan, and catches up with Dylan in his present life as a freelance music journalist with a black girlfriend to mark the maintenance of the street credibility that made him such a success at the upper-crust Camden College before he dropped out. The novel culminates in Dylan's unsuccessful attempt to use the ring to break Mingus out of prison. In the end, Dylan lives and moves in the free world, while Mingus remains incarcerated. The ring is passed off to another imprisoned childhood friend/enemy, Robert Woolfolk, who kills himself trying to make an escape, and the closing juxtaposition between Dylan and Mingus seems to signal the inevitability of the social forces of race and class.

In response to a similar question about the organization of the novel in two different interviews, Lethem says that "at the start I meant to write a book of two halves," and that "in the first half of the book, though the characters are suffering, there's a golden glow that makes everything okay. Whereas the feeling in adulthood, in the second section, is that nothing is okay. In the last part of the book, everyone seems so estranged and inconsolable that you want to make them go back to the way they were. But rescue is impossible."[42] The novel as a whole seems poised to take on the social themes of racial and class inequities. Yet if we turn from race and class as social categories, as orientations for reading the novel, and focus instead on the ring, a new vista opens briefly. If the characters will just recognize the material associations that form the larger categories that seem to govern their lives, then we might understand those categories differently. But readers cannot seem to figure out how to engage the ring. Is the ring actually magical? Do the boys truly fly, become invisible, and swim like fish under water? What we decide to do with the ring influences how we read the text as a whole, but also influences how we understand the networks of relation that are attempted but ultimately doomed to failure in the world of the novel.

The reviews of Lethem's novel are representative of the confusion surrounding what to do with the ring. In the pages of *Time*, Lev Grossman almost dismissively mentions the "magic ring that intermittently" gives the boys superpowers as a "risky element of magical realism." Like Grossman, Jason Picone reads the ring as a mere literary convention that might seem at first to violate the "book's ground rules," but ultimately does not because of *Fortress*'s underlying commitment to the fantastic. Whereas Grossman and Picone rely on the genre of magical realism to explain the phenomenon of the ring, A. O. Scott, writing for the *New York Times Book Review*, reads the ring as a metaphor symbolic of the book's nearly allegorical message: "the ring may, then, seem like a distraction or a crutch, a bit of game playing to soothe the novelist's well-established postmodernist allergy to realism [. . .] I prefer to think of it as a sign of utopian possibility." Peter Bradshaw's entertaining reading in Britain's *New Statesman* moves away from both the language of magical realism and from Scott's metaphorical reading as he recalls his initial discovery of the ring's magic powers: "I absorbed this only after much rereading and goggling and eye-knuckling, so casually does Lethem introduce the revelation, in a storyline that often seems ancillary to the rest of the novel [. . .] I found myself gasping: 'Is it a metaphor? Is it delusion? No, it's really happening!'" But it is Michiko

Kakutani's "White Kid, In a Black World" in the *New York Times* that goes furthest in separating the narrative of the ring from the rest of the novel by branding it as "Coover-esque allegor[y] and high jinks" and as "a vestige of the postmodernist techniques" Lethem employs in earlier works. She characterizes the passages devoted to the ring as "awkward interludes" and "cutesy pyrotechnics."[43] The ring transgresses the laws of nature in the novel so passive-aggressively that reviewers either wave it away as a gimmick or chalk it up to some generic convention, calling to mind the ways in which Latour says we use the term "social" to explain away phenomena that require deeper and more sustained examination.

I would suggest that the ring creates such a problem for readers because it closes what appears to be a rupture between the natural order of the novel and the social order of the novel. And yet, similar to reviewers like Kakutani, most scholars have preferred to divorce the ring from the rest of the novel's material domain. Without a single reference to the ring that transforms Dylan and Mingus into Aeroman, Marc Singer dwells in the world of metaphor, arguing, "Lethem renders the impossible feat of becoming the flying superhero Aeroman and the mundane occurrence of pubescent sexual awakening as equally mysterious, equally prone to create private new selves that supplant old ones."[44] Matt Godbey's illuminating reading of gentrification as a symptom of the novel's treatment of race, class, and authenticity ignores the ring altogether. Although he charts Dylan's and Mingus's diverging trajectories over the course of the novel to explain how Dylan is granted "a sense of agency denied Mingus and other Gowanus residents," Godbey, like Singer, never mentions the ring.[45] Each of these critics offers insightful readings of the novel, Singer focusing on the Dylan/Mingus relationship to illustrate how the realities of adulthood dismantle childhood superhero metaphors, and Godbey explaining how white urbanites envision the consequences of gentrification as a product of their own alienation rather than as a product of the racialization of others. But these essentially "social" arguments depend on the ring in unacknowledged ways. The gap between how Dylan and Mingus relate to one another as youths and as adults, for instance, is enacted in how the ring operates differently when Dylan picks it up again after many years. The racialization of the novel's characters of color and the neutralization of whiteness in the project of gentrification are carried out in the development of a character like Dylan, who can go years without using a ring that gives him the powers of flight and invisibility.

How would the novel be different without the ring? What if Lethem had simply composed a straightforward narrative in which we follow the friendship, maturation, and growing apart of a young white boy and a young black boy in the heart of Brooklyn? That seems to be the story that Kakutani wants to read, and the story that other critics actually read. But much like the opal ring that comes in at the end of Morrison's novel, the material object that turns two teenage boys into magical superheroes is as vital to the juxtaposition of their respective narratives as it is to our understanding of what Lethem is doing at the level of the novel by calling on the specter of the comic book and critiquing the racializing process of gentrification. The ring is just as significant an actor in the novel as Dylan or Mingus, and its particular significance lies in its capacity to dissolve the nature/culture divide. For a time the boys are able to resist, even defy, what are presented as the logics of nature and culture. Yet, following the logic of the nature/culture binary, what we find at the novel's end is that race is natural for Mingus and cultural for Dylan. The ring offers a third way, a materialist marriage of nature and culture in which a category like race is not a priori or static, but a materially constructed thing. For Dylan and Mingus, what is most important is that the possibilities of this third way ultimately go unclaimed.

The subtlety with which Lethem introduces the power of the ring into the text stands in stark contrast to Morrison's abrupt insertion of the opal ring into her narrative. The appearance of the magic ring is overshadowed by the racialization of an exchange of money, pushing the miracle of flight into the shadows of racial tension. Dylan stands in an empty lot, trying to assert himself as a graffiti tagger with his own unique identity, "but this isn't going to happen today. Because today is the day the flying man falls from the roof." Next, there is "a shadow flashing at the corner of the boy's eyes [. . .] Flight, reversed. Then a collapsing thud, someone thrown, and the wheezing sigh, the exhale thrown from a body by force of impact" and all of this followed by a voice: "Little white boy," groans the voice. "Whatchoo doin'?" (99). The narrator consistently refers to the falling person as "flying man," but the flying man is homeless, filthy, and smells of urine. The straightforward characterization, descriptions, actions, and words of the flying man in the larger context of a realist novel all point toward an ironic portrayal of a drunken derelict who is much more a falling man than a flying man. When asked if he has any money, Dylan gives the man two quarters and then a dollar as the man "turns a silver ring on his pinky finger" and explains to Dylan that he "used to fly good" (101). When Dylan responds that he has seen the man fly, we are inclined to read him as humoring the derelict out of fear. Thus, the first revelation of the ring and its powers can be completely missed because it occurs one hundred pages into the novel, it is located on the finger of a man who could easily be read as mentally unstable, and it is all but lost in the ritual racial tension in which the scene is couched.

While it might seem that race is only an ancillary concern to a young boy confronted by a homeless man described as "huge," the ritual the two engage in, whereby Dylan gives the man his pocket change, is an example of a racialized exchange called yoking that recurs throughout the novel: "Sixth grade. The year of the headlock, the year of the yoke, Dylan's heat-flushed cheeks wedged into one or another black kid's elbow, book bag skidding to the gutter, pockets rapidly, easily frisked for lunch money or a bus pass" (83). The ritual is one in which blackness is asserted as appropriational or commandeering, while whiteness is construed as acquiescent. The logic is simple: hand over something of value and ease the tension, then we'll all laugh uncomfortably. The yoke is not always physical. When the flying man asks Dylan for a dollar, the boy is "almost relieved to shift to such familiar turf. On automatic, he digs in his pocket" (100). Dylan's fear of the derelict acts as a yoke, and so when the man asks him for money the dynamic of black and white is restored and he can breathe easier. The comfort of this ritual is unsettling. Dylan reaches in his pocket "on automatic," as if by instinct understanding that handing over money to the black man will release him from the yoke. Race overshadows the ring. The homeless man has an object that gives him the power of flight, and yet he is homeless and dirty, pressed into borrowing change from a kid.

One way to read the flying man scenes is as a commentary on the impotence of the ring in the face of race, but another approach would be to acknowledge the absurdity of the characters' continued faith in race in the face of the ring's properties. On some level it is true that race might be used to explain why the homeless man is homeless, or why Dylan hands over his money to the man. But Lethem is not satisfied with such "social" explanations insofar as they would take race for granted. Instead, he has the derelict give the ring to Dylan, reversing the yoke. By undoing the ritual, Lethem begins to build a different conception of race, one in which race is neither a static fact of nature nor an artificial product of culture, but a way of being that is made out of materials and associations, an ongoing product of the interactions of persons and things. So what does it mean to value things on an equal ontological plane as characters in this novel? For starters, it means that the features of the text we might typically consider postmodern—its magical realism, shifting narration, rhizomatic structure, and complicitous critique—are catalyzed by the thinginess of the ring.

Unfortunately, the recurring pattern of Lethem's novel is to reveal social categories as fluid processes, only to show how these possibilities go unrealized by characters who are unwilling or unable to embrace the social as a product of the interaction of both humans and nonhumans. Dylan's ruminations on the powers of the ring serve as a case in point. Dylan first discovers these powers during a game of stoopball in which he is suddenly transformed into a master outfielder, able to snag home runs out of the air in a single bound. After a few amazing catches, the narrator muses on Dylan's state of mind in which he sees "the ring and the ball in some kind of partnership of magical objects" (160). He even finds himself outjumping the amazing Mingus as the two leap for the same fly ball and Mingus "f[a]ll[s] short, minus the advantage of the flying man's ring" (163). Dylan goes unaccountably unhassled at a block party later in the summer, and the narrator voices Dylan's internal questions: "maybe this night's just lucky, maybe he's passed through some flame and come out the other side. Maybe it's the ring. Maybe the ring has made him invisible. Maybe the ring has made him *black*. Who can say?" (166). Dylan only thinks in terms of white and black; they are the categories through which he rationalizes everything. To be athletic and cool is to be black. To be unathletic and uncool is to be white. But the ring's powers suggest that these categories are not as static as they seem to Dylan. The ring can break through the various circumferences of Dylan's Gowanus-becoming-gentrified-Boerum Hill neighborhood, but rather than capitalizing on these possibilities, he consistently subjects them to the dead ends of race and class.

The gaps created between individuals and groups by such social categories present themselves as irreducible and impassable when they are, in fact, constant products of material processes. Again, this assertion does not dismiss the referential significance of such categories as white folks or black folks, but it challenges the tendency to rely on such rubrics as wholesale explanations for the very phenomena that shape these categories in the first place. In his analysis of *Fortress* alongside Lethem's rewriting of the Marvel comic *Omega: The Unknown*, David Coughlan compares these impassable gaps to the "gutters" that separate the individual panels in a comic. Coughlan argues that Lethem's Brooklyn in *Fortress* is a "city laid out like a comic book page, where each block of houses can be seen as a panel, and the streets are the comic's gutters." He interprets the gutters of Gowanus as representative of "the ever present possibility of failure, the unbridgeable abyss between a series of isolated individuals."[46] For Coughlan, this impassable gap applies not only to race relations but also to Dylan's connections with his father, mother, and his hometown in general. But to reinforce the various gaps and gutters in the novel as impassable is to ignore the ring, which regularly empowers Dylan and Mingus to defy the various gutters of the neighborhood social code. The first time Mingus takes up the ring, he does so to prevent two young black boys from harassing a white boy. In this instance the ring intensifies Mingus's predisposition to flaunting the mores of racial etiquette, much as he has done in boosting Dylan's reputation by sharing his graffiti handle. The unified identity that Dylan and Mingus forged through the graffiti tag "Dose" now takes active form in the person of Aeroman, as the two boys become each other's crime-fighting alter egos.

But something begins to change. The familiar narratives of black-kid-bound-for-prison and white-kid-bound-to-leave-the-neighborhood begin to take shape. The division starts innocently enough. Mingus excels in the acrobatic feats made available by the ring, while Dylan slowly takes up the position of audience: "they'd meant to swap it back and forth, the changing from black to white one of Aeroman's mystifying aspects, another level of secret identity, but it had always been Mingus in the costume, always Dylan crouched behind a parked car or dangled as bait" (238). In a heroic feat gone bad, however, it is Mingus, not Dylan, who gets arrested as Aeroman for trying to break up a drug deal that was actually a drug sting. Soon, Mingus has begun "fluffing cushions for change, palming pennies from the dish Abraham kept at the front door, scraping up enough for a nickel bag" (196). Dylan, on the other hand, finds out from his science teacher Mr. Winegar that his test scores have made him the only kid in I.S. 293 to be accepted into Stuyvesant, a competitive academic high school. When Dylan expresses hesitation about attending Stuyvesant because of his desire to go to Sarah J. Hale, he can see in Mr. Winegar's eyes that he "might as well have said *I think I'll just go straight to the Brooklyn House of Detention* [. . .] *You're white!* Winegar wanted to scream. *Man can fly!* Dylan wanted to scream" (200–201). The dissonance between Winegar's and Dylan's unspoken exclamations illustrates the instability and inconsistency in the division of culture and nature, the social and the material. Winegar follows the logic of race as a natural phenomenon that drives Dylan's choice of schools and reinforces the American cultural logic that says black boys go to jail, white boys go to school. Dylan, on the other hand, has flown and has seen Mingus fly.

The miracle of flight brought on by the ring enables the boys to see just beyond the various racialized schisms and class hierarchies that organize their world, but the taxonomies of everyday life have so overwritten their more fundamental constituents that they have come to appear irreducible and thus inevitable. The unrealized potential of the material domain is palpable when Dylan returns to Mingus's house before leaving for college and buys back a bunch of his comics from Mingus, along with the ring. The scene concludes with a fight erupting between Mingus's father and grandfather, which we later discover ends with the shot that kills Barrett Rude Senior and lands Mingus in prison. Mingus shouts Dylan out of the house, protecting him one last time. The novel then breaks in half. We get Dylan's liner notes to a re-release of an album by Barrett Rude Jr.'s group The Subtle Distinctions, followed by the final section, "Prisonaires," which rivals "Underberg" for length.

Critics such as Singer and Coughlan have read the shift from the first to the second half of the novel as a reassertion of the "literal over the symbolic,"[47] and as a critique of "relations, ritual, identity, marginalization, consumption, and capitalism."[48] Focusing on the ring, however, it does not seem like a stretch to point out that the fading glow of the first half of the book coincides with the many ways in which nature and culture begin to take their courses. Lethem signifies this shift by transitioning from a third-person narrative voice in the first half of the novel to a first-person narration, voiced from Dylan's perspective, in the novel's second half.

The move from a third-person voice to a more limited first-person perspective demonstrates the reduction of possibilities available to the boys in the first half of the novel. Throughout "Underberg" multiple focalizing points of view are possible, but in "Prisonaires" Dylan's view has become the sole perspective. The effect of this change is less than flattering for Dylan's characterization. After dropping out of college, becoming a music journalist, and moving to Berkeley, where he maintains his Brooklyn street cred by living with his black girlfriend, Abby, Dylan's view of the Gowanus of his youth reeks of nostalgia.[49] He assembles a small shrine in their apartment consisting of the "ring, Mingus's pick, a pair of Rachel's earrings, and a tiny, handmade, hand-sewn book of black-and-white photographs" (316). Preparing for a flight to Los Angeles to meet his father, Dylan fights with Abby, who lashes out, "What *happened* to you? Your childhood is some privileged sanctuary you live in all the time, instead of here with me. You think I don't *know* that?" Dylan explains his obsession with his childhood with the revealing tautology, "'My childhood is the only part of my life that wasn't, uh, overwhelmed by my childhood'" (316–17). Unconcerned by the social stratifications of Brooklyn that had so attracted his mother, Dylan longs for a return to the real Gowanus, not the Boerum Hill of Isabel Vendle's dreams, which has become a reality. He imagines himself as a victim of the gentrification that has rendered his childhood haunts all but unrecognizable. But as Godbey points out, Dylan's "victimhood becomes less tenable when one places his crisis of alienation and dislocation alongside the actual, physical alienation and dislocation of Gowanus/Boerum Hill's poor black,

Puerto Rican and Dominican residents and his role in facilitating gentrification."⁵⁰

While a typical postmodern reading might turn on the deconstruction of a monolithic whiteness here, the material domain of Lethem's novel precludes any such monolithic view in the first place. Most obviously, Rachel Ebdus, Isabel Vendle, and Dylan have three dramatically different views of the old neighborhood. For Rachel, the neighborhood is a badge of courage, a way to distance herself from the previous generation of white women with their concerns about safety and their children's schools. For Isabel, it's a project, something to be remade, restored, even purified. This tension is palpable in an early conversation in which Isabel tells Rachel she should pull Dylan out of public school: "'He'll be with children who'll never learn,' said Isabel, feeling impulsive and a little cruel. The fact was undeniable. Let Rachel squirm now. 'Maybe he'll teach them,' Dylan's mother said easily, then laughed. "'It's a problem for him to solve, school. I did it, so can he'" (19). Isabel imagines herself appealing to a mothering instinct that Rachel either will not own or at least wants to revise. The neighborhood is the proving ground. If Isabel can remake the neighborhood in her image, it becomes the Boerum Hill of every white, middle-class family's dreams and her property value skyrockets. Whiteness is constructed, literally, through construction. The renovation of the neighborhood will create clear racial demarcations, displacing nonwhite residents and drawing new white residents. If Rachel can withstand the onslaught of what she calls the "Vendlemachine," if her son thrives in public school, then she validates her own cultural rebellion. Whiteness is constructed through contrast, as with Isabel's gentrification project, but also through appropriation.

Dylan's shrine of objects suggests at least a third form of whiteness, a whiteness of nostalgia and memory, constructed out of the selective stories he pulls from the objects themselves. The ring enacts the story of his fusion with Mingus. The ring had enabled him to jump higher, run faster, even question whether he himself might be black. Like Mingus's comic books, which he says are "in a box in my closet, mingled with mine," the ring and Mingus's pick allow Dylan to reconstruct his childhood in a new place. The problem here is that Dylan's nostalgic view of the neighborhood renders the things into objects. They become mired in human determination in their roles as items in Dylan's collection. Abby senses this in the heat of their argument when she accuses him of treating her as "the official mascot of all the shit you won't allow yourself to feel. A featured exhibit in the Ebdus collection of *sad black folks*" (315). The agency of these collected objects, their thingness, has been subsumed as they have been used to construct a whiteness of nostalgia that imagines itself as fixed. His visions of himself as the exception, the white kid who could hang with the black kid, have set his whiteness like the concrete slabs of sidewalk that line the Gowanus streets. Whiteness is not only established through contrast and appropriation, but also through a selective memory, a hegemony that Dylan sustains in the objects in his collection.

The ring asserts its own agency once again when Dylan removes it from the shrine. As Dylan argues with the girlfriend he seems unlikely to keep, he slips the ring into his pocket and sets out to free Mingus from prison. In an ironic twist, he discovers that the ring no longer enables flight but now makes its wearer invisible, recalling his wonder on the night of the party so many years earlier when he had gone unhassled among the older, cooler, blacker crowd. At the Watertown facility where Mingus is locked up, the guards sift through his pockets, asking "What's this ring?" Dylan lies and says that it is his mother's wedding ring, and they allow him to keep it. When Dylan tries to give the ring to Mingus, Mingus tells him to put it away. Dylan insists, "'You could use it to break out of this place,' I said quietly. His laugh now was bitter, and authentic. 'Why not?' 'You couldn't even use that thing to break *into* this place.' The rest, until my time was up, was small talk. [. . .] A wall had fallen between us" (444–45). The reality of a flat ontology—one in which all things exist equally and thus even the most mundane objects can have serious effects on the arrangements of larger collectives—is finally unrealized. Mingus dismisses the ring's capacity to change his situation, but perhaps even more unaccountably, Dylan has had the ring for years while it gathered dust on a shelf next to other objects mired in nostalgia. Dylan's privileged status as a middle-class white man has made any need to understand the material domain of his day-to-day life unnecessary, and Mingus's disenfranchised status as a poor black man has rendered any impulse he may have had to consider his material circumstances seemingly pointless. Thus, both characters ignore the material realities of the ring, albeit for drastically different reasons, and the "social" explanations of their lives go unchallenged.

Nowhere is this bifurcation more obvious than in Dylan's ability to sneak back into the prison while invisible, spend hours talking with Mingus, and then leave the ring with another inmate before walking out completely visible to the guards. Having heard from Mingus the long rap sheet of his childhood friend/enemy Robert Woolfolk, Dylan finds Robert and gives him the ring. The exchange ends no differently than the many yokings Robert visited on Dylan when they were kids: "'Yo, Dylan?' 'What?' 'Fuck you, motherfucker'" (493). Pretending to have been locked in the visitors' room all night, Dylan bluffs a corrections officer into escorting him back to the parking lot. His whiteness acts as the ultimate natural phenomenon here, as it certainly helps him sell the guard on his story and also shows itself as the cultural product of his circumstances: clothing, fake press credentials no one had asked twice about, and his condescending tone of voice when he says to the guard, "'Surely you remember me, young man'" (494). On their way out, Dylan asks about an uproar he had heard during the early morning hours, and the young officer tells him that an inmate had killed himself leaping off the prison roof. Robert Woolfolk had not known the ring no longer enabled flight. "Craziest thing I've ever seen," the guard says to Dylan, "his arms got tangled under his body, so he sort of crumpled up and broke in half as he slid down that bank. Didn't even look human by the time he came to a stop" (497). Dylan's hasty decision to utilize the ring's power has had disastrous consequences.

Lethem never explains how or why the ring's properties change over time. We might speculate that the ring has taken on the properties of its owner. Dylan's ability to walk in and out of the prison, once with the ring and once without, suggest that he might as well have been invisible both times. His whiteness operates as a kind of power that renders him invisible when he wants to be and visible when he needs to be, as in "Surely you remember me, young man." Having been subjugated to the social as a substance for so long, the possibilities of the material domain are cowed into effects when, in fact, the things that constitute the material realm of everyday life are also always causes. They may have more or less agency, be more or less influential, or their properties may alter with time, but they can never be dismissed as the mere effects of "social" causes, even when they are sorely misunderstood, as with Robert Woolfolk. The closing chapters of *The Fortress of Solitude* demonstrate the consequences of preferring a vision of the social as a substance over an understanding of the social as an ongoing process. Robert Woolfolk's death is one consequence of this view.

There is, somewhere between nature and culture, what Dylan calls a "middle space" that cannot be entirely reduced either to the determinism of nature or the open-endedness of culture and thus resists the binary completely. Morrison actualizes such a middle space at the end of *Jazz*, when Joe, Violet, and Felice reassemble the love triangle formerly constituted by Joe, Violet, and Dorcas. Unfortunately, such middle spaces are only available to Dylan via the phantasmagoria of memory. Lethem's characters fall short of Morrison's reimagining of the social because they are beaten down by so-called "social" realities that separate nature from culture and subjugate each to the other whenever it is necessary to maintain familiar structures of relation without revealing the material foundations of those structures. Remembering the music that he loved enough to make himself into a music writer, Dylan listens to Brian Eno's *Another Green World* and considers how what "he once loved in this record, and certain others—*Remain in Light*, 'O Superman,' *Horses*—was the middle space they conjured and dwelled in, a bohemian demimonde, a hippie dream." But that same space has become a point of embarrassment in the face of "music that would tell it like it is," music that Dylan says would tell it "like I'd learned it to be, in the inner city" (507–508). Notice the conflation of telling it "like it is" with telling it "like I'd learned it to be." This subtle confusion embodies the ultimate nature/culture paradox by validating the social, what he learns to be the case, by reading it as natural, "like it is." That is, the binary insists on having it both ways: insisting on the separation of nature and culture while simultaneously imposing the features of both on familiar social categories whenever it is most convenient.

The middle space is a domain of possibility—the possibility of recognizing culture as natural. He recognizes the hippie farm for which his mother had left him and his father as a middle space, along with Camden College, and his old neighborhood during its time between being Gowanus and becoming the gentrified Boerum Hill. Each of these spaces is densely populated, not only with human but with nonhuman actors. In fact, the last glimpse of a middle space in the novel occurs in the final pages, as Dylan remembers a trip to Camden to retrieve his things after being dismissed from the college: "I'd been forced to return to the campus once more, to collect my belongings—books, bedclothes, stereo" (506). On the way home, father and son are caught in a dangerous blizzard:

> Abraham and I let ourselves be swept through the blurred tunnel, beyond rescue but calm for an instant, settled in our task, a father driving a son home to Dean Street. There was no Mingus Rude or Barrett Rude Junior with us there, no Running Crab postcard or letter from Camden College pushed through the slot. We were in a middle space then, in a cone of white, father and son moving forward at a certain speed. Side-by-side, not truly quiet but quiescent, two gnarls of human scribble, human cipher, human dream. (509)

Having become so mired in the social as a substance rather than a process, even the middle space that Dylan recalls on that return trip is marred by the "cone of white" that shelters them in the violence of the storm. And yet, I would not argue that Lethem is making a case for the social or for the inevitable bifurcation of nature and culture. The predominance of race along the familiar fault lines of white and black, the class structure that so sickens Dylan's mother and confuses his own view of Brooklyn—these categories win out in the narrative at the painfully obvious expense of the middle spaces in which we are reminded by the ring that "*Man can fly!*," as Dylan so desperately wants to scream but does not.

When considering *Jazz* and *Fortress* as texts that acknowledge the significance of actors, only to take that significance in two entirely different directions, I chose to end this chapter on ontological perspectivism with Lethem because *Fortress* seems to me indicative of postmodern fiction's final attempt to communicate in any way possible that when the social is validated as irreducible, then the material possibilities of everything we take for granted are overlooked. The work of postmodernism is to reveal that culture is natural. At the root of the disconnect between these realms lies language. Is language a part of nature, or is it a cultural phenomenon? Do we use language or does it use us? Postmodernism has most typically been represented as an aesthetic that enacts the infinite deferral of poststructuralism. But is postmodernism synonymous with poststructuralism? How can we reconcile the representations of things with the things themselves? Rereading the language-obsessed fiction of John Barth and David Foster Wallace from a neomaterialist perspective opens up new productive and reparative possibilities for these texts and for postmodernism as a resolutely materialist aesthetic.

Chapter 3

Rewriting Language

In their academy-award winning film *Eternal Sunshine of the Spotless Mind* (2004), director Michel Gondry and screenwriter Charlie Kaufman assemble a cinematic narrative that tests the boundaries of memory and consciousness. Protagonist Joel Barish (Jim Carrey) falls in love with the zany and mercurial Clementine Kruczynski (Kate Winslet), but the relationship eventually turns sour and Clementine undergoes a memory-erasing procedure to forget Joel. When Joel discovers he has been erased, he decides to reciprocate and have Clementine erased from his memory. The doctor instructs Joel to go home and retrieve every object, memento, and keepsake that might remind him of Clementine so that these items can be used to construct a map of Joel's brain, which will enable the doctor and his technicians to locate the relevant memories of Clementine and delete them. Joel returns with art supplies, coffee mugs, potatoes that he and Clementine dressed as people—two garbage bags full of things. The technician sits Joel in a chair topped with a brain scanner that resembles a hair dryer at a salon, sets the first object down in front of him—a snow globe—and asks him to "react" to the object. Joel begins by explaining that there is a funny story that accompanies the snow globe, but the technician interrupts and says he will actually get a better readout if Joel refrains from any verbal explanations of the thing and simply focuses on the memories. Joel apologizes, looking slighted. The objects have become essential to Joel's memories because they were central to the actions and events from which those memories were formed. The stories contained in those objects do not need to be articulated, however, in order for Joel's brain to reform their attendant memories. Language, it seems, is not necessary when the objects are present. This scene enacts one of the principal concerns of postmodernism: the relationship between word and world.

The literature typically identified as postmodern has taken on many names over the last half century, including metafiction, surfiction, the literature of exhaustion, and the literature of silence. Each of these monikers points in some way to the prominent trend of making writing itself the subject of postmodern narrative. They raise the questions: How does the language of fiction relate to experience? Does language simply describe the world or actually affect it? What is the relationship between words and the actual things they are supposedly meant to represent? Can language represent the world at all? Just as these fictional forms began to build momentum in the 1960s, two influential philosophical approaches to language gained influence in literary studies. The first, commonly referred to as the "linguistic turn," is explored in Richard Rorty's 1967 collection of the same name in which he defines his topic as "the view that philosophical problems are problems which may be solved (or dissolved) either by reforming language, or by understanding more about the language we presently use."[1] The second, poststructuralism, made its way from Continental Europe to the United States via the work of Jacques Derrida and then Paul de Man, among others, asserting that signifiers have no fixed relation with signifieds and that the language of literary texts, therefore, cannot be reduced solely to any kind of referential meaning. These linguistic-centered philosophies were on a collision course with the aesthetic of fiction writing as metacognition throughout the 1970s when, in 1979, Jean-François Lyotard's *The Postmodern Condition* clinched the connection with its "incredulity toward metanarratives" enacted through "many different language games."[2] Lyotard's postmodernism transposed the problem of meaning from the realm of textual analysis to "cultural life," which, as David Harvey explains, comes to be "viewed as a series of texts intersecting with other texts, producing more texts."[3]

The implications for literature are that linguistic play becomes a hallmark of postmodern fiction and that, consequently, postmodern fiction comes to be seen as open-ended, immaterial, abstract—like much of the literary theory that was coming into its own at the same time. Geoffrey Galt Harpham explains the significance of both the linguistic turn and poststructuralism to postmodernism when he suggests that "for many postmodernists and fellow travelers, the defining discovery of the era was that language determines or structures society rather than the other way around."[4] Society, then, is best understood in terms of language, but language, having been processed through structuralism and poststructuralism, is an endlessly self-referential system that can never connect signifiers to the concepts they signify, let alone the actual things they once seemed to reference. The division between word and world that preoccupies postmodern fiction has led to an understanding of postmodernism as an aesthetic caught up in ceaseless signification. But what if language itself is a thing? What if word is world, and not in the sense of making all world into word, but in understanding all word as world? So much postmodern literary criticism has been filtered through the linguistic-centered approaches of the linguistic turn and poststructuralism; perhaps a non-linguistic-centered analysis can reveal a different dimension of postmodern fiction. In the preceding chapters I have avoided this orthodoxy of postmodernism in hopes of establishing a more material foundation for reading that emphasizes the agency of human and nonhuman actors in post-1960s fiction. Now that this foundation has been established, I want to turn to a few texts that overtly engage in the linguistic and metafictional play that has become a trademark of postmodernism and reread them as works of postmodern materialism to show that, although they may in fact be obsessed with language, they conceive of language as a fundamentally material thing and not merely a hall of mirrors.

John Barth and David Foster Wallace stand out as canonical postmodernists whose work is especially interested in language. Barth's classic work of metafiction *Lost in the Funhouse* (1968) has been a staple in discussions of postmodernism's self-reflexive wheel-spinning over more than four decades. Wallace's story "Westward the Course of Empire Takes Its Way" (1989) rewrites the Ambrose cycle of stories from *Lost in the Funhouse,* casting Barth's protagonist Ambrose as a professor of creative writing at East Chesapeake Trade School in Baltimore, Maryland. The layers of formal meta-awareness within and between these texts create a *mise-en-abyme,* drawing attention to themselves as transporters of content while simultaneously frustrating our ability to arrive at any final resolution. When Joel's last memories of Clementine have been erased, he receives a tape recording of his therapy sessions from a disillusioned office worker at the memory-erasing facility. He and Clementine have met and hit it off again as total strangers, and they listen to the tape together in confusion and pain. Knowing from what they hear on the tape that a breakup is imminent, they forge ahead anyway, and viewers are pulled into the infinite regress of their love. The trace of affection they feel for one another is not abstract. It is visceral. The abstract version of their relationship—their memories—has been erased, and they are left with concrete attractions, emotions, and desires. New objects will replace the discarded ones, and their love will take shape once again, even if only to be erased. The tape recording and the voices it projects are significant, not for the particulars of what they say but because their very existence constitutes Joel's and Clementine's erased connection. The tape is their love. The medium is the message.

If material objects contain stories in the sense revealed by Silko's narrative, then how much more might the language that constitutes those stories be material? In the analyses of Barth and Wallace that follow, I mean to consider language and the conventions of metafiction not as abstract enterprises, but as resolutely material phenomena. If all actors, both human and nonhuman, are significant in postmodern fiction, as we saw in the work of Foer, Morrison, and Lethem, and if all networks of relation are literally made out of those actors, as we saw in Silko, then all actors count in the formation of human communities. Language, too, is an actor in this sense. It is material, like a ring or a calendar or a steel folding chair. Language is what Latour calls a "mediator," rather than an "intermediary." An intermediary is an actor that "transports meaning or force without transformation," whereas a mediator "cannot be counted as just one."[5] Halfway through *Reassembling the Social*, Latour composes a dialogue between an imaginary student and a professor in which the student declares that his work is about "finding the hidden structure that explains the behavior of those agents you thought were doing something but in fact are simply placeholders for something else." The professor responds, "Placeholders, isn't that what you call actors?" The professor expands this initial response a little later when he says, "either you have actors who realize potentialities and thus are not actors at all, or you describe actors who are rendering virtualities actual."[6] Language renders virtualities actual in postmodern fiction. Language is a mediator, not a placeholder.

In the Western tradition from which postmodernism arises, language has historically been figured as either a system of meaning or a set of actions and practices. Under the latter position, language philosophers such as J. L. Austin have theorized language as a series of speech acts, rescuing it from abstraction by grounding it in human actions. We might think of Wittgenstein's famous argument that meaning is use in *Philosophical Investigations*. Neomaterialism's view of all actors as mediators can add an even more material dimension to this philosophy of language by asking what it would mean to consider words as actors in Latour's sense. Language, in this view, becomes more than an interplay of human actions or behaviors; it becomes a materialized actor in its own right. Although my neomaterialist methodology takes me in a decidedly different direction, I am building here on a theoretical foundation laid by critics such as Andreas Huyssen and Marianne DeKoven, who stand among the thoughtful few who do not consciously or unconsciously conflate postmodernism with poststructuralism.[7] For poststructuralism, language is certainly more than a medium. However, the presences constituted by signs play a secondary role to the absences that make those presences meaningful in the never-ending process of deferral and difference.

While any number of critics have insightfully examined how postmodern fiction enacts this process by focusing on absence—a necessary byproduct of following the path of literary theory that invariably leads back to Saussure—I argue that what makes fiction postmodern is its emphasis on the presence of language. The Saussurean view of language as a social construction, Harpham argues, undergirds the thinking of postmodern literary theory. Chomsky, he suggests, provides a different view of language as a biological component of human beings—a view that has been all but ignored by literary studies.[8] I am not advocating that literary approaches to postmodernism adopt a Chomskyan view of language over and against a Saussurean view, although one can see why Chomsky's notion of a "biological endowment that makes it possible for a grammar of the required sort to develop in human beings" would be appealing to my particular brand of neomaterialism.[9] To do so, however, would be implicitly to juxtapose Saussure's so-called "social construction" view of language as immaterial with Chomsky's "biological" view as material, and as I spent the last two chapters explaining, constructed does not mean artificial or immaterial. Early Marxist critics, most notably Raymond Williams, have addressed the possibilities and pitfalls of Chomskyan linguistics for materialist approaches to literature.[10] I want to go in a different direction and read language as a thing, a mediator, an object.

One central goal of this study is to demonstrate how social/natural distinctions do not always hold for post-1960s fiction, hence the flattened ontology I explored in Chapter 2. The differences that do exist in the debate between the so-called social and natural views of language predate Chomsky's departure from Saussure, surfacing and resurfacing throughout the history of linguistic and literary thought. In the Middle Ages, for instance, scholastic philosophers battled over the status of language as a posteriori or a priori. Nominalists "held that only particular physical items constitute reality, and that general or 'universal' terms (such as *man, horse, red*, etc.) designate mere abstractions." On the other hand, realists "held that these are not abstractions, but have a reality which is prior to that of any physical particulars."[11] What if language could be approached as a "particular physical item," but one that is not "prior to that of any physical particulars"? What if language can be a thing just like a ring or a rock? Is it possible that postmodernism is not concerned with the relationship between word and world as two separate realms, but simply as two different things?

In Chapter 1, I asked, if the social is constructed, then constructed out of what? The Speculative Realist and object-oriented ontological perspectives can help us reframe this question for language. In the opening chapter of *After Finitude*, Meillassoux points out that after Kant, and especially in the twentieth century, language was consistently theorized in such a way as to subject all nonhuman actors to human perception by galvanizing all nonhumans as exterior to human consciousness: "Consciousness and its language certainly transcend themselves toward the world, but there is a world only insofar as a consciousness transcends itself towards it. Consequently, this space of exteriority is merely the space of what faces us, of what exists only as a correlate of our own existence."[12] This correlationist view of language cannot account for words as things. It may allow for a view of language as formative and not merely a conduit; it may be able to realize meaning as use and reject meaning as static, hidden, or embedded. But it does not leave room for imagining the possible outcomes of language as a thing apart from human use. Bogost begins to carve out such a space for language in *Alien Phenomenology* when he explores "the list" as an ontographical mode, that is, a mode for describing ontology. He draws examples from, among other things, IKEA assembly instructions, Roland Barthes's autobiography, *Moby-Dick*, a Coca-Cola ad, François Blanciak's series of 1,001 rectilinear architectural sketches *Siteless*, the photography (both process and product) of Stephen Shore, an exploded diagram of a Shimano bicycle gear assembly, the Nintendo DS handheld's *Scribblenauts* video game, and a card game called *In a Pickle*. "Lists remind us that no matter how fluidly a system may operate, its members nevertheless remain utterly isolated, mutual aliens."[13] He ultimately asks us to consider language as a building material for lists and lists as evidence that language can function as a thing:

> Philosophers, literary critics, and theorists spend so much of their time dealing with textual material that they risk forgetting about the ordinary status of such material. When made of language, lists remind the literary-obsessed that the stuff of things is many. Lists are perfect tools to free us from the prison of representation precisely *because* they are so inexpressive.[14]

I have suggested that postmodern fiction assembles the social out of everyday objects, but the fiction itself is also assembled out of something: language. One question it seems we must consider, then, is how a neomaterialist view of language might recalibrate our reading of language in postmodern fiction. What happens when we try for a noncorrelationist view of language?

When the disconnect between word and world seems to present an impassable chasm, postmodern fiction materializes language, closing the gap. John Barth quite literally makes language physical, converting words into people and coins in *Lost in the Funhouse*. Rather than representing a mere re-enactment of poststructuralist language play, postmodern fiction values all human and nonhuman actors, including language, to account for the processual nature of our networks of relation and to decenter the individual as the reason for which even language exists.

WORDS AND THINGS

In the "Author's Note" to *Lost in the Funhouse*, Barth calls his unique collection a "series" of stories "meant to be received 'all at once.'"[15] Consisting of fourteen stories in total, the series opens with the interactive "Frame-Tale," before moving into six stories that bounce back and forth between inventive narrative experiments and a straightforward account of the birth, early childhood, and coming-of-age of a character named Ambrose. The final seven stories comprise a self-reflexive meditation on the complex relationship between artist, text, subject matter, and audience, focusing especially on the process of generating fiction. This latter half of the series comes to fruition in Barth's rewriting of a handful of figures and events from ancient Greek mythology that has received much critical attention. From the experimental "Frame-Tale," to the blurring of the lines between author, narrator, and audience, Barth's funhouse of fiction interrogates the mediating influence of its characters, things, and language, echoed even in the book's subtitle: "Fiction for print, tape, live voice." As Barth explains, some stories

> take the printed medium for granted but lose or gain nothing in oral recitation, [while others make] somewhat separate but equally valid senses in several media: print, monophonic recorded authorial voice, stereophonic ditto in dialogue with itself, live authorial voice, live ditto in dialogue with monophonic ditto aforementioned, and live ditto interlocutory with stereophonic et cetera.[16]

In fact, Barth's earliest explanation of these stories is that they were written to be delivered live on a reading tour.

Throughout the year before *Funhouse* was published in 1968, Barth spent time on the road reading selections from his earlier novels in various public forums. In *The Friday Book* he includes some short introductory remarks originally prepared when he decided to introduce a few excerpts from *Lost in the Funhouse* into the set lists for these readings. There, Barth writes that in all of the pieces, "for better or worse, the process of narration becomes the content of the narrative, to some degree and in various ways; or the form or medium has metaphorical value and dramatical relevance. The medium really is part of the message." He goes on to say that most of the stories "exploit, one way or another, ambiguities of language and narrative view point."[17] In other words, *Lost in the Funhouse* takes writing itself as its subject but also as its object of inquiry. Thus, it should be no surprise that the vast majority of critical attention paid to Barth's experiment has zeroed in on its playful structure and its preoccupation with the power of language to construct the world in which we live, perhaps attempting to answer what Charles Harris figures as the central question in Barth's work: "Can words and world resolve themselves into a unified harmony?"[18] Although my own neomaterialist reading builds on the three most common approaches to *Lost in the Funhouse*, it also differs substantially by arguing that the effect of Barth's language play is to reimagine language itself as something more than a medium that is the message. The result is a much broader expansion of the poststructuralist dogma that all signifieds are themselves necessarily signifiers. Barth pushes us to reconsider the more obvious, and thus more overlooked, idea that all signifiers are also signifieds. That is, all things are, of course, signs, but signs themselves are also things.

Two approaches have dominated the conversation about *Lost in the Funhouse*, both revolving around Barth's obsession with language in general and writing in particular. Much of the early criticism focuses on Barth's rewriting of classical and eighteenth- and nineteenth-century narratives. Charles Altieri, for instance, proposes that for Barth, "reader, writer, and material remain moving about in a closed system which is nonetheless in continual motion and offering, on its uninterrupted surface, an infinite field of possible recognitions and interrelationships" and that this mode takes its cue from "Ovid's *Metamorphoses* where for the first time a writer clearly accepted and turned to his own purposes the field for free play created by the utter fictiveness of the myths he inherited."[19] Perhaps best represented by critics such as Christopher Morris, Jerome Klinkowitz, and artist-critic Raymond Federman, the other prominent approach to *Funhouse* focuses on Barth's manipulation of and play with language. Morris argues that "the funhouse world resembles the universally neurotic one described by the French poststructuralist Jacques Lacan" in which "the Moebius strip becomes a symbol of the paradox by providing an image which is simultaneously one and two and also asserts that the signifiers which compose it have no connection with anything outside themselves (*i.e.* the 'signified' is nothing at all)."[20] With regard to writing specifically, Klinkowitz points out that "for Barth, it seems, fiction should forever be an imitation of an action, and not an action itself."[21] Federman situates Barth among a host of writers who demonstrate that "the real world is now inside language, and can only be recreated by language" and who reveal that "words and things—*LES MOTS ET LES CHOSES*, as Michel Foucault so well demonstrated—no longer stick to each other, because language too is an autonomous reality."[22] Each of these critical approaches begins and ends with language.

A third approach has emerged in which a few critics have begun to challenge the conclusions of these earlier readings on the grounds that they inevitably result in the denial of "any dimension beyond language."[23] Deborah Woolley recounts the spirit of contemporary criticism that has grown up around the work of writers like Barth: "The 'text' heroically foregoes the old securities of presence—signification, thematic unity, totalizing form—and accepts the existentialist challenge to confront the lack of a center at the heart of language and to dwell in that void." She says of Barth in particular that his fiction is often cited as an "example of the 'empty' postmodern 'text.'" Woolley counters that while postmodern fiction writ large may very well seem "preoccupied with the deterioration of language in general and of narrative forms in particular," it "does not follow that self-reflexive fiction [. . .] is devoid of 'presence.'"[24] Max Schulz contends that while *Funhouse* may appear to be "the ultimate instance of metafiction forever adrift in the mirrored reflections of its own and its literary predecessors' words, forever imitating 'its own processes,' there is a pattern discernible that questions and inverts, if it does not outright reject or deny, what critics superficially have taken Barth to represent."[25] Both of these critics insist that Barth is, in fact, breathing life back into language and into the Western literary tradition. While Woolley and Schulz continue to rely on Saussurean *langue*, their insightful dissatisfaction with the idea of Barth's playfulness as somehow solely linguistic, or as offering an abstract poststructuralist critique as an end in itself, opens the door for a reading of Barth that does not have to begin and end with language, at least not with language as it has been figured in the post-Saussurean tradition. Beginning with "Frame-Tale," I want to examine a handful of passages in which Barth materializes language and allots it the kind of agency we have seen enacted in other nonhuman actors throughout post-1960s fiction.

"Frame-Tale" is actually a Moebius strip the narrator instructs us to cut out of the book, twist into a circle, and fasten end to end. The resultant text endlessly reads, "ONCE UPON A TIME THERE WAS A STORY THAT BEGAN" (1–2). While the Moebius strip is certainly a circuitous language game, an overtly closed system, I would point out that it comes to us unclosed. That is, in order for the strip of paper to become a true Moebius strip, it must be literally cut from the text by the reader. We do the closing; we create the ceaseless cycle. The only way to close this system is to remove it from the book, and even then some might object that "ONCE UPON A TIME THERE WAS A STORY THAT BEGAN" does not constitute a narrative at all.[26] Although Schulz, among others, has argued that the "Frame-Tale" represents one of two "binary support system[s]" in the book that "confirm the hold on Barth's imagination of a searching skeptical faith in the central tradition of storytelling,"[27] the material circumstances through which the actual Moebius strip is produced suggest that Barth is at least as interested in the rupture of such binaries and systems since his narrator asks the reader to excise a physical portion of the text. The Moebius strip acts as a material obstacle to our reading whose instructions, if followed, render the reader complicit in the composition of her own cultural myths as she enacts the vicious circle of the idyllic fairy-tale opening: "Once upon a time." What seems like a language game becomes a material interruption in the text that, whether intended or not, calls our attention away from the words and toward the paper, a pair of scissors, and perhaps some tape. Language, in this instance, acts. That act can either be followed or resisted, misconstrued or ignored; it can even simply be. Anyone who experiences the "Frame-Tale" instructions must engage their action in some form.

"Frame-Tale" is just the first in a series of examples from the Ambrose stories in which Barth materializes language. He anthropomorphizes words in the story "Ambrose His Mark," sets language on the same ontological plane as a glass bottle in "Water-Message," and converts it into a defunct currency in "Lost in the Funhouse." Along the way, Barth's notion of what language is and does seems at turns Saussurean and Chomskyan, sometimes figuring words as components of some grand system, sometimes suggesting that they might be biological phenomena. My point is not to settle on a theory of language. Rather, my point is to demonstrate that postmodern fiction in general and metafiction in particular conceive of language as material. When language becomes material, we can see that the open-endedness of postmodern fiction is not purely abstract, theoretical, or indeterminate. Morrison's *Jazz* closes with the word "now," defying an ending by stopping in the reader's present. Silko's *Ceremony* concludes with "Sunrise," ending with a beginning, and we will see that both Barth and Wallace frustrate our desire for closure at the ends of their stories. But if the open-endedness of these conclusions is effected in language that is resolutely material, then what becomes clear is that we are left not with some precocious ambiguity or lack of direction but with the materials we need to account for the ongoing formation, reformation, and transformation of the networks formed through reading.

"Ambrose His Mark" explores the gap between signifier and signified that we typically imagine as the cornerstone of language play in postmodern metafiction. The story is narrated by Ambrose himself as he looks back on his early childhood. He challenges our good faith as readers immediately when he explains the "hectic circumstances" of his own birth, but what is important for our purposes is that the infant goes many months without a proper name (14). His family refers to him sometimes as *"Honig,"* German for "honey," and other times as "Christine." The final decision to award him a name is the byproduct of the central conflict of the story: a fight between Ambrose's grandfather and a beekeeping neighbor named Willy Erdmann. The two elderly men are in a contest to woo a swarm of bees to their respective hives. The swarm arrives one Sunday morning as Ambrose's mother Andrea lies in the backyard hammock with her little *Honig*. The bees alight on Andrea's breast, covering her and the baby. The older men each attempt to lure the bees, and the scene erupts when the bees go wild. The men fight and are eventually separated by congregants from the church across the street. In the aftermath of the mayhem, Aunt Rosa points out that the baby's birthmark resembles a bee: "'All the time he was our *Honig*, that's what drew the bees. Now his mark'" (32). Uncle Konrad declares the mark a "naming-sign"; thus, the relationship between the baby and the experience with the bees takes shape in the birthmark, which is imagined as a sign that will lead them to a name (which is itself a sign).

To recalibrate our understanding of the postmodern view of language is not to claim that the baby's name is somehow not a sign, not referential or representative. Instead, my point is that the signs themselves are also things. In the chain of signification under poststructuralism, when we want to understand a signifier we examine its signified only to realize that the signified is, itself, a signifier, and so on, perhaps barely grasping the trace of each signifier in the next or previous. When it comes to naming Ambrose, however, it is not the signification of signifiers but the signifiers themselves that influence his mother's decision. Uncle Konrad spends the afternoon consulting *The Book of Knowledge*, whereby he comes up with "a number of historical parallels to [the child's] experiences in the hammock" (32). His book turns up Plato, Sophocles, Xenophon, and Saint Ambrose as potential namesakes who all were said to have been marked by bees in some way: "'For instance, a swarm of bees lit on Plato's mouth when he was a kid. They say that's where he got his way with words.'" Andrea detests the first three names: "'No kid of mine is going to be called Plato'" (33). The names themselves, not their signified concepts, concern Andrea most, mirroring Aunt Rosa's exclamation that it was "'our *Honig*, that's what drew the bees." The name they finally agree on, "Ambrose," is a combination of two signifieds; it is both the ambrosia or honey and, simultaneously, a tribute to a great thinker of the Western world. At the same time, Ambrose himself is the honey, the *Honig*, that draws the bees. He is the thing. Yes, the name is a word, but it is also Ambrose himself: "Vanity frets about his name, Pride vaunts it, Knowledge retches at its sound, Understanding sighs; all live outside it, knowing well that I and my sign are neither one nor quite two" (34). The sign seems immaterial, separate from the person: "Yet only give it voice: whisper 'Ambrose,' as at rare times certain people have—see what-all leaves off to answer!" (34).

If language operates as an actor in a manner similar to the pair of scissors you might use to cut "Frame-Tale" from Barth's book, or like the bees that swarm Ambrose as an infant, then it can organize the existence of other actors in very real, material ways. Uncle Konrad's reading of naming practices and the significance of bees from a variety of cultures in *The Book of Knowledge* reveals that signs mediate; they do not merely serve as placeholders or intermediaries. "The American Indians, he declared now, had the right idea. 'They never named a boy right off. What they did, they watched to find out who he was. They'd look for the right sign to tell them what to call him.'" Far from imagining language as an abstract system that follows material particulars, as Grandfather intones—"'How can you tell what name'll suit a person when you don't know him yet?'"—this approach demonstrates how names can shape a person. "'There's some name their kids for what they want them to be. A brave hunter, et cetera,'" Uncle Konrad explains (17). Later, he expounds on the differences between how different cultures understand the swarming of bees as a sign: "'A swarm on the house was thought by the Austrians to augur good fortune, by the Romans to warn of ill, and by the Greeks to herald strangers; that in Switzerland a swarm on a dry twig presaged the death of someone in the family, et cetera'" (22). In each case the swarming operates as a sign, a signifier whose signified is good fortune, a warning, or an announcement. But the different interpretations of the same sign actually constitute the differences between these cultures. How else can such abstract cultures be distinguished, other than by considering how similar phenomena operate differently in a given context? The signs are things that shape the culture.

For language to organize the lives of other actors, it must be present to those actors. It cannot, therefore, be understood primarily in terms of the absences that divide signs. Harpham points out that "Saussure is ritually invoked by the thinkers of postmodernity as the genius who first articulated the two principles on which postmodernism is founded, the system without a center, and differences without positivity."[28] Barth certainly figures language as a system, but is the center of that system absence? The answer, I argue, is no. Postmodern writers like Barth can be read as constructing language as a system of presence. "Water-Message" recounts Ambrose's early adolescence. He and a friend, Perse, walk along the Eastern Shore's tidewater one afternoon and find a clear glass bottle containing a note:

> the sea-wreathed bottle was an emblem. Westward it lay, to westward, where the tide ran from East Dorset. Past the river and the Bay, from continents beyond, this messenger had come. Borne by currents as yet uncharted, nosed by fishes as yet unnamed, it had bobbed for ages beneath strange stars. Then out of the oceans it had strayed; past cape and cove, black can, red nun, the word had wandered willy-nilly to his threshold. (55)

The bottle is an emblem, a sign containing a message the boys desperately want to know. But the object resists their attempts to acquire, much less decipher, the message. They remove the cap only to be unable to extract the note from the bottle. Finally, Perse shouts: "For pity's sake bust it!" (55). At once the bottle and its message assert their agency as signs. Their presence frustrates the boys' attempts at interpretation.

The note itself may, at first, seem to confirm the idea that postmodern fiction concerns itself with language as a system without center. After three violent swings, Ambrose shatters the bottle and retrieves the note:

> On a top line was penned in deep red ink:
> TO WHOM IT MAY CONCERN
> On the next-to-bottom:
> YOURS TRULY

Apart from the salutation and the closing the note is blank: no message, no name. Thus, the heart or center of the note seems to be an absence. And yet, as Ambrose shifts the note in his hand, he stares at it and thinks to himself, that "those shiny bits in the paper's texture were splinters of wood pulp. Often as he'd seen them in the leaves of cheap tablets, he had not thitherto embraced that fact" (57). These are the final lines of the story. At the center of language lies not a void but a substance that Ambrose has never considered before. The letter's open-endedness, apart from the basic form of salutation and close, has led some to conclude that "the message consists in the fact of its occurrence,"[29] and that "the content of a message is irrelevant in comparison with the importance of the act of writing that message."[30] Both of these approaches make an effort to account for the presence of language, but might be enhanced by claiming that the opening and closing of the letter are present to Ambrose not because of the seemingly absent center but because of the material space that separates them. Practically, this material space is as present as the bottle itself, which now litters the water's edge in the form of a hundred sparkling shards. Every time Barth creates a potential void at the center of language, he invariably fills that void. The bottle contains the note. The empty space in the note contains the "shiny bits" of wood pulp. Thus, the endless chain of language divides signifiers not by absence but by other presences. There is no void.

And yet, if there is no void in the language system, how does Ambrose come to be "lost in the funhouse"? The final story in the Ambrose cycle, which is also the title story of the collection, has commonly been read as a "gradual confrontation with the absent center of language," as Morris explains.[31] As Barth's narrator puts it, Ambrose takes "a wrong turn, stray[s] into the pass *wherein he lingers yet*" (97). Woolley leans less on the rhetoric of emptiness, but argues nonetheless that "as the self-reflexive language undermines language's reference function, it undermines our sense of the narrator as person."[32] If we will accept for just a moment the possibility that language is built at least as much on presence as it is on absence, we might look up to realize that "Lost in the Funhouse" is overrun with material objects: "Under the boardwalk, matchbook covers, grainy other things" (79); "*El Producto* cigar butts, treasured with Lucky Strike cigarette stubs, Coca-Cola caps, gritty turds, cardboard lollipop sticks, matchbook covers" (80); "the world winks at him through its objects, grabs grinning at his coat" (88). One object in particular materializes language, rendering it as present and palpable as a Lucky Strike cigarette stub: a name-coin. The story follows a now-thirteen-year-old Ambrose on a family trip to the boardwalk at Ocean City, Maryland, with his father, mother, Uncle Karl, brother Peter, and their neighbor Magda. A boardwalk and amusement park staple, the name-coin is explained by the presence of "a machine that stamped your name around a white-metal coin with a star in the middle: A____" (85). The presence of these many nonhuman actors, and of the name-coin in particular, revises our reading of the funhouse as the endless hall of linguistic mirrors, and reimagines it as the kind of material interruption that Barth explores in "Frame-Tale." Language becomes another nonhuman actor whose presence constitutes the material out of which our networks of relation are constructed.

From the very outset there is no reason that language must be read as the all-consuming presence, or I should say absence, of "Funhouse." After all, while Ambrose gets lost in one version of the ending, Barth crafts another ending in which "[t]he family's going home. Mother sits between Father and Uncle Karl, who teases him good-naturedly" (97). Why linger with Ambrose in the funhouse and not in the car on the way home? But if we follow Ambrose on his path to and through the funhouse, it becomes clear that even the most abstract of sign systems has the material capacity to interrupt our lived experience, give us access to community, or deny us access. The name-coin represents two of the most abstract sign systems: names and money. Names are by nature referential, and yet, as we saw with Ambrose's name, they can also be read as resolutely material. Money is also referential. There is nothing inherently valuable about most currencies. The US dollar is not tied to any referential standard in the way it once was, and the coins of US currency have not been made out of the metals from which they were once forged for decades. Barth merges these two systems in the name-coin, rendering Ambrose's name in material currency. Such an object is surely in keeping with the many readings of the funhouse as a manifestation of the trap of language in which its occupants long for return to some pre-linguistic state that is impossible, as Harris points out: "Man simply cannot leap outside language."[33] And so we might expect it to gain him entrance to the funhouse. But when Ambrose approaches the ticket woman and "inadvertently [gives] her his name-coin instead of the half dollar," the woman rebuffs him and remarks on his birthmark to Magda, "'Watch out for him, girlie, he's a marked man!'" (92). The layers of signification point not to absence but to presence. The faulty coin is not valid currency, and it holds up the line as Ambrose presumably digs out the half dollar that gains him admittance to the funhouse. Its presence is palpable; it stops the line, but moves the story along.

So then what to make of the funhouse itself? If the funhouse is a metafictional metaphor for language, as so many have claimed, then Barth is not embracing the funhouse but exposing it as a farcical trap for those who get caught up in searching for some hidden structure to explain everything. The funhouse exposes and rejects language as a system abstracted from the rest of the world. If language is not privileged as something wholly different from other things, then one conclusion we might draw is that it is a thing, an actor, just like other things, and so it can play a vital role in the construction of human networks, much like the nonhuman actors investigated in previous chapters. "For whom is the funhouse fun? Perhaps for lovers" (72). These opening lines of "Lost in the Funhouse" point toward Barth's theory of language as much as the stranding of Ambrose within its walls. The young boy's whole problem with the funhouse is that he does not understand that it is a place where young lovers can chase each other and flirt. He boldly asks Magda to accompany him, naively relieved when his older brother scrounges up a quarter to come along. The older boy and girl quickly run off together in the funhouse, while Ambrose is left behind to fend for himself. Barth's metadiscourse amps up as Ambrose takes one wrong turn after another: "A long time ago we should have passed the apex of Freitag's Triangle and made brief work of the *dénoument*; the plot does rise meaningful steps but winds upon itself, digresses, retreats, hesitates, sighs, collapses, expires" (96). Finally, Ambrose "wishes he had never entered the funhouse. But he has. Then he wishes he were dead. But he's not." Whether blithely unaware of the unexplored angles and dimensions of the funhouse, like Magda and Peter, or cripplingly self-aware of every loose plank, like Ambrose, the funhouse is not separate from the rest of the world. Word and world are one. Ambrose both lives out his days wandering the funhouse and rides home with his family, wondering whether or not "he will become a regular person."

Barth's introductory remarks from the earliest readings of these stories suggest that language is of no more significance than emotion: "If these pieces aren't also *moving*, then the experiment is unsuccessful, and their author is lost in the funhouse indeed."[34] Barth's reticence at the thought of being "lost in the funhouse indeed" betrays his dissatisfaction with endless language play and, perhaps more important, shows that the funhouse is not necessarily a world apart. The funhouse is a fantastic attraction but not a place to dwell. There is no reason to get lost there. When signs are understood as things, their mediating capacities become more evident. Ambrose's name, or lack thereof, can affect his status as surely as the glass bottle can resist the boys' attempts to break it open. Postmodern fiction's obsession with language can be read as a preoccupation with the actors that shape the social, and not just as a meditation on the impossibility of meaning. David Foster Wallace's rewriting of the story points us toward the possibilities of a non-linguistic-centered reading of postmodern fiction that accounts for the world by attending to the materiality of language in everyday experience and addresses questions such as, How does language operate as an actor? If it is a mediator like other nonhuman actors, how does it affect human actors? If the funhouse is for lovers and Ambrose is no lover, then is he representative of a person who experiences a different relation to language than others?

THINGS AND PEOPLE

> For whom is the funhouse fun? Perhaps for lovers.
> —John Barth, *Lost in the Funhouse*

Taking the opening lines from "Lost in the Funhouse" as an epigraph, the final story of Wallace's 1989 collection *Girl with Curious Hair* revisits the sights and sounds of Barth's classic metafictional story en route to what James Rother calls a "sendup-*cum*-homage that is nearly six times as long as its source text."[35] "Westward the Course of Empire Takes Its Way" spins itself out of the creative writing workshop taught by Professor Ambrose at East Chesapeake Tradeschool, and much like Barth's Ambrose and his family in "Lost in the Funhouse," Wallace's main characters, D. L. Eberhardt, Mark Nechtr, and Tom Sternberg, embark on a journey to a fantastical destination: "the scheduled Reunion of everyone who has ever been in a McDonald's commercial, arranged by J. D. Steelritter Advertising and featuring a party to end all parties, a spectacular collective Reunion commercial, the ribbon-cutting revelation of the new Funhouse franchises' flagship discotheque."[36] D. L., a self-proclaimed postmodernist, and Mark, a trust fund college student with a heart of gold, seem an unlikely romantic pairing. They are polar opposites in nearly every way, and yet when Mark witnesses D. L. fleeing the scene after writing something nasty about Professor Ambrose on the chalkboard one day prior to class, he does not rat her out, and somehow a connection is forged. D. L. claims to be—but is in fact not—pregnant, and Mark marries her out of a sense of noble obligation and accompanies her on the reunion journey, along with Tom Sternberg, a fellow commercial alum and friend of D. L. Through a series of unlikely events interlaced with various characters' memories and narrative interjections, the group arrives in Illinois, where they are to be picked up and transported to the reunion via helicopter by advertising mogul J. D. Steelritter and his hapless son DeHaven, another unlikely pair. The story bogs down soon after, along with DeHaven's car, before the group ever arrives at its destination, marked by huge golden arches that can be seen towering over the endless cornfields of the Midwest.

The novella-as-rewrite of Barth's "Lost in the Funhouse" has been the primary focus of the few studies of "Westward," but critics tend to disagree as to Wallace's feelings toward the so-called "first generation" postmodern writers such as Barth, Coover, and Pynchon.[37] Rother reads "Westward" as both tribute and critique. Paul Giles proposes, "Wallace's story suggests that Barth's notion of ironic reflexivity has become thoroughly institutionalized, as much a syndicated brand as McDonald's itself."[38] Other critics have recognized in Wallace's Professor Ambrose a fictional version of Barth himself, "presented as the foremost theorist of postmodernism in *Westward*—which draws heavily on Barth's seminal story 'Lost in the Funhouse' in order to unmask the often shallow strategies of metafiction."[39] In one of the few book-length treatments of Wallace's work, Marshall Boswell says outright that "*Westward* should be read as a metafictional critique of metafiction that seeks to demolish even metafiction's own claim to imperious self-consciousness."[40] Across this range of perspectives on Wallace's relation to Barth, the common ground appears to be that the novella critiques the early metafiction of

Barth and his cohort as coming up empty. Boswell characterizes this critique as Wallace entering the "prison house of postmodern self-reflexivity" while maintaining a firm hold on "the world of the real, the world outside the text, that is, the text's transcendent referent."[41] Rather than continue to depend on the binary opposition of world to text, inside to outside, a neomaterialist reading suggests that Wallace asks us to embrace the paradoxical conflation of inner and outer to view language, not as an abstract system that ultimately depends on absence and precludes touching, but as a sincere (perhaps overly sincere) facilitator of connections between actors.

Wallace merges word and world most tangibly through an arrow given to Mark Nechtr as a gift. A wedding present from his former YWCA archery coach, the Dexter Aluminum Target Arrow intervenes in the story by preventing Mark, D. L., and Tom from meeting Steelritter and DeHaven on time at the helipad when they arrive at Central Illinois Airport: "The LordAloft pilot, a Polynesian in a just bitching three-piece and mirrored glasses, wouldn't allow Mark's disassembled bow or quiver on the helicopter. [. . .] Target arrows are deadly weapons, after all" (248). The circulation of this object throughout the novella uncovers a Zeno's paradox between text and world. The choice of an arrow reminds us of Zeno's arrow paradox in which motion is impossible because everything is motionless at any given instant and time is essentially a series of instants. The Zeno's paradox between text and world is that the characters never arrive at their destination, and so it would seem that readers cannot finish the story, and yet, of course, we do finish the story, just as I will argue that the characters do reach a destination. Wallace's use of the arrow compels this connection, but it also insinuates that the metafictional language play of early postmodern fiction is less abstract and more corporeal than the likes of Pynchon, Coover, and even Barth may have realized. Language is tangible. Language is a thing, like a target arrow or a glass bottle. It can pierce or shatter, convey or resist, much like any other actor, human or nonhuman.

Wallace takes postmodernism on directly by making much of the fact that D. L. self-identifies as a postmodernist: "she actually went around *calling* herself a postmodernist. No matter *where* you are, you Don't Do This." Wallace has Professor Ambrose, Barth's fictional incarnation, condemn this style by characterizing it as having a "certain 'Look-Mom-no-hands quality'" (234). Wallace associates the infinitely playful poststructuralist experimentation with language with those who claim to be postmodern, but he dissociates his Barthean character from that crowd. Whereas Barth was trying to explore the ultimate connections and ruptures between things, people, and words, Wallace represents those who follow in his footsteps for the sake of some abstract idea of the artist as "coldly fertile" (234). In other words, Wallace's gripe seems to be with the critical conversation surrounding "Lost in the Funhouse," not with the story itself, because Barth is not invested in the infinite deferral of meaning, but in the material interruption of what we take for granted as the immaterial process of reading (think "Frame-Tale"). If Wallace is postmodern, then postmodernism is not poststructuralism; postmodernism names a way of seeing and being that is in process, open, and focused on language as an actor.

This reading of Wallace is in keeping with the general claim that his work represents a return to sincerity amidst the pervasive irony of postmodernism and with Adam Kelly's more specific claim that Wallace was "returning to literary narrative a concern with sincerity not seen since modernism shifted the ground so fundamentally almost a century before."[42] Kelly's reference to modernism returns our focus to the gap between word and world. Channeling Lionel Trilling's view of sincerity as bound up with irony in modernism, Kelly observes that "what Trilling could not anticipate in 1972 was that irony was in the process of taking over, and with the rise of poststructuralism in the academy, and postmodernism in the arts, the surface/depth model of the self assumed by both sincerity and authenticity would soon be superseded by the privilege afforded to the inaugurating powers of capital, technology, culture, and especially language."[43] While some might argue that Wallace's sincerity is what distances his work from postmodernism and perhaps even inaugurates some new *ism*, I would counter that the sincerity evinced by Wallace's view of word and world is representative of postmodernism given its dependence on the materiality of language.

Wallace reveals the materiality of language as mediator by using the arrow to accomplish in "Westward" what Barth accomplishes with words in "Funhouse." Throughout "Funhouse," Barth punctuates his prose with unfinished sentences: "The smell of Uncle Karl's cigar smoke reminded one of" (74). The period that follows "of" signals the grammatical end of the sentence, but Barth does not complete the thought and explain what the smell calls to mind. It could be anything: another smell, a memory, a taste, a radio program, anything. This playfulness is a textbook example of the open-ended and seemingly endless cycle of signification that language supposedly represents for postmodernism. But the point here is that the smell reminded "one," not Uncle Karl, of something unknown. That is, the narrator does not leave anything out so much as refuse to fill in the blank for others. There is a gap between what the smell reminds Uncle Karl of and what it recalls to my mind, but that gap is not an absence, as we saw with Ambrose's message in a bottle. Cigar smoke might remind someone of her father and remind someone else of poker. Wallace uses the target arrow to demonstrate that what seems like an absence, or empty space, at the heart of language is actually a trick of perception that can be overcome. Here is how the narrator of "Westward" describes Mark's mastery of target shooting:

> As you stand shoulder-first across thirty orthogonal meters between you and the red thing that encloses the gold chroma, [...] the point of your arrow, at full draw, is somewhere between three and nine centimeters to the left of the true straight line to the bull's-eye, even though the arrow's nock, fucked by the string, is *on* that line. The bow gets in the way, see. So logically it seems like if your sight and aim are truly true, the arrow should always land just to the left of target-center [...] But the straight-aimed and so off-angled target arrow will stab the center, right in the heart, every time. It is an archer's law that makes no sense. How is this so? (294)

The answer, our narrator explains, "lies in what happens to the well-aimed arrow when it's released; what happens *while it's traveling* to the waiting target" (294). Much like we all know the ending of Barth's unfinished sentences in our own ways, so too can we know that the gap between where the arrow is aimed and where it actually strikes the bulls-eye is a trick of the eye. A space separates the off-center mark and the heart of the target, and yet there is no space at all, "the bow gets in the way, see." Like any other object, a bow for instance, language gets in the way of its own existence. As the bow delivers the arrow and yet skews our perception, so language connects us and mediates our communication. The distance between bow and target is not empty; it is occupied by the arrow itself.

Barth's unfinished sentences and Wallace's off-target arrows suggest that postmodern open-endedness is not so much a matter of meaning deferred as it is a matter of leaving the text open to the world in which it operates. After all, we do communicate with language as surely as an arrow aimed and shot at a target will hit the target. The gap between where the archer aims and the bulls-eye represents a correlation, not a separation. The bulls-eye is clearly to the left, and yet. Words clearly do not touch their concepts, referents, the world, and yet. Wallace's narrator recalls Mark's attempt to lose the arrow:

> The thing cannot be lost. Even shot it at the sea once. Off an old wharf. Except it *floated*, though, glinting; hung in the water by its cedar knock; came in on the sluggish tide within hours. And Mark had waited for it. On the crumbled wharf that smelled of fish. The fact that the arrow can't disappear is both a comfort and a worry. It makes Nechtr feel special, true. But from special it's not very far to Alone. (308)

The arrow signifies. It is a sign for comfort, worry, uniqueness, and loneliness. In the chain of signification it is a signifier and a signified. If an object like the arrow can be a signifier as surely as it is a signified, then why not an object like this sentence? If this sentence, even this word, can be a thing like an arrow is a thing, then the materials out of which we construct our networks of relation might also include language. All communities, Latour contends, are more "worknets" than networks because "it's the work, and the movement, and the flow, and the changes that should be stressed."[44] Language is the material of social construction as well as a tool, not in the sense of a mere intermediary, but in the sense of a thing that affects the formation of another thing. Language constitutes, and we just as surely use language to construct. For Latour, "if you stop making and remaking groups, you stop having groups."[45] If the entire story is a meditation on the shortcomings of the "prison house of postmodern self-reflexivity," as Boswell says, then perhaps material manifestations of poststructuralism such as the "archer's law that makes no sense" can also be read more positively as alternative models of how postmodernism figures language.

Language is not so much a prison house or an infinite deferral as it is an assemblage of parts whose use, while faulty, does convey and constitute meaning with the agency and material force of an arrow let loose or a car broken down. We should not be afraid of saying that language conveys. One can also convey with a gift, a look, a gesture, and yet we would not reduce these things to mere vehicles of conveyance. When the reunion crew is denied passage on the helicopter, J. D. and his son DeHaven come to pick them up from the airport in DeHaven's quirky car: "I built this baby from scratch. It's not technically an anything." When D. L. refuses to ride in anything but a Datsun, J. D. compromises: " 'Tell you what, Eberhardt [. . .] we write DATSUN in the shameful no-pride dust on the kid's rear window, here' [. . .] It both relieved Sternberg and gave him the creeps. 'An instant Datsun?' " (298). A name brand would locate the car along a hierarchy of carmakers, and D. L. seems a prisoner to that particular system of signs. But the fact that DeHaven's car isn't "technically an anything" means her imprisonment does not correspond to the actual order of things in the world of the story. Correspondence is not a bad word here. There is no "Datsunness," in a Platonic sense, for Wallace. Instead, he is critiquing D. L.'s "postmodern" understanding of meaning as merely constructed, as in artificial. She thinks meaning is as simple as writing "Datsun" into the dust on DeHaven's rear window. Wallace knows that language is not some world apart, but one mediator among many others that has been assembled in very specific orders to shape Datsun as a brand and to form individual Datsuns. The word is another actor, like the shape of a headlight or the line of a fender that would help us identify a Datsun. The narration, the language, the words—like the car in the story—have conveyed us to this moment. When the car eventually bogs down in the Illinois mud a few short miles from the Reunion site, the narrator says, with still thirty pages left to go, "This is pretty much the climax of the whole journey, by the way, pending arrival" (345). The arrow and car have brought us to the *"while it's traveling"* of the narrative, the literal rising action that Wallace treats as the climax of the story in Freitagian terms.

Much has been made of Barth's inclusion of a literal Freitag's Triangle in the text of "Lost in the Funhouse."[46] As "Lost in the Funhouse" spins out of control, Barth's narrator explains, "[a] long time ago we should have passed the apex of Freitag's Triangle and made brief work of the *dénouement*; the plot doesn't rise by meaningful steps but winds upon itself, digresses, retreats, hesitates, sighs, collapses, expires" (96). Similarly, as DeHaven's car fails to reach its goal and instead "digresses, retreats, hesitates, sighs, collapses, expires," the abusive father who has demeaned and bullied DeHaven throughout the story seems to soften toward his son, and D. L. "can tell DeHaven Steelritter and J. D. love each other, deep down, and this affects her" (345). According to the paradox, the arrow does not arrive at its target, the group does not make it to the reunion within the bounds of the narrative, but do we not arrive anywhere at all? We arrive in-process as DeHaven seeks assistance from a local farmer to pull the car out of the mud, thus growing the strange little community again by one—well, two if we count the horse the farmer brings to help extract the "instant Datsun." What Wallace emphasizes in this simultaneously penultimate and ultimate moment of his narrative is the very fact of process. The ragtag band of travelers in "Westward" does not arrive, does not enjoy the reunion, "but in time, they'll arrive at what's been built" (372).

To arrive at an ending that is process rather than product is not abstract, immaterial, or devoid of meaning. The wheels of DeHaven's car spin in the Illinois mud, and it wouldn't be out of line to stop and explain how Wallace is critiquing postmodern metafiction and poststructuralism as abstract, immaterial, and unproductive. But Wallace himself does not stop. The wheel spinning leaves the narrative open to its reader, whom Wallace's narrator addresses directly: "So trust me: we will arrive. Cross my heart. Stick a needle. To tell the truth, we might already be there. [. . .] But the wheel! Bound by nothing, the Goodyear spins and spins, has lost its ringing hub, has disclosed a radial's spokes" (373). The center, or hub, is lost, but this absence discloses the presence of the wheel's spokes. Rather than one unifying center, we find a multitude of centers.

The narrator speaks in the imperative: "Hold rapt for that impossible delay, that best interruption: that moment in all radial time when something unseen inside the blur of spokes seems to sputter, catch, and spin against the spin" (373). When the center is not missing but broken, the infinite reaching tendrils of the individual spokes sprawl out of radial time and erode any inner/outer binary by refusing that inevitable "[n]ot only . . . but also" that Latour decries as perpetuating the false distinction between subjective and objective reality in which "objectivity is always on the other side of the fence" (145). What I hope has become clear through these first three chapters is that in post-1960s fiction there are no sides, only fence. All things, including words, are, well, things. We pick words up and set them down. They resist our usage. They refuse to bend to human will, as any writer from Barth to Wallace knows.

Wallace abandons both sides of the fence and sets the stage for "Westward" in an earlier installment from *Girl with Curious Hair* by collapsing the distance between story and narrative discourse.[47] Among the earliest pieces of fiction Wallace ever published, the story "Here and There" does not contain any narration. That is, there is not a single word in the story outside quotation marks. There is literally nothing outside the story, no narration, no commentary. Furthermore, the entire story is a session of so-called "fiction therapy" in which the protagonist Bruce, a brilliant MIT graduate in electrical engineering, recounts the dissolution of his relationship with a young woman by speaking in both his own voice and his ex-girlfriend's voice in an attempt, as his therapist says, "'to construct an instance in which for once your interests are to be subordinated to those of another'" (153). However, what may seem at first like the ultimate incarnation of Derrida's *il n'y a pas de hors-texte* is, in fact, something else. Rather than making all the world into an abstract and semiotic text, Wallace materializes all textual constructions by rejecting representation in favor of direct discourse and by focusing on a stove at the story's end that contains all of Bruce's fears and anxieties. It should come as no surprise that the second story of Barth's *Lost in the Funhouse*, the "Night-Sea Journey" of a sperm fertilizing an egg, also takes place entirely in direct discourse. In the world of "Here and There" there is only story, only action; there is no separate world of narration. Bruce finds himself spiraling down into the labyrinth of language, only to have the semiosis of the system disrupted by the stubbornness of a 1960s electric stove.

Similar to the way in which the Moebius strip in Barth's "Frame-Tale" requires the material intervention of the reader in order to complete its work, "Here and There" asks us to piece its story together without the help of any narrative discourse. Throughout the story we follow Bruce's obsession with the erosion of language as a "correlative" system. Bruce explains, "Words as fulfillers of the function of signification in artistic communication will wither like the rules of form before them. Meaning will be clean" (155). He describes his ideal vision of the language-meaning system as "the icy beauty of the perfect signification of fabricated nonverbal symbols and their relation through agreed-on rules" (167). As he goes on to recreate the dissolution of his romantic relationship in the fiction therapy session, Bruce recalls a trip he takes to his aunt's and uncle's house in Maine, where he begins to feel a separation between his emotions and the source of those emotions, which he describes as "something outside" himself. He explains that he is overcome with "an urge to 'write it all out,' to confront the past and present as a community of signs, but this requires a special distance I seem to have left behind. For a few days I exercise instead—go for long, shambling runs in jeans and sneakers, move some heavy mechanical clutter out of my uncle's backyard" (165–66). Instead of turning to language, or to the other characters, who seem to draw their very breath from language, Bruce turns to physical activity, to manual labor and material experience.

In fact, Bruce seems to see no marked difference between things and people in his attempts to understand himself, but his valuation of the material renders all things intermediaries, not mediating actors. He calls his brother Leonard on the phone and gives an "involved and scrupulously fair edition" of his breakup, and subsequent unhappiness. Leonard insists that, like their mother, Bruce suffers from "an unhappy and basically silly desire to be perfect," the fulfillment of which would ultimately render a person's life boring (166). When Bruce responds that being boring is an imperfection and "would by definition be impossible for a perfect person," Leonard retorts that his brother has "always enjoyed playing games with words in order to dodge the real meanings of things," which Bruce thinks "segues with suspicious neatness into [his] intuitions about the impending death of lexical utterance" (166). Bruce's therapist counters that Leonard was simply trying to point out the impossibility of perfection, but Bruce retorts, "There is no shortage of things that are perfect for the function that defines them. Peano's axioms. A chameleon's coat. A Turing Machine" (167). The therapist points out, "Those aren't persons," but Bruce insists, "No one has ever argued persuasively that that has anything to do with it. My professors stopped trying" (166–67). For Bruce, all human and nonhuman entities are mere placeholders in "systems of information and energy-transfer" (154). In his language-dominated world, actors do not count for more than just one, and thus the agency of language is foreclosed.

Bruce is the ultimate Ambrose teetering on the edge of an earth-shattering revelation in his subsequent encounter with his aunt's stove. The interruption of Bruce's theory of the "icy beauty of the perfect signification" occurs as the result of what Brown has called "the suddenness with which things seem to assert their presence and power."[48] As Bruce waits for his uncle to get home from work one day, his aunt asks him to take a look at their old stove because it is not working properly. With an electrical engineering degree from MIT, fixing an electric stove shouldn't be that complicated, but Bruce quickly makes a mess of the stove's wiring. He understands the workings of the circuits, jacks, and burners, but has never "personally bound a system of wire." Instead, he explains, "the work that interests me is done with a pencil and a sheet of paper. Rarely even a calculator. At the cutting edge of electrical engineering, almost everything interesting is resolvable via the manipulation of variables. I've never once been stumped on an exam. Ever. And I appear to have broken this miserable piece-of-shit stove" (170). Bruce's frustration is grounded in his lack of assurance about what he can and cannot know. He cannot adjust for all the variables necessary to fix the stove without information that is unavailable to him, in part, because of the age of the appliance. He laments, "There is *no way to know* without data on the resistance ratios in the metal composition of the burners" (170–71). The therapist interjects, "You're unable to fix an electric stove?" The stove resists Bruce's ideal world in which all things, people, and words count for just one, where we are all intermediaries. This stove, a relic of the

Kennedy era, as Bruce is often reminded, is composed of numbers, systems, and functions, and should be a sure fix. Instead, the gap Bruce has created between word and world renders him not only unable to mend the stove, but also oddly fearful of the thing itself in its resistance. This fear is an important crack in the foundation of Bruce's personal funhouse of signification as his frustration gives way to fright: "Suddenly the inside of this stove is the very last place on earth I want to be. I begin to be frightened of the stove" (171). This fear drives Bruce to begin behaving strangely, putting on a performance that only multiplies his agitation: "I rattle a screwdriver against the inside of the stove so my aunt thinks I'm doing something. I get more and more frightened" (171). At this point we experience a fast-paced exchange between Bruce, his imagining of his ex-girlfriend's voice, and the therapist, in which Bruce's fascination with the systematization of knowledge through signification finally crumbles altogether in the face of his fear. He explains, "I'm so scared behind this dirty old stove I can't breathe. I rattle tools" (171). The ultimate merger of knowledge and experience, word and world, subjective and objective takes place as Bruce's aunt kneels down next to him "to lay her hand on [his] shoulder," and he concludes, "I'm afraid of absolutely everything there is" (172). More than just a fracture in his theory of the world, Wallace characterizes this fear as an invitation to the world. The final line of the story belongs to the therapist, who responds to Bruce's fearful confession with the simple phrase, "Then welcome" (172). Thus, the failure of Bruce's attempts to treat all words, things, and even people as mere placeholders in the galaxy of his life simultaneously constitutes his entrance into what it means to be in the world.

Bruce's fear in "Here and There" recalls the opening sentences from "Lost in the Funhouse," the first of which Wallace employs as an epigraph to "Westward": "For whom is the funhouse fun? Perhaps for lovers. For Ambrose it is *a place of fear and confusion*" (*Funhouse* 72). In "Lost in the Funhouse," Ambrose gets turned around and caught up in the funhouse and spends his time telling stories and looking for the cracks in the walls he ran across earlier in his journey. D. L. Eberhardt, Mark Nechtr, and the rest of the gang in "Westward" are all bogged down in Wallace's purposefully unending rewrite of Barth. Finally, in "Here and There," Bruce is mired in the "icy beauty of the perfect signification"

(167). What becomes apparent if we read each of these stories in light of Barth's question, "For whom is the funhouse fun?" and in light of the possible answer, "perhaps for lovers," is that none of the main characters featured in these stories is a lover. Instead, like Ambrose, they are all either fearful, or confused, or both. The funhouse can be fun for lovers because lovers have a form of relation that is not dependent on the funhouse. They do not come to the funhouse for the sake of the funhouse itself, but to heighten the effects of their already existing relationships. Barth's narrator explains Ambrose's realization of this fact as he scrambles along the floor of the funhouse: "shamefaced he saw that to get through expeditiously was not the point" (92). For lovers, the funhouse represents an opportunity to perform their love in new ways, but for those who focus on the amusement itself, the funhouse represents an endless preoccupation with the funhouse.

Most readings of Barth and Wallace as postmodern writers have fixated on language in what Meillassoux would call a correlationist fashion. That is, they only imagine language in terms of its relation to humans. If my own reading of Barth and Wallace in this chapter seems like something of a stretch, it's because I am trying to theorize the possibilities of language, beyond the gravitational pull of human significance. Wallace does this himself in *Infinite Jest* when he sketches "the night-noises of the metro night":

> Horns blatting off in the harbor. Receding sirens. Confused inland gulls' cries. Broken glass from far away. Car horns in gridlock, arguments in languages, more broken glass, running shoes, a woman's either laugh or scream from who can tell how far, coming off the grid. Dogs defending whatever dog-yards they pass by, the sounds of chains and risen hackles. The podiatric click and thud, the visible breath, gravel's crunch, creak of Green's leather, the *snick* of a million urban lighters....[49]

The list goes on, calling to mind Bogost's view of the list as a form for recognizing the thingliness of language. For my purposes here at the end of this chapter, it's the "arguments in languages" that stand out, or, rather, that do not stand out as any different from the other things in the list.

All of these things, "arguments in languages" included, signify here in ways that cannot be reduced to human perception. If all things exist on a flat ontological plan, and if all social networks are constructed out of things, then the final and most difficult step to take in a neomaterialist reading of postmodernism is to consider what it would mean to let go of language as somehow entirely coterminous with human meaning.

At the risk of overstating the case, Barth's seminal story can be read as a cautionary tale against approaching fiction, society, love, language, or fear as entirely understandable in relation to humans. To do so is to cut the Moebius strip from the "Frame-Tale" and spend the rest of our lives riding its circuitous contours, as opposed to acknowledging the reconstructive possibilities it represents. Wallace's rewriting of "Lost in the Funhouse," then, is a critical correction to the misreading of Barth as a sage who demonstrates that language is all that is the case, when, in fact, what makes writers such as Barth and Wallace postmodern are the ways in which they view language as a thing, as one material mediator among others. If, as Barth suggests and Wallace echoes, the funhouse is fun for lovers, then the final lines of "Westward" are especially significant:

> See this thing. See inside what spins without purchase. Close your eye. Absolutely no salesmen will call. Relax. Lie back. I want nothing from you. Lie back. Relax. Quality soil washes right out. Lie back. Open. Face directions. Look. Listen. Use ears I'd be proud to call our own. Listen to the silence behind the engines' noise. Jesus, Sweets, *listen*. Hear it? It's a love song. For whom? You are loved. (373)

Wallace's narrator, like Morrison's in *Jazz*, closes with a final appeal to readers, opening the narrative to us and explaining that we are loved. If we will only recognize our status as lovers, then we will also come to understand that the funhouse can be fun for us, not as an end in itself as it is for the fearful and confused such as Ambrose and Bruce, but as one component of our experience, one means of adding dimensions to our in-process lives as lovers. Wallace ends "Here and There" with the word "welcome" because realizing the mediating properties of material actors like the stove is only the first step in recognizing the in-process nature of all "worknets."

Just as Wallace closes the gap between his fictional world and the world of the reader, so too does postmodernism close the gap between word and the world. Neither word nor world can be understood in static terms. Both are always in process. A non-linguistic-centered analysis of Barth and Wallace reveals that metafiction does not view language as mired in human signification, but rather as a thing in its own right. "Even as textual entities," Latour insists, "objects overflow their makers, intermediaries become mediators."[50] Barth's title story closes with Ambrose constructing funhouses for others. "Westward" ends with the second-person admonition, "You are loved." "Here and There" concludes with an invitation: "Then welcome." In each of these instances, language is an other-oriented process. It is never an entity that can be cordoned off from other entities in a neat binary mode (i.e., word and world). Thus, if Derrida's over-quoted and under-considered *il n'y a pas de hors-texte* applies to postmodern fiction, then it must be understood not as claiming that everything is textual, or wrapped up in some abstract system of signs. First off, as James K. A. Smith explains, this famous phrase is better translated, "there is no outside-text." Smith continues: "To say that there is nothing outside the text is to say that there is nothing outside of textuality—there is no engagement with or inhabitance of a world which doesn't live off the mediation of signs."[51] If language is not separate from the world but operates as other things operate, then of course there is no outside-text. To say that there could be anything outside of the mediation of signs would be like saying a person could live and move in the world without having her experience mediated by things like the ground, water, cars, trees, phones, or chairs. Postmodern fiction is not so much preoccupied with the seemingly absent spaces in the endless chain of signification as it is with the ways in which our experiences of those spaces constitute common material presences. Language is a mediator that shapes the non-stop process of forming worknets.

This notion of being in-process resonates with Rita Felski's claim that postmodernism is not the "end" of anything,[52] and I would go further and say that postmodernism is the *in medias res* of everything. The open-ended nature of many of the texts treated at length in this study points to the fundamental ethic of postmodernism's interest in the ever-increasing complexity of everyday life. While the untraversable funhouse and the wheel of DeHaven's car that "spins and spins" may seem indicative of an endlessly playful aesthetic, they also enact a fluidity that allows actors to change the nature of their relations to one another. Postmodernism has typically been understood as grounding these relationships between actors in the idea of otherness, or difference. Given the recalibration of the absence and presence of language, however, and given the material foundation laid by these first three chapters, the next chapter re-examines otherness as an orthodoxy of postmodernism. Otherness, I argue, is actually the product of a more basic set of material relations. Don DeLillo's *Underworld* (1997) and Julia Alvarez's *How the García Girls Lost Their Accents* (1991) offer opportunities to explore how writers not only envision the social as a process, but also structure narratives so as to accentuate the significance of texts themselves as actors.

Chapter 4

Collapsing Otherness

Nearly twenty years before Ihab Hassan asked whether postmodernism should be considered a social phenomenon or "perhaps even a mutation in Western humanism,"[1] Leslie Fiedler argued that the new generation associated with "post-Modernist" fiction was rising in protest to "that bourgeois-Protestant version of Humanism, with its view of man as justified by rationality, work, duty, vocation, maturity, success."[2] Originally delivered as a lecture at Rutgers University, Fiedler's oft-cited 1965 essay, "The New Mutants," specifically analyzes "the effort of young men in England and the United States to assimilate into themselves (or even to assimilate themselves into) that otherness, that sum total of rejected psychic elements which the middle-class heirs of the Renaissance have identified with 'woman.'"[3] Although Fiedler's early contribution focuses especially on how WASP males buck the Enlightenment narrative of their sex, this idea of differentiation from tradition through "otherness" works its way into the larger discourse of postmodernism and develops into a defining trait in postmodern theories of sociality. Otherness has become the legacy of postmodernism. Even harsh critics of the postmodern aesthetic, such as Fredric Jameson and Terry Eagleton, praise its "celebration of difference and differentiation" in which, ideally, "cultures around the world are placed in tolerant contact with each other in a kind of immense cultural pluralism,"[4] and claim that the enfranchisement of previously voiceless groups is the "trend's most precious achievement."[5]

Difference, otherness—how do such negative, or absent, qualities evolve as positive, or present, defining traits? "The manufacture of Otherness," K. Anthony Appiah maintains, is the product of Enlightenment rationality and commodity culture, as it is for Lyotard, who also pitched postmodernism as a response to the hegemonic metanarratives of Enlightenment modernity.[6] For Appiah, postmodernism reappropriates commodity culture's multiplication of difference to challenge the hegemonic social imaginary of Enlightenment modernity typified by Max Weber.[7] In other words, the rise of modern commodity culture created the need to define through distinction in order to clear a space in the marketplace, and postmodernism simply takes this idea of "the manufacture of otherness" to its absolute extreme as a means of critiquing the monolith of modernity. After all, how can we believe that we live in a world defined by the unifying pervasion of reason and secularization when every day we witness the effects of authoritarian regimes and religious fundamentalisms? Given the undeniable proliferation of a vast array of different cultures, Appiah notes that "the beginning of postmodern wisdom is to ask whether Weberian rationalization is in fact what has occurred historically."[8] This question gestures toward the basic problem with postmodern theories of the social—the idea that cultures can be clearly defined through differentiation from one another. It is this idea of difference, or otherness, that has been understood incompletely in postmodernism's attempts to redress the hegemonic social imaginary of Enlightenment modernity.

In this chapter I argue that postmodern fiction is just as interested in the common material conditions out of which otherness is constructed as it is in otherness itself. As with the re-examination of postmodernism's orthodoxies in each of the preceding chapters, there is a significant gap between the ways in which postmodern fiction enacts the social and the ways in which it has been theorized. Eagleton looks back on the rise of postmodernism in *After Theory* to explain that on the path to postmodernism "whatever linked us—whatever was the *same*—was noxious. Difference was the new catch-cry."[9] In his landmark "Mapping the Postmodern," Andreas Huyssen describes the postwar social imaginary as made up of "various forms of otherness [. . .] constitutive of postmodern culture."[10] However, as we saw in the novels of Silko, Morrison, and Lethem, opposing cultures, races, and genders to one another necessarily ignores the in-process nature of so-called social markers. That is, to conceive of the social as grounded in otherness alone is to risk assuming that the categories being differentiated from one another are, at some point, not in-process. In turning once again to nonhuman actors that populate Don DeLillo's *Underworld* (1997) and Julia Alvarez's *How the García Girls Lost Their Accents* (1991), this chapter asks what we might learn by moving away from otherness as foundational to the postmodern construction of the social. The objects in these texts reveal that postmodern fiction is marked by an intrinsic interest not solely in otherness, but also—and perhaps more than one would think—in "inclination," or in what Jean-Luc Nancy calls the clinamen of fundamentally relational beings toward one another in an "inoperative community."[11]

For Nancy, there is a vital distinction between a social collective identified as a community and one identified as a society. A society is an organized (or operative) association of individuals, maintained through work, and a community is "the exposure of singularities."[12] By "exposure of singularities," Nancy means that community is not the gathering of autonomous individuals under an operative structure. Rather, building on Heidegger's idea of *Dasein*, Nancy envisions community as a kind of *being-with* or *being-in-common*. Thus, for Nancy, community is the mere inclination of singular beings toward one another, and, at base, these beings are relational, not individual. Inclination is not a novel concept for Nancy or for Western philosophy by any means. Its roots can be followed back at least as far Lucretius's two-thousand-year-old poem *On the Nature of Things*, in which the entire material universe is explained by the atom's power "to swerve from its normal path, plus its power to cling together with other atoms both like and unlike itself."[13] Stephen Greenblatt defines this "swerve" or, in Lucretius's Latin, this clinamen, as "an infinite number of atoms moving randomly through space, like dust motes in a sunbeam, colliding, hooking together, forming complex structures, breaking apart again, in a ceaseless process of creation and destruction" and later as "an unexpected, unpredictable movement of matter."[14] Greenblatt's book, *The Swerve: How the World Became Modern* (2011), charts the influence of this theory of matter throughout the European Renaissance, whereas Nancy culls it from Heidegger's later discussions of being.[15] The parallel theme in both treatments of the concept is that there is an unaccountable movement common to all matter that brings things into contact with one another. Without the clinamen, swerve, or inclination of atoms falling through the void, matter would never come into contact with other matter. There would be no difference because there would be no staging of difference. While postmodern fiction is certainly invested in valorizing difference, I contend that it is at least as interested in the inclination of actors that makes this difference possible.

There may seem, at first, to be a conflict between my emphasis on the importance of inclination in postmodern sociality and Latour's insistence that the social is best understood as a worknet: "no work, no group."[16] After all, Nancy distinguishes between a community, which is the mere "exposure of singularities," and a society, which is the result of work. However, we must keep in mind that Latour is talking about the formation of groups that we would typically identify as "social," or as recognizable societies. These two modes of thought do not contradict one another so much as they stress different ontological dimensions. Throughout this study, I have investigated the interactions of actors to demonstrate how even mundane things and actions shape the larger groups we typically think of as given, or social. In this chapter I am interested not only in the materials out of which collectives are built, but also the nature of the relations between those materials prior to and during their interactions, the environment in which the work of constructing the social takes place. The tension between inclination and work is in keeping with the flat ontology that values all actors equally and provides the materials out of which postmodern fiction builds worknets. Inclination is the state of things, all things. The social is the ongoing work of actors. Otherness is produced when actors incline together and work to establish groups. Inclination is foundational.

What makes literary texts postmodern in terms of their view of the social, then, is not so much the fetishization of difference, as Eagleton posits, or the manufacture of otherness, as Appiah proposes, but the foregrounding of the inclination of what Nancy calls "singularities" or "singular beings." Postmodern writers such as DeLillo and Alvarez do not merely enact the idea of clinamen, but also take it in a new direction by including nonhuman actors in the genus of "singularities." Otherness has been misunderstood as primary when it is actually only definable in the view of the inclination of actors toward one another. The obsession with otherness that has dominated the critical discourse of postmodernism arises, in part, out of a legitimate need to engage with the ethical implications of the differences we encounter when actors are exposed to one another, but these theories of otherness have become the foundation upon which our understanding of the postmodern is built. In the process, the inclination that precedes otherness has been pushed to the side and, more often than not, ignored altogether. If Silko, Morrison, Lethem, Barth, and Wallace enable us to see the significance of all actors, from a calendar to a prison, then the material domains of DeLillo's and Alvarez's novels help us see how these actors incline toward one another in the first place. These texts suggest that when we widen our critical gaze to include nonhuman actors in the construction of the social, we can ultimately move away from a reliance on otherness that dictates a view of the social as static substance.

Recasting otherness as part and parcel of inclination is especially important now, at a time when astute criticism is being leveled at the preoccupation with difference that postmodernism shares with two other important *isms*: poststructuralism and multiculturalism. Rey Chow begins an analysis of critical theory by arguing that difference has become the ultimate foundation for most philosophies of identity:

> In the increasingly globalized realm of theoretical discourse, a habitual move may be readily discerned in critical discussion regarding marginalized groups and non-Western cultures: the critic makes a gesture toward Western theory, but only in such a way as to advance the point that such theory is inadequate, negligent, and Eurocentric. As a consequence, what legitimates concern for the particular group, identity, or ethnic culture under discussion [...] is its historical, cultural, gendered difference, which becomes in terms of the theoretical strategies involved, the basis for the claim of opposition and resistance.[17]

Building on earlier critiques of postmodernism's interest in difference, such as bell hooks's "Postmodern Blackness," as well as Chow's argument and others like it, critics such as Sue J. Kim have argued that "Otherness postmodernism, then, is the hegemonic idea that, by describing the anti-hegemonic in a formal way as difference, recuperates it back into the hegemony" and that "it fails to provide a concrete means to move beyond that sameness-difference binary."[18] Thus, postmodernism has finally been charged with committing the same crimes of Enlightenment modernity that it originally set out to fight. That is, in resisting the hegemonic social imaginary of Weberian rationalization, postmodernism has relied on heterogeneous narratives to the extent that it generates and perpetuates essentializing naturalizations of these different groups against some monolithic idea of sameness. But postmodern fiction, with all its rich material domains, offers us alternatives. When we foreground the treatment of everyday objects in postmodern fiction, these texts uncover an inclination of various actors that ultimately *produces* the otherness that has been understood as foundational.

The basis for a more productive understanding of the inclination of postmodern otherness has been present all along. In the same essay of Appiah's that I referenced earlier, he proposes that one key feature of modern commodity culture is the need to "clear a space in which one is distinguished from all other producers and products—and one does this by the construction and marking of differences." A little later he defines postmodernism as "a retheorization of the proliferation of distinctions that reflects the underlying dynamic of cultural modernity, the need to clear oneself a space."[19] Just as Jameson, Hutcheon, and others saw in postmodernism unlimited potential to critique familiar social categories, but could not see the reconstructive agency wrapped up in that critique, critics have recognized postmodernism's ability to challenge hegemony by focusing on otherness, but missed out on the all-important idea that what postmodernism actually does is clear space for gathering, not differentiating, by revealing the social as a process. In *The Inoperative Community*, Nancy declares that a community is "neither a work to be produced, nor a lost communion, but rather [. . .] space itself."[20] And in *Reassembling the Social*, Latour, who repeatedly cautions us never to begin with what should be our result, proclaims that the social "is no more than an occasional spark generated by the shift, the shock, the slight displacement of other non-social phenomena."[21] The word "social"—along with its various satellite terms that come out of the identity politics and multiculturalism associated with postmodernism—has been used to paper over the fact that for any two actors to be considered *in relation* to one another, they first must *be in relation* to one another. This chapter explores the presence of Nancy's space, the shift, the shock, the slight displacement of Latour's non-social phenomena, ultimately demonstrating how the unaccountable circulation of everyday things exemplifies the nature of the relations out of which actors construct their social networks.

DeLillo's magnum opus *Underworld* follows the trajectory of a famous baseball across nearly half a century as it circulates through the lives of numerous characters, clearing space that draws actors together. DeLillo develops the worknets in his novel out of common interactions and not out of contrasts between ready-made "societies." Alvarez's *How the García Girls Lost Their Accents* features a series of objects—culminating with a toy drum brought from the United States to the Dominican Republic—that can help us further reconcile Nancy's theory of inclination with Latour's theory of the social as always constituted by work. Alvarez illuminates and extends both approaches by focusing on the image of the hollow space contained by the toy drum, demonstrating that these two processes—inclination and work—are complementary. This reconciliation is essential to the novel's overall goal of spinning diverse communities out of common material experiences. Both authors use narrative structure to gather communities of actors, including their readers, into unexpected societies. Both novels finally make a metafictional move similar to the one made by Silko, Morrison, Barth, and Wallace, turning to their readers in the end and making us complicit in the process of constructing their ongoing fictional worlds. This turn to second-person point of view demonstrates how the trademark formal experimentation of postmodernism can be read as a call that we choose to answer or ignore. Either way, it is an invitation, an offer that opens our eyes to the inclination that drew us to the novel in the first place.

WHAT DOES INCLINATION LOOK LIKE?

Originally published in the October 1992 issue of *Harper's*, DeLillo's "Pafko at the Wall" recounts the final game of the 1951 pennant race between the New York Giants and the Brooklyn Dodgers, in which Bobby Thomson hits a walk-off home run to put the Giants in the World Series. The "Pafko" in the story's title is the Brooklyn Dodgers outfielder who watches as the home run ball sails over his head and into the grandstands of the ballpark at New York's Polo Grounds. When the story reappears five years later as the prologue to *Underworld*, however, it is retitled, "The Triumph of Death." This title is taken from a sixteenth-century painting by Pieter Bruegel the Elder, depicting a variety of violent and horrifying deaths in a war-torn landscape. Bruegel's masterpiece shows up in the story as FBI Director J. Edgar Hoover sits watching the pennant game and a reprint of the painting torn from a magazine floats down over him in pieces while the crowd throws various items onto the field. Since the Bruegel reprint appears in both the 1992 and the 1997 versions of the story, why change the title? To complicate this question further, the story was also republished as a novella under the original title, "Pafko at the Wall," in October 2001 to commemorate the fiftieth anniversary of Thomson's home run, whose reputation as "The Shot Heard Round the World" serves as the novella's subtitle. The most obvious answer to why DeLillo changes the title is also the most significant: the prologue serves a different purpose in relation to the novel than it does in the more isolated context of a periodical like *Harper's* or as a novella.

Most of the critical attention paid to DeLillo's retelling of this famous game has focused on the contrast between blissful postwar America and the looming Soviet threat, covered up by the baseball game, or on baseball itself as an allegory of American society. As John Duvall notes, "Pafko at the Wall" presents a problematized view of American society in the postwar era. Duvall asserts that, in the ballpark, DeLillo exposes but fails to transcend a faulty "series of 'us-them' binaries of the early 1950s," especially that of race relations.[22] In other words, DeLillo demystifies the mythic social categories of postwar America, but does not offer a means of moving beyond these myths. I agree with Duvall's assessment of "Pafko at the Wall," which resonates with Hutcheon's notion of postmodernism as complicitous critique. However, in its rebirth as "The Triumph of Death,"

DeLillo's story of that monumental day in baseball history is only the beginning of a much longer work, and therefore I would argue that it must be reconsidered in light of its function in relation to the novel. In that context, "The Triumph of Death" is perhaps most important to *Underworld* because it provides the object—a baseball—whose movement throughout the rest of the narrative reveals the inclination of actors in the formation of a vast social network. The movement of the baseball throughout the text might be said to develop Lucretius's unaccountable swerve, the inclination of actors, and Nancy's theory of the "inoperative community," but what it also accomplishes at least as convincingly is the formation of relations between actors that cannot be explained by what Latour calls the "sociology of the social."[23] In other words, the inclination of various human and nonhuman actors around the baseball results in an association of actors that can only be understood in terms of how they are gathered together, not in terms of their fundamental differences or otherness.

The scope of DeLillo's longest novel provides the baseball ample space and time to circulate widely, and he draws actors together across vast distances and numerous years. In a 1997 interview with DeLillo, Gerald Howard declares that *Underworld* belongs on a "short list of books that [. . .] attempt to grapple with the subterranean history of postwar American life."[24] Howard places *Underworld* alongside novels such as William Gaddis's *The Recognitions* (1955), Thomas Pynchon's *Gravity's Rainbow* (1973), and David Foster Wallace's *Infinite Jest* (1996), to point out that a number of the most important texts to address the postwar era are "behemoths." DeLillo's response to this observation is both telling and useful:

> The novel is a very open form. It will accommodate large themes and whole landscapes of experience. The novel is here, the novel exists to give us a form that is fully equal to the sweeping realities of a given period. The novel expands, contracts, becomes essaylike, floats in pure consciousness—it gives the writer what he needs to produce a book that duplicates, a book that models the rich dense, and complex weave of actual experience. The novel goads the writer into surpassing himself.[25]

In the tumult of *Underworld*'s sheer size and its exhibition of all the formal elements DeLillo mentions in his interview with Howard, the baseball acts as a constant force, enduring when other objects wane and connecting the disparate narratives that constitute the novel. As the ball passes from one owner to another, its movement connects actors across space and time whose lives would never have overlapped otherwise.

This inclination results in a fluid network that stands in sharp contrast to the crowd contained within the Polo Grounds where the ball is first introduced. The crowd gathered in the ballpark of "Pafko at the Wall" is representative of the static and stratified categories of race, class, gender, occupation, and so on, that we typically accept as constitutive of society. The Polo Grounds stadium is ringed by ticket booths and turnstiles, inhabited by announcers, fans, players, coaches, any number of autonomous individuals playing predetermined roles. Even the sidewalks and streets outside the stadium are worked by vendors and "scraggy men hustling buttons and caps."[26] There are security guards, police officers, symbols of law and order, "black kids and white kids up from the subways or off the local Harlem streets [. . .] a mick who shouts *Geronimo*" (12). Each of these individuals fits securely into a larger category, and the stratification of these categories forms the society of the ballpark. But as we have seen in the other narratives included in this study, when we imagine any collective group as a lowest common denominator, we obscure the agency of its constituent actors. As Nancy points out, "The community that becomes *a single* thing [. . .] necessarily loses the *in* of being-*in*-common. Or, it loses the *with* or the *together* that defines it. It yields its being-together to a being *of* togetherness."[27] When we imagine the social in terms of categories—black, white, Irish, Indian—then we lose sight of the "*in*," the "*with*," the movement or inclination of the actors that actually forms the social itself. Starting with the social further instantiates such categories as foundational and thus reduces groups and individual actors to the differences that seem to define them.

This reduction appears accurate, at first, in the case of Cotter Martin, one of the many "black kids" who leaps over the ticket turnstiles and steals his way into the game. The entire group is skipping school, and as Cotter evades Polo Grounds security guards he "runs up a shadowed ramp [...] Then you lose him in the crowd" (14). While in the crowded stands, Cotter is befriended by a middle-aged white man named Bill Waterson. Like Cotter, Bill is ducking his responsibilities for the day, and the two become fast friends. Their words and actions are bathed in the ritual of America's pastime, complete with what Bill calls the "law of manly conduct," in which Cotter shares his peanuts with Bill, and Bill must reciprocate by buying the young man a soda (22). However, after Bobby Thomson hits the famous home run, there is a mad dash and struggle to retrieve the baseball. Cotter comes up with the object, and as he runs from the stadium he realizes that the arm he wrenched to win it was Bill's. In the scenes that follow, we see DeLillo performing what critics have called a demythologizing of American society in the romanticized afterglow of the postwar era, as the jovial relationship formed by Cotter and Bill during the game falls apart on account of the baseball.[28] Bill follows Cotter through the streets, trying to persuade him to give up the ball. The man becomes steadily more aggressive toward the boy, not realizing that Cotter is leading him farther and farther into "unmixed Harlem" (57). It is only when Bill notices that Cotter is becoming cocky, showing off with the ball, that he realizes where he is and backs off. Bill's slow but powerful realization of his surroundings acts as what we might think of, appropriately, as a dramatic shift in home field advantage. Cotter skips home triumphantly, and "Pafko at the Wall" comes to an end. Thus, as Duvall has pointed out, DeLillo exposes the ballpark as an idealistic view of America-as-society, and offers a problematized representation of, among other things, race relations in the 1950s.

When placed in the context of *Underworld*, however, "Pafko at the Wall" becomes "The Triumph of Death," and much more than an exercise in demystification. While we might read the stand-alone "Pafko" as a fictional rendition of one of Roland Barthes's brilliant *Mythologies*, "The Triumph of Death" does not merely demythologize postwar American society, but, as Nancy would say, it literally interrupts this myth. Nancy distinguishes between demythologizing and interruption when he characterizes the former as a critique that ultimately "leaves the essence of myth untouched," while the latter recognizes itself as myth and is subsequently "cut off from its own meaning."[29] Removing the ball from the Polo Grounds and unraveling the relationship between Cotter and Bill, DeLillo interrupts the romanticized myth of convivial race relations by demonstrating that the gap between white and black cannot simply be overcome through good feeling over peanuts and Coke at a baseball game. He then moves beyond that revelation in the novel to show both how it was made and how it can be remade. Bill beams at the young man in the stands, but later fumes as Cotter begins to feel safe in his own neighborhood and "holds the ball chest-high and turns it in his fingers, which isn't easy when you're running—he rotates the ball on its axis, spins it slowly over and around" (57). However, what makes the novel so important is what it does in the wake of interrupting this myth. DeLillo does not reduce the opposition between Cotter and Bill to race. After shaking the white man, Cotter walks home through Harlem and, at one point, "sees four guys from a local gang, the Alhambras, and he crosses the street to avoid them and then crosses back" (58). Cotter maneuvers to avoid the Alhambras just as he did to avoid Bill. His own father later steals the ball from him and sells it for himself. "The Triumph of Death" can be read as an interruption of myth because DeLillo is not content to expose the problems of black/white relations in the characters of Cotter and Bill. He goes on to explore Cotter's fear of other black characters and his mistreatment by his father, as well as vast cultural and economic differences between white characters like Bill, the Texas Highway Shooter, and Charles Wainwright Sr., suggesting that race itself is not a monolith. But if race, among other collectives, is interrupted, then how does DeLillo understand the phenomenon that we talk about when we talk about race? Like any other collective, race is a matter of "being-*in*-common" in unique ways, but these ways are constantly changing. The novel is therefore not merely interested in any category, but in the more fundamental sense of community in which actors incline toward one another.

The social network that gets constructed as we trace the movement of the ball also stands in stark contrast to the bedlam of the ballpark in the aftermath of Thomson's famous home run. As J. Edgar Hoover sits in the stands and the crowd goes crazy, someone tears a two-page printing of Bruegel's *The Triumph of Death* from the pages of a magazine and the two halves come floating down into Hoover's lap. Hoover assembles the pieces to reveal "the meatblood colors and massed bodies, this is a census-taking of awful ways to die. He looks at the flaring sky in the deep distance out beyond the headlands on the left-hand page—Death elsewhere" (50). Hoover's interpretation of the painting as a "census-taking" of death speaks to the sociological and political implications of gathering a mass of individuals together in one location. He looks at the glossy pages and sees the crowd that surrounds him. The overwhelming triumph of death in the painting corresponds to the madness in the ballpark as races, classes, and generations clamor over the monumental souvenir. But as the ball leaves the Polo Grounds in Cotter Martin's hands, the narrative leaves the ballpark behind, jumping more than forty years forward in time and jettisoning the ready-made microcosm of the society of the ballpark.

The structure of the narrative is roughly reverse chronological, a trait *Underworld* shares with Alvarez's *García Girls*. Divided into a prologue set in 1951, six main parts that work backward from the narrative present of 1992 to the night following the famous pennant game in 1951, and an epilogue set in 1992, *Underworld* is essentially organized around revealing whether or not a baseball owned by protagonist Nick Shay in the novel's present is in fact the authentic "shot heard round the world" that Bobby Thomson blasted into the stands and Cotter Martin pulled from the fray. While the main parts of the narrative move back through time, there are three smaller sections devoted to Cotter Martin's father, Manx, at the end of parts one, three, and five, which recount the initial sale of the ball. Manx's narratives cover the few hours left unaccounted for by the man from whom Nick purchases the ball. Although DeLillo organizes the narrative in reverse-chronological order to "create plot tensions that simply would disappear if one were to retell the story by reconstructing a conventional timeframe,"[30] I want to reconstruct the movement of the ball in chronological order as a way of emphasizing the ball's trajectory through time and the formations that result from its various "swerves."

The ball's trajectory is unpredictable. Like Lucretius's atoms, "at certain times / and at uncertain points, they swerve a bit—"[31] On the very night of Cotter's unlikely escape with the object, the ball is stolen by the boy's own father: "Manx steps into the room and sees the baseball almost at once. It is sitting in the open on the unused bed. This is what gets him every time. They obtain a valuable thing and don't even bother to hide it. Trust fairies to watch over their valuables" (149). Piecing together the three narrative sections devoted to Manx, we follow him out of the apartment, down into the street, where the super accuses him of stealing shovels from the basement of the building, and over to the Polo Grounds where a line is already forming at the box office as fans wait to buy tickets to the upcoming World Series. DeLillo bookends each of Manx's sections in the novel with pages that are solid black, both front and back. Manx is a man who views race as foundational; he is hemmed in by it on all sides, like Mingus at the end of *The Fortress of Solitude*. When brooding over how to approach the sale of the ball, he reasons that he will not be successful if he approaches another black man as a potential buyer:

> Black man's not gonna believe anything he says. Think I'm some fool running a penny hustle. Black man's gonna look him down with that saucy eye he's got for outrageous plots against his person. No. Got to go white. Only way to go. Besides, the numbers mostly white, so it's the percentage play. (642)

However, in the exchange that results in the sale of the ball, what takes precedence is not the fundamental otherness that Manx feels between himself and the white buyer, but the "cooperation" he encounters in the white man, Charles Wainwright Sr., who is looking for an excuse to purchase a ball whose significance will be all but impossible to authenticate.

DeLillo privileges inclination over otherness by foregrounding the ways in which the two men seem to be of one mind as they talk about the ball in straightforward terms, both acknowledging that Charles has a much better chance of convincing anyone of its authenticity than Manx. Manx facilitates the sale by doing his best to anticipate and answer the potential objections to the ball's authenticity that Charles will inevitably encounter. He explains that his son convinced him of the ball's genuineness and that while Cotter might lie about skipping school or going to the dentist, he would not lie about this because, as Charles says helpfully, "'this is baseball' [. . .] And baseball. This counts.' Manx takes heart from the man's cooperation because he doesn't want to suffer another bringdown. But at the same time he doesn't want to think of Charlie as a sucker, a rube in a duffle coat, falling for an easy line" (647). Charles finishes Manx's sentences. There is a bond between them that precedes their seemingly a priori racial otherness, and that bond is baseball, in this case an actual baseball. Manx "calls him Charles now, for the social aspect, gentlemen drinkers at the club, and the two share a drink from Charles's flask" (650). Charles "Doesn't even wipe off the rim. Just flips the flask and drinks, too deep" (650). The fact that Charles puts his mouth on the flask after Manx and drinks only seems significant because of their racial difference, but ultimately even that difference is the product of their proximity, their inclination toward one another in relation to the ball. If Charles does not move toward Manx, take up the flask, and drink deeply, the weight of his gesture as a reaching across distance would not be so heavy. Ironically, this gesture highlights the production of whiteness, even as it reifies whiteness as a concept constructed in opposition to blackness—as if either concept could somehow be a priori.

While some have argued that the ball is a mere commodity in this moment, that it "condense[s] and reif[ies] the game's lore into something with exchange value rather than mythical value" and that "myth has been replaced by commerce,"[32] such interpretations overlook the agency of the ball itself. The ball is not merely symbolic in its existence, like a hundred-dollar bill. When Charles Wainwright Sr. buys the ball from Manx Martin, the emphasis is not on the amount of money, which DeLillo describes as "[a] ten, two fives, another ten, two singles, a quarter, two nickels and a tiddlywinks dime," but on the fact that Wainwright gives "every nickel in [his] pocket above and beyond" (652). The ball has not been commodified in the sense that it has a particular exchange value. Just the opposite is true; the ball can never be authenticated, and thus can only ever be worth everything (as in Wainwright's case) and nothing at once. The ball is truly an invaluable object. DeLillo washes the ball clean of both its utility—as Charles Wainwright Sr. would certainly never use it to play catch with his son—and its exchange value—as its genuineness cannot be verified. In doing so, he frees it from the human determination that makes the "thing" an "object."

Neither is the ball a mere nostalgic symbol. In the narrative present of 1992, protagonist Nick Shay contacts a baseball memorabilia collector by the name of Marvin Lundy who is said by Nick's coworker Brian Glassic to be in possession of the famous ball. Brian had visited Marvin Lundy impulsively while on a business trip and heard the entire convoluted history of the older man's lifelong quest to locate the "shot heard round the world." Lundy purchases the ball from the estate of a man named Rauch, whose wife says she purchased it from the ex-wife of a man named Charles Wainwright Jr., who inherited the ball from his father. Lundy can trace the ball all the way back to the night of the pennant game, but does not know about Manx or Cotter and thus cannot connect Wainwright Sr. "to the ball making contact with Bobby Thomson's bat" (181). Brian returns home and tells Nick about Marvin Lundy. When Nick calls Marvin, he can't quite articulate why he wants the ball. The narrative is focalized through Marvin's thoughts as he listens to Nick: "This was good. Marvin liked this. It was good to hear from someone who was not palpitating in his mind for the old Giants or the old New York" (191). Marvin's relief at Nick's lack of nostalgia is explained by his own search for the ball: "This was Marvin's exact status. For years he didn't know why he was chasing down exhausted objects. All that frantic passion for a baseball and he finally understood [. . .] it was some terror working deep beneath the skin that made him gather up things, amass possessions and effects" (191). Neither man can quite articulate why he wants the ball. Their reasoning cannot be attributed to any one motivation or cause. This sense of longing, or inclination, drives complex series of connections between characters and forms unexpected associations among a host of seemingly unrelated actors, especially in the case of Marvin Lundy.

Marvin Lundy's search for the ball takes him to Long Island, San Francisco, Texas, Detroit, Eastern Europe, and beyond in a frustrating and fruitless attempt to find a man named Charles Wainwright Jr., last known to be in Greenland. Material objects are no respecters of geography, nation, race, or creed. When Marvin hits a dead end in his search for Wainwright Jr. and fails to trace the ball backward through time, he tries instead to start from the ballpark and work up to Wainwright Jr. He amasses photographs of the crowd that were taken in 1951 during the mad scramble for Thomson's home run ball:

> At one point Marvin hired a man who worked in a photo lab and had access to special equipment. They studied news photographs of the left-field stands at the Polo Grounds taken just after the ball went in. They looked at enlargements and enhancements. They went to photo agencies and burrowed in the archives. Marvin had people sneak him into newspaper morgues, into the wire services and the major magazines. (175)

Not only does Marvin's search take him around the world and into archives and morgues, but it also leads him to look at "a million photographs because this is the dot theory of reality, that all knowledge is available if you analyze the dots" (175). In Marvin's self-styled "dot theory," DeLillo explains the relationship of the thousands of individual dots that make up a photo to the photo as a whole. While the photo is viewed as a totality, its existence as such does not negate the singularity or the significance of its constituent "dots."

Similarly, the social network that gets constructed around the movement of the baseball—that so far consists of Bobby Thomson, the bat, Ralph Branca, the turnstiles, Cotter Martin, Bill Waterson, peanuts, soda, Manx Martin, the shovels Manx is supposed to have stolen, the Wainwrights, the flask, Genevieve Rauch, Judson Rauch, Marvin Lundy, his vast collection, and all the people, places, and things these various characters encounter in their interactions with the ball—may be legible as "American culture" or even "America," but it is also the constant product of the inclination of all these actors in relation to the movement of the baseball. Extending Marvin Lundy's "dot theory of reality," we might think here of photomosaics. A mosaic is "an image traditionally composed of small pieces of material," while a photomosaic is "a digital image made up of other digital images."[33] For instance, a popular style of photomosaic is the picture of a famous historical figure made up of hundreds of smaller pictures, each depicting a specific moment in that person's life. As Marvin Lundy investigates pictures of the grandstands in the Polo Grounds during the scramble for the ball, he develops his "dot theory," which is synecdochical for the larger network that gathers around the ball over the course of the entire narrative. The dot theory provides another perspective for understanding the phenomena that social categories such as race and class have typically denoted by calling our attention away from the assemblage as a totality and toward the importance of the actors involved in the actual assembly of those groups.

In this perspective, the differences that mark larger groups as distinctive are secondary to the more fundamental inclination of the singular actors that make them possible in the first place. In other words, the inclination of all actors has an effect on the groupings that get made. Each dot, or actor, is a mediator, and even the most seemingly insignificant outliers can play a role in shaping the assembly. As we track the ball forward in time from Charles Wainwright Sr., who leaves it to his son, we discover that the ball falls into the hands of Wainwright Jr.'s ex-wife, Susan, and eventually winds up in a family by the name of Rauch. The narrative focalizes through Lundy's memory again:

1. The mother of twins in what's that town.
2. The man who lived in a community of chemically sensitive people, they wore white cotton shifts and hung their mail on clotheslines.
3. The woman named Bliss, which he was younger then, Marvin was, and maybe could have, with eyes as nice as hers, done a little something, in Indianola, Miss.
4. The shock of lives unlike your own. Happy, healthy, lonely, lost. The one-eighth Indian. Lives that are blunt and unforeseen even when they're ordinary.
5. Who knew a Susan somebody who spoke about a baseball with a famous past. Marvin forgets the tribe. (317)

The list goes on and on to include "a hippie Christian cluster," "the bone cancer kid in Utah," "the woman with the chipped tooth," and "the chemicals in the core of the ball that made the man run in place after breakfast every day" (317). But perhaps the most notable outlier to affect the construction of a social network around the ball is the serial killer whose actions ultimately bring the ball into Marvin Lundy's possession. Without the demented deeds of this character who seems, at first glance, utterly cut off from the community of the baseball, Marvin would never find the ball, Brian would never learn of its existence, Nick would never call Marvin, the whole narrative would be different.

I want to examine the serial killer more closely here to show how the group that forms around the ball cannot be accounted for by any familiar category, and to suggest that the collectives we typically identify in categorical terms may also be formed as much by the unaccountable inclination of actors as they are by so-called social markers. DeLillo devotes a number of sections of the novel to Richard, the Texas Highway Killer, who shoots motorists while they drive their vehicles across Texas highways. Richard never comes into contact with the ball, he does not know anyone personally who does come into contact with the ball, he seems completely outside the social network being constructed by the inclination of a host of actors in relation to the ball. And yet, when recounting the breakthrough in his quest, Marvin Lundy explains that he had lost years in the 1970s looking for "Judson Jackson Johnson" until a woman named Genevieve Rauch contacts him out of the blue and says that she was once in possession of the ball, but the lead goes nowhere. Then, one day, "[a] man's driving along in his car, someone shoots him dead. Turns out the victim is the long-lost former husband of Genevieve Rauch. Turns out further his name is Juddy Rauch, Judson Rauch. So the two rivers meet. Took homicide to reveal the connection" (179). Lundy's daughter goes on to explain how Marvin had gone to Deaf Smith County, Texas, to hire a lawyer on behalf of Genevieve Rauch "and finally located the baseball sealed in a baggie and vouchered and numbered and stored in the property clerk's office. Impounded by the police along with the body, the car, all the things in the car, of which this was one, crammed in a cardboard box filled with junky odds and ends" (180). Thus, it is Richard, the serial murdering Texas Highway Killer, who finally brings the ball out of obscurity. While it is tempting to emphasize the disturbing otherness of this murderous character to heighten the importance of all actors in the formation of the social, that otherness is ultimately revealed as a product of Richard's stress over his place in society.

The Texas Highway Killer's concern for social categories overshadows the more everyday experiences he shares with others. In fact, Richard's problem is not some inherent difference between himself and others. When alone he worries about a copycat crime in which someone else has been shot by a driver. He is an "early riser" who leaves "food for a stray cat" and cares for his aging parents (271–72). When we discover that he has purchased an electronic device to disguise his voice from "a mercenary magazine," the narrator explains that "this was not a publication Richard normally perused. He was not a surveillance man or gun lover" (269). His problem seems to be rooted in his preoccupation with how others see him. He lives in constant fear of how others view him, so he avoids others as much as possible. The only person he ever talks meaningfully with is a television news anchor named Sue Ann who "gave him the feeling he was taking shape as himself, coming into the shape he'd always been intended to take, the thing of who he really was" (269). Richard persistently worries about the category into which he fits. He repeatedly prefaces his statements to Sue Ann with phrases like, "let's set the record straight." He is concerned about being incorrectly labeled a child who grew up in a dysfunctional home with head trauma (215–17). He insists that he is not a "sniper" because he is not "an individual with a rifle working more or less long-range. You're mobile here, you're moving, you want to get as close to the situation as humanly possible without bringing the two vehicles into contact, whereby a paint mark might result" (217). He fears that "contact" with others will reveal something foundationally different and troubling about himself, so he gets as close as possible without actually touching others. But Richard creates the difference. His resistance to contact produces violence, revealing the consequences of subjugating inclination to otherness.

The ball connects every single one of the numerous narrative threads of the novel, from the prologue, to the six main parts narrating Nick Shay's reverse chronology, to the sections devoted to Manx, to the chapters set aside for Richard the Texas Highway Killer, to the epilogue in which the narrative voice briefly shifts to Nick's first-person perspective. The ball resembles a *deus ex machina* or the existential feather that floats around in Robert Zemeckis's *Forrest Gump* (1994). DeLillo himself says in an essay that writers sometimes stretch the bounds of believability: "It is almost inevitable that the fiction writer, dealing with this reality, will violate any number of codes and contracts. He will engineer a swerve from the usual arrangements that bind a figure in history to what has been reported, rumored, confirmed or solemnly chanted. It is fiction's role to imagine deeply."[34] DeLillo engineers the many swerves of the baseball throughout *Underworld* to establish connections between a wide array of human and nonhuman actors. Some of these actors search fervently for the ball, while it fortuitously intersects with the lives of others. The ball sits in storage for years with the other things that occupied Judson Rauch's car when he was shot by Richard. All of these entities, from Nick Shay to Richard's voice-altering device, ultimately find themselves in relation. If Silko reveals that the social is a process and not a substance, then DeLillo demonstrates that this process cannot be explained by some "specific social ties revealing the hidden presence of some specific social forces" because "associations are made of ties which are themselves non-social."[35] There are no social forces, only actors inclining. The community of the ball is one of unrecognized relation until Marvin Lundy does the work to form what we might legitimately call a "social history" of the object. The ball's "social" history is social because it can be seen from Marvin's point of view as the product of actors coming together, not as a ready-made assembly, and because its community remains in process. Some of these actors—Manx Martin, for instance—remain unaccounted for in Marvin's history, maintaining the centrality of the swerve.

In an essay written following the tragic events of September 11, 2001, DeLillo reimagines the significance of memorable days like the one that took place at the Polo Grounds in 1951 through the lens of global terror when he says that "[f]or the next 50 years, people who were not in the area when the attacks occurred will claim to have been there. In time, some of them will believe it. Others will claim to have lost friends or relatives, although they did not."[36] But what is most evocative of Thomson's home-run ball is DeLillo's interest in the objects of September 11. After rattling off an entire paragraph of items like cell phones and box cutters, DeLillo says, "These are among the smaller objects and more marginal stories in the sifted ruins of the day. We need them, even the common tools of terrorists, to set against the massive spectacle that continues to seem unmanageable, too powerful a thing to set into our frame of practiced response."[37] These objects, much like the baseball in *Underworld*, serve as reminders that no actor is reducible to any single association or event. All actors have the capacity for mediation and the inclination to assemble in unexpected formations.

The social history of the baseball is built, much like the social history of 9/11, in the space cleared by the movement of objects. The ball leaves Branca's hand, blasts off Thomson's bat, and moves through time and space, gathering various actors in its wake. A complex host of world events led the 9/11 hijackers onto planes and into a terrible act of violence on that late summer morning. Now a monument to those who died and to the memories of those who survived has been constructed where the towers once stood in lower Manhattan. I do not mean to imply any scalar similarities between these two historical moments. What seems clear, however, is that the myriad differences that appear essential between characters in the novel are secondary to the more intriguing question of what draws these actors together in the first place. In the aftermath of 9/11 many were, and continue to be, rightly concerned with the ideological differences that could create such a cataclysmic event. These differences, however, are always differences in relation to some shared experience. In other words, the disagreements that cause one group to view another as "other" are necessarily disagreements over how to interpret, approach, and respond to shared experience. Postmodern fiction not only interrogates such differences but also foregrounds the more fundamental fact that the otherness produced by these different reactions always takes place in relation—in relation to common experience, in relation between actors. The very notion and occurrence of relation is the necessary state of things for any differences to be constructed. I call this state of things "inclination," and inclination looks like the movement of a baseball as it changes hands over the course of fifty years. If postmodern fiction is more concerned with what draws actors together than what distinguishes them, then its aesthetic function is not to deconstruct existing social categories but to construct them. The question inclination leaves us with, then, is this: How can we read postmodern fiction constructively?

BUILDING ON INCLINATION

In the Introduction I explained that the radical anti-anthropocentrism of thinkers such as Ian Bogost, Graham Harman, and Levi Bryant would be important insofar as it could help push the limits of how we think about nonhuman actors in fiction, but that I would ultimately follow Latour more closely in focusing on the roles of nonhumans in the formation of networks we typically think of as unique to humans. In Chapters 1–3, I demonstrated the value of even the most mundane things in postmodern narrative by showing how all actors are mediators in the material construction of the social, and how even language itself is a material actor. Along the way, my hope is that we have come to see new possibilities in the orthodoxies of postmodernism. But there is a recurring theme throughout much of this literature that ultimately suggests postmodern fiction is most invested in how actors relate to one another, a phenomenon I am calling "inclination." The metafictional collapse of distance between writer and reader is one common formal approach to enacting this inclination. Nearly every writer I have examined in this study turns her or his narrator toward the reader at some point, often at the end of the text. And some, like Barth, ask the reader to intervene in their texts. Such moves further break down the ontological distinction between word and world, as I have argued, but also paradoxically imply a fundamentally common form of communication. That is, these narratives seem to say, "based on our shared understanding of the world, our differences are secondary, beautiful, damning, negligible, monumental," or whatever else texts may insinuate. Even this shared understanding, or whatever we might call postmodern fiction's view of essence, is mediated by nonhuman actors and assembled in the spaces cleared by these objects as they circulate throughout narratives like Julia Alvarez's *How the García Girls Lost Their Accents*. To read postmodern fiction constructively, or, as Brian McHale might say, to construct postmodernism, we must attend both to the spaces cleared by actors circulating through texts and to the ways in which those spaces come to constitute the experiences, memories, and relations of human actors.[38]

García Girls follows the family of Carlos and Laura García from the Dominican Republic to the United States in the midst of the political turmoil that plagued the island throughout the long reign of Rafael Trujillo. In 1960, Carlos is implicated in a plot to unseat the Dominican dictator, and when two inspectors show up at the García house to question him, a friend from the American Embassy is forced to intervene. The García family flees to the United States, where the four young daughters, Carla, Sandra, Yolanda, and Sofía, learn English, grow up, attend US schools and universities, and settle themselves as adults. Throughout the years after their departure, the girls frequently visit their birthplace, but with each successive trip the disparity between life on the island and life in the States becomes more prominent. The novel tells this story in reverse-chronological order over the course of three major sections, each of which is subdivided into five smaller chapters. Each of these chapters begins with a title and a name or series of names that denotes which character or characters focalize the chapter. The first section crawls back in time from 1989 to 1972, and includes four chapters narrated in the third person and one in the first person by Yolanda. The second section covers the years 1970–1960, and includes three chapters narrated in the third person and two in the first person: one seemingly by all the sisters together, and the other by Yolanda. The third section covers the years 1960–1956, and includes one chapter narrated half in the third person and half in the first person by Sofía, and four narrated in the first person: two by Yolanda, one by Carla, and one by Sandra. The steady movement from a predominant use of the third person to a prevailing multiplicity of first-person narrations as the narrative moves back in time enacts the postmodern view of the social, which I have described here as the inclination of various entities as the voice of the novel is unpacked into its constituent pieces and then those pieces are gathered into a common space.

Whereas I read against the reverse-chronological structure of *Underworld* to emphasize the baseball's movement forward through time, I want to follow Alvarez's reverse chronology back in time to demonstrate how she organizes the novel by steadily tracing the entire narrative present back to a single thing: a toy drum. The hollow of the drum renders the object both an absence and a presence in the construction of Alvarez's narrative. The danger in following the García girls back in time is that we might come to consider the novel purely a story of origins, a juxtaposition of Dominican Republic as homeland and United States as foreign land. In fact, Catherine Romagnolo has investigated the complexity of Alvarez's "narrative beginning" alongside those of Toni Morrison in *Beloved* and Zora Neale Hurston in *Their Eyes Were Watching God*.[39] Because the text is deeply invested in examining the Garcías' struggle with what their Tía Carmen calls "American ways," critics have often approached the text as an examination of the complexities of bicultural, international, and hybridized experience. The earlier criticism especially echoes the binary language of multiculturalism. Jacqueline Stefanko, for instance, sees Alvarez and other Latina writers as "hybrid selves who cross and recross borders of language and culture [and] create hybrid texts in order to 'survive in diaspora,' to use Donna Haraway's term."[40] Maribel Ortiz-Márquez turns to Homi Bhabha to blur the lines between various binaries in the novel, such as that between the private and public sphere, but ultimately reasserts a sharp division between "that social reality which lies not at the core of the text, but at its margins."[41] Other critics focus on language in the novel as the "borderline" on which "Alvarez situates her characters," as Julie Barak has argued,[42] and as the source of the sisters' conflicts "with their bicultural surroundings," according to Ricardo Castells.[43] Such approaches tend necessarily to begin where they should finally end because they rely on social categories such as nation and culture, and terms such as "hybrid" that unavoidably reinforce these categories as substances, in the way many self-styled postmodern readings do with novels like *Ceremony*.[44]

While many otherwise insightful readings remain beholden to the "between two worlds" narrative,[45] more recent investigations into Alvarez's first novel have taken a turn toward showing how the text pushes beyond this reductive framework. Sarika Chandra convincingly claims that while older immigrant narratives depict immigrants grappling with their identities in a US culture that homogenizes diverse individuals into oversimplified ethnic categories, "more contemporary narratives such as [. . .] Julia Alvarez's *How the García Girls Lost Their Accents* (1991) present immigrants who conduct similar negotiations but in a much more interconnected world."[46] Such critics typically employ the language of globalization or transnationalism, as opposed to that of hybridity or multiculturalism. Katarzyna Marciniak, for instance, asserts that writers like Alvarez compose "characters who transgress the boundaries of established nationhood by moving across national borders, languages, cultures, and competing ideologies. In doing so, [...] they show how liminal identities, with their shifting subject positions, complicate the dichotomous hierarchy of citizen-legal subject/stranger-illegal other."[47] The difference between much of the earlier and later criticism can be found in the move away from binaries and dichotomies and in the direction of "interconnectedness" and the "trans-" national, cultural, and so on. Building on this evolving critical conversation, a materialist reading of *García Girls* can help realize the type of interpretation that Chandra, Marciniak, and others imagine as ideal. Chandra reasons that newer "immigrant/ethnic" texts like *García Girls* "should dispel the notion that a culturalist identity politics can, on its own, become a refuge from and provide critical resistance to the contemporary forces of globalization."[48] Chandra eschews the binary, dichotomous language of earlier readings, but ultimately relies on the somewhat nebulous "forces of globalization" to explain social changes that require the political intervention of novels like Alvarez's.[49] To read *García Girls* constructively is to replace the "forces of globalization" with the inclination of everyday things, even a thing as simple as a guava.

The guavas that fill the foothills of the Dominican Republic serve as materials out of which Alvarez constructs more global forces, in this case, class, gender, nation, and race. In the novel's opening section, Yolanda returns to the Dominican Republic from the United States to visit her family and borrows a Datsun to go collect guavas. The battle she must wage against her aunts to get permission to drive out into the foothills demonstrates that the family's upper-class status is less a ready-made category than a constant task, an ongoing process. In the narrative present of 1989, Yolanda has not lived permanently on the island for nearly three decades, and when she expresses her desire to go pick guavas, her aunts' disagreement over the prospect serves as an inventory of the language, attitude, and things that constitute class. One aunt offers the use of a family car, another exclaims, "have you lost your mind? A Volvo in the interior with the way things are!"[50] Yolanda breaks the tension by offering the even more laughable alternative of taking the bus: "'A bus!' The whole group bursts out laughing. [...] 'Can't you see it!?' [Lucinda] laughs. 'Yoyo climbing into an old *camioneta* with all the *campesinos* and their fighting cocks and their goats and their pigs!'" (9). The name brand of the car, the language of the "interior," and the laughter all seem to designate an established line that Yolanda should not cross, but she leaves the protection of the compound in the morning in the less-impressive Datsun and makes her way into the hills, where she stops at a small cantina. The woman who runs the cantina becomes "the long arm of [Yolanda's] family" and volunteers a young boy to gather the fruit for her: "The doña will get hot, her nice clothes will get all dirty. José will bring the doña as many guavas as she is wanting" (16). Before the woman can react, Yolanda gathers a whole troop of boys into the car and they set out on their expedition. They are successful and "Yolanda eats several right on the spot, relishing the slightly bumpy feel of the skin in her hand, devouring the crunchy, sweet white meat. The boys watch her" (17). Her inclination toward, or desire for, the guavas materializes class in both her aunts' conversation and in the distance that separates the "doña" from the cantina owner and the young boys.

The guavas also materialize gender, race, and national identity. That is, they reveal these groupings to be under construction. When the Datsun blows a tire, Yolanda sends José for help, but before the boy returns, a group of men walk out of the guava grove with machetes in their hands and ask if the señorita is all right. The narrator notes specifically that one of the men is "no taller than Yolanda," seeming to intimate that the biological differences of sex are not so acute, but the difference in their genders becomes stark considering the fact that "anywhere else, Yolanda would find [his companion] extremely attractive, but here on a lonely road, with the sky growing darker by seconds, his good looks seem dangerous, a lure to catch her off guard" (20). She freezes with fear and the men take her silence for incomprehension: "The handsome one smiles knowingly. [. . .] 'Americana,' he says to the darker man, pointing to the car" (20). The chasm between her and the men grows when they replace the tire for her and she insists on paying them for their trouble. After overcoming their refusal, she reaches for their hands: "The shorter man holds his back at first, as if not wanting to dirty her hand, but finally, after wiping it on the side of his pants, he gives it to Yolanda. The skin feels rough and dry like the bark of trees" (22). The man's hand recalls the rough, "bumpy feel" of the guava skin and is juxtaposed with a Palmolive advertising poster illuminated by Yolanda's headlights as she drives José back to the cantina. On the dish soap ad the "Palmolive woman's skin gleams a rich white" (23). The contrast between the "rough" and "gleaming" skin is heightened by the commodification of leisure and color in an effort to sell a product that will ostensibly make one smooth and white. Thus, the ad actually manufactures this distinction in its effort to achieve a more singular goal: to have everyone share the common experience of buying the soap. The social, that which seems fixed, is revealed here as processual. Race becomes racialization, national identity becomes nationalization, both constructed out of the guavas, headlights, and advertisements that Yolanda encounters.

The point is that such associations, and thus the differences between them, require constant work to be made, but also that they are built out of and around actors that exist in relation. The tension between Nancy's notion of merely existing in relation and Latour's insistence on the necessity of work arises here once again. How can the social be a constant work in progress that reveals differences if the state of all actors is one of inclination? Alvarez can help us negotiate this paradox. The final object in her novel reconciles gathering and differentiating, absence and presence, being and work. The novel's last chapter opens with Yolanda's recollection of a favorite childhood present: "It was a drum Mamita brought back from a trip to New York, a magnificent drum, its sides bright red, criss-crossed by gold wire held down by gold button heads, its top and bottom white. [. . .] 'Ah,' I sighed, for in the hollow at the center, two drumsticks were stored" (275). The drum provides Yolanda with an entire day's worth of entertainment. Late in the afternoon she discovers a litter of kittens in the coal shed and decides to adopt one. She drops the kitten into the hollow of the drum and commences to beat on the top mercilessly. The kitten is dazed when Yolanda removes the top, and the "accusing sound of meow" it makes generates an odd combination of guilt and anger in the young girl: "I wanted to dunk it into the sink and make its meowing stop. Instead, I lifted the screen and threw the meowing ball out the window. I heard it land with a thud, saw it moments later, wobbling out from under the shadow of the house, meowing and stumbling forward" (288). The hollow of the drum has served as home to the drumsticks, to the kitten, and now to young Yolanda's fear and guilt as she fastens the top in place, and the voice of the narration begins to shift and fly back through the narrative toward the future.

The narrative structure indicates that the hollow space between the sides, top, and bottom of the drum comes to contain the entire series of stories that make up the various chapters that Alvarez has followed back in time to this final moment: "The cat disappeared altogether. I saw snow. I solved the riddle of an outdoors made mostly of concrete in New York. My grandmother grew so old she could not remember who she was. I went away to school. I read books. You understand I am collapsing all time now so that it fits in what's left in the hollow of my story?" (289). The story of the drum is the narrative space from which all of the other stories in the novel flow, and the drum itself is therefore the thing that contains all of these stories. After all, the hollow space of a drum is the absence that produces the sound the drum makes when struck. This absence brings us back to Heidegger's jug once again and how it is the hollow space that makes the jug a thing. The narrative structure of *García Girls* is arranged in such a way as to lead us against the chronological current of time, back to its source in the story of the drum—or it might be more appropriate to say the story in the drum. All of the complex and nuanced relations of the novel's earlier chapters can be traced back to the hollow space of the drum. The space cleared at the heart of this novel ultimately reveals that communities arise out of a common material domain, not out of differentiation based on fundamental otherness.

How is the social built on inclination? Nancy says that community "cannot arise from the domain of *work*. One does not produce it, one experiences or one is constituted by it as the experience of finitiude."[51] Latour, on the other hand, maintains that "if you stop making and remaking groups you stop having groups. No reservoir of forces flowing from 'social forces' will help you."[52] In short, as Nancy himself recognizes, community and society are not the same. Theoretical orthodoxy has read postmodern fiction as being primarily concerned with social categories, the deconstruction or demystification of those categories in particular. My point is that postmodern fiction is just as interested in community, in the inclination, relation, or being-in-common of the actors that work to construct the social. Alvarez's drum holds these two concepts in cooperative tension. It represents the social in that its sides, top, bottom, strap, and sticks are certainly made. Just so, the sound a drum makes requires work. If you stop hitting the drum, you stop creating sound. At the same time, as I have mentioned, the drum contains a space, and it is the space that actually produces the sound, gives the drum its purpose or worth. The novel imagines such a space as the epicenter of the entire social world when Yolanda turns directly to her reader and imperatively asks, "You understand I am collapsing all time now so that it fits in what's left in the hollow of my story?" The hollow is the site of all the events and entities that populate the complex chronology of the novel. Alvarez pulls us back through time to show that everything comes from this gathering; the entire narrative emanates from this one space. All of the work that has gone into constructing the García girls' nationality, race, culture, class, and gender can be traced back to the idea that all things exist in a state of relation.

At the level of the narrative discourse, the drum plays as central a role as DeLillo's baseball. If we follow Yolanda back through time and end up with/in the drum, then the drum seems to be the thing that catalyzes her retelling of the entire series of stories we have just read. Like many of the other writers I have examined, Alvarez chooses this final moment of her narrative to break down the barrier between the novel itself and the world in which the novel intervenes. Like Morrison's ambiguous narrator or Barth's "Frame-Tale," the drum creates a narrative moment that troubles the too easily demarcated worlds of writer, text, and reader. Both *Underworld* and *García Girls* turn to their readers in the final moments of narration, addressing us directly and gathering us all into the hollow spaces of their stories. Such self-conscious narrative tropes have become hallmark postmodernism for their ironic preoccupation with writing as an end in itself, an orthodoxy I have examined in Chapter 3. In *The Friday Book*, Barth characterizes his own work as representative of that group of texts described by critics such as Irving Howe and Susan Sontag as "novels which imitate the form of the Novel, by an author who imitates the role of Author." It is this self-conscious obsession with form, or what Barth calls the "technical," as inseparable from content or theme that renders postmodern fiction especially well suited to demonstrate the material construction of our social networks and narratives and to perform as a material actor in the construction of those networks and narratives.[53]

Alvarez collapses the otherness of her fictional world and our own and constructs an entirely new world. Her fictional narrator turns to her reader and presumes, "You understand. . .." The sentence is both an imperative command to comprehend or identify with the narrator and an interrogative. Who exactly is the "you"? Situated as this sentence is in the center of the novel's last paragraph, in which nearly every other sentence begins with the first-person singular pronoun, "I," the odd "you" stands at the heart of Yolanda's final narration, and appeals to her audience as if seeking our affirmation, or perhaps even our assistance in finishing the narrative. The end of the narrative is, however, the beginning of the story because we have been reading back through time. The invitation to understand, then, recalls the way *Ceremony* ends with sunrise and "Here and There" ends with a welcoming. These endings are also beginnings. The narrative does not end so much as it continues to process. While beginning *in medias res* may be a classic literary trope, postmodern fiction makes a habit of ending *in medias res*.

When DeLillo shifts to the second-person point of view in the final pages of *Underworld*, he does so to set up the novel's one-word conclusion: "Peace." This single word can be read as a diagnosis of the present, a prayer for the future, a statement about the history he has just crafted, or a description of the state of things, but at its core this peace is for whoever embodies the "you" of the penultimate paragraph:

> And you can glance out the window for a moment, distracted by the sound of small kids playing a made-up game in a neighbor's yard, some kind of kickball maybe, and they speak in your voice [. . .] and you try to imagine the word on the screen becoming a thing in the world, taking all its meanings, its sense of serenities and contentments out into the streets somehow, its whisper of reconciliation, a word extending itself ever outward, the tone of agreement or treaty, the tone of repose, the sense of mollifying silence, the tone of hail and farewell, a word that carries the sunlit ardor of an object deep in drenching noon, the argument

of binding touch, but it's only a sequence of pulses on a dullish
screen and all it can do is make you pensive—a word that spreads
a longing through the raw sprawl of the city and out across the
dreaming bourns and orchards to the solitary hills. (827)

The narrator's presumption of our experiences and our ability to relate to these "serenities and contentments," in Roland Barthes's terms, "try to abolish (or at least to diminish) the distance between writing and reading, in no way by intensifying the projection of the reader into the work but by joining them in a single signifying practice."[54] Thus, at the heart of postmodernism we find a joining or inclination, not a disjunction or otherness. We find a hollow that is not a space of absence, but a space of presence, of gathering. The final words of *Underworld*, "Peace," *Ceremony*, "Sunrise," *Jazz*, "now," and "Here and There," "welcome" are processual. They indicate and enact emotion, experience, and time in such ways as to create a commonality in the moment that stretches into time. DeLillo characterizes this sense as "a longing," which I might repackage as an inclination.

Constructing social networks necessarily produces otherness. Postmodern fiction, as many have argued, interrogates this otherness, often elevating it as a primary element of cultural identity. But the postmodern aesthetic also valorizes the being-in-common, or the state of inclination in which actors exist in the construction process. If inclination is just as important as otherness, then postmodernism is not only interested in the negative space of difference, but also in the fundamental similarity of all actors as actors. Returning to my introduction to Chapter 1 and my argument in Chapter 2, this juxtaposition of community and society does not contradict a flat ontology because it does not hold inclination up as real/natural and social categories as somehow fake/cultural. Both are real. Both are natural. Both are cultural. The key here is that both are simultaneous. Actors always exist in a state of relation and are also always at work forming worknets that we typically think of as social categories. The larger significance of this foregrounding of both inclination and otherness is that it allows us to value the construction of social categories, acknowledge their processual nature, and keep in mind that differences are constantly being produced out of material circumstances. If difference is produced, then there is also the possibility that it can be produced differently. The fundamental inclination of all matter suggests that the present configuration of actors can be understood in terms of the work that has gone into producing the social as it is currently in process. There is the potential that this social process could be redirected, reassembled, remade in some other configuration. Nothing, not even historical groupings that are thought of as social, is fixed.

Afterism

The Promise of Postmodernism

Despite its unfortunate name, postmodernism is not an *ism* at all. I have used the refrain "what makes fiction postmodern . . ." throughout this study to synthesize my revisions of postmodernism's orthodoxies. But what should be clear by now is that what makes fiction postmodern is that it cannot be defined by any static set of orthodoxies at all. Postmodernism is less a name for a unified aesthetic, as its *ism* implies, than a description of the state of being *after* unified aesthetics. Postmodernism is not an entity. Postmodernism, ironically, is not a thing. McHale states this as a matter of fact in the opening line of *Constructing Postmodernism*: "No doubt there 'is' no such 'thing' as postmodernism."[1] But where McHale's solution to understanding postmodernism is to concatenate it "into coherent larger units, such as 'periods,' 'schools,' 'genres,' etc.," I want to consider a slightly different approach.[2] I want to explore postmodernism as more of a setting, a space, or, as I have said, a state of being. To be sure, proceeding in this way re-raises some important obstacles and objections to theorizing the postmodern, especially as interpreted by Lyotard and Jameson. But this perspective can enable a new narrative of postmodernism's place in literary history; it can help us see why postmodernism is not dead and why it cannot die.

Postmodernism's zombie-like resistance to death is perhaps best illustrated in an essay Jonathan Lethem first published in *The New York Times Book Review* in 2009. In "Postmodernism as Liberty Valance: Notes on a Ritual Killing," Lethem allegorizes the unkillable spirit of postmodernism using John Ford's 1962 film *The Man Who Shot Liberty Valance*. This classic western features Jimmy Stewart as the righteous Ransom Stoddard, who is praised for gunning down Lee Marvin's evil character Liberty Valance. In the end, however, we discover it was actually John Wayne's prickly hero Tom Doniphon, located somewhere off camera, who pulled the trigger. In Lethem's allegory, Stoddard represents realist writers like Raymond Carver who seemed to stand toe to toe with the reckless and destructive postmodernism (Valance), but it is the literary critic (Doniphon) who actually brings the outlaw down. The allegory falls apart when Lethem insists that postmodernism, unlike Liberty Valance, does not die. Why won't this evil *ism* just die? For starters, it's difficult to aim at something when no one agrees on the target: "In literary conversations," Lethem points out, "the word is often used as finger-pointing to a really vast number of things that might be seen as threatening to canonical culture," and then he goes on to enumerate the so-called orthodoxies of postmodernism, including those I have discussed here and more. "The reason postmodernism doesn't die is that postmodernism isn't the figure in the black hat standing out in the street squaring off against the earnest and law-abiding 'realist' novel against which it is being opposed. Postmodernism is the street. Postmodernism is the town," he reasons.[3] Postmodernism, for Lethem, is the setting of the film, the space in which the action unfolds. The writers and the critics are all winging shots at one another in the air of postmodernism.

But if postmodernism is not dead, neither has it ever been alive—well, not as an *ism* anyway. Literary history typically casts romanticism, realism, and modernism as historic and aesthetic markers. The waxing and waning of these *isms*' hallmark characteristics demarcate their rises and falls, demonstrating, for instance, that romanticism was the prevailing ethos of mid-nineteenth-century US literature before it was usurped by a realist commitment to life as it is actually lived in the years following the Civil War. No literary scholar would claim that we are currently living in the age of romanticism. Romanticism was alive and now it is dead. In contrast, postmodernism was never alive because it is not a set of hallmark characteristics but the very atmosphere in which such characteristics play out. Postmodernism, unlike romanticism, cannot end.

It does not distinguish itself or separate itself out from other *isms*; it has no self, no unique set of criteria. Its *-ism* belongs to the word "modern," as McHale points out,[4] and so its most important feature is its "postness." Postmodernism is the state of being after modernism, or after the last *ism* in conventional literary history. It is a certain way of being, or a space without *isms*. I am not arguing that we have always been postmodern. The revelations I associate with postmodernism are historically emergent. But what postmodernism reveals is that things have always been in process. Postmodernism is the impossible term we have used to talk about the space, or vantage point, from which these processes become visible.

Lyotard introduces but misapprehends postmodernism's atmospheric quality in "Answering the Question: What Is Postmodernism?" While his own theorization of postmodernism as an aesthetic that cannot be judged by "applying familiar categories to the text or to the work" clearly anticipates my own, he identifies this phenomenon as the "nascent" and "constant" state of modernism.[5] He seems to be rejecting conventional periodization here, but he addresses postmodernism after first working his way through realism and modernism, logically positioning postmodernism as next in line. The distinctive move of his argument is to relocate postmodernism at the beginning of modernism by insisting that the postmodern aesthetic can be understood as the impulse within the modern that seeks to make the unpresentable palpable: "The postmodern would be that which, in the modern, puts forward the unpresentable in presentation itself; that which denies itself the solace of good forms [. . .] but in order to impart a stronger sense of the unpresentable."[6] Here is where we part company. Although I do not figure postmodernism as an *ism* either, I do see it as emergent in the sense described by DeKoven and Huyssen. It is made possible by realism and modernism because of their opposing views of the unpresentable. For postmodernism there is no unpresentable. The work of art is not "looking for" the categories that have typically been used to define it, as Régis Durand translates Lyotard's claim; it is creating them out of the available materials. Postmodernism is not a set of criteria that can be added up to the unpresentable or aligned to demonstrate its absence. The unpresentable is not on the map of the postmodern.

Postmodernism is thus an atmosphere, a space that provides a certain way of seeing. Trying either to kill postmodernism off or to stand in the way of the bullet perpetuates the kind of periodizing thinking that leads to the dominance of such monstrous and reductive *isms* as postmodernism in the first place. But what would it mean to be without *isms*? Gao Xingjian offers an answer that resonates with the neomaterialist resistance to pre-existing social categories that I have explored in postmodern fiction:

> To be without isms is to some extent more positive than being a nihilist, because there is at least an attitude towards events, other people and the self. Yet this attitude is one of refusing to acknowledge the existence of irrefutable *a priori* knowledge. It may be regarded as a form of rationality—although where this leads does not concern us here—but it is at least not blindly and superstitiously believing in religion or power, and not feeling any need to follow some authority, trend or fashion and thus being led by the nose; nor is it allowing oneself to be shackled to an ideology and thus constructing a prison around one's own feet.[7]

Postmodernism refuses a priori knowledge as a determiner for how actors interact with one another. Postmodernism examines the processes through which knowledge is made. Xingjian's argument that to be without *isms* is an "attitude" or "a form of rationality" adds another dimension to Lethem's theory of postmodernism as a setting, or space. The many unsatisfactory attempts to nail postmodernism down—and they are legion—reveal more than the fact that postmodernism is not "nail-downable." They suggest that postmodernism is not a *thing* to be nailed down or hammered out. It is a space, or, at most, a form of rationality. Its lasting value may in fact be that it models a way of thinking about literature that is once again attuned to language and human relations in such a way as never to take the material domain for granted. The most mundane objects are of vital significance to the work of postmodern fiction. This move away from *isms* may be a potential horizon for literary studies, a horizon without *isms*, a horizon in which each and every actor, including the work of art, can *be* for itself and for the relations it experiences and establishes with other actors.

Xingjian's theory of thinking about literature without *isms* comes out of a long and complicated history of Chinese culture in the twentieth century in which the work of art must always serve some political purpose. He longs for an aesthetic perspective that "does not depend upon philosophical speculation or scientific methodology," but rather "is merely a form of understanding." His insights are not exclusive to the political limitations of the historically oppressive Chinese government. Writing in exile, he insists that "[f]or a frail individual, a writer, to confront society alone and utter words in his own voice is, in my view, the essential character of literature, which has changed little from ancient times to the present, whether it be in China or abroad, in the East or in the West." Recalling, to my mind, Barth's aversion to *isms* as "more or less useful and necessary fictions," Xingjian maintains that "endowing the will of these abstract collectives with authority can only strangle literature."[8] Postmodernism does not divest modernism or romanticism of their *ism*-driven authority. That seems an altogether unlikely and unproductive endeavor. After all, while such *isms* may be more or less useful, as Barth says, they are also necessary, or, at least, they have been necessary. Postmodernism does, however, strike out in a new direction as it names an eclectic, disjointed, and inchoate attempt to think literature without the authoritative structure of an *ism*. It does not live up to the stature of other *isms*, but this lack of development is not a failure. Postmodernism's persistent incoherence marks its greatest success: the primacy of the particular, the material, the everyday, the mundane.

The actors, both human and nonhuman, that occupy the material domain of postmodern fiction relate to one another in constant states of flux. Their singular properties and their collective relations are always in process. Postmodernism is the space and the process of change that takes place within space. Change is at once both a state of being and a resistance to any one state of being. Similarly, postmodernism is at once a state of being after *isms* and a disavowal of any set of fixed features of its own. Perhaps the best illustration of this notion of change comes from Octavia Butler's unfinished Parable Trilogy. In the two completed novels, *Parable of the Sower* and *Parable of the Talents*,

Butler's protagonist and primary narrator Lauren Olamina records her experiences in a not-so-distant apocalyptic future where the infrastructure of the US government has withered and the rule of law has become legend. After her walled neighborhood is attacked and burned by local drug addicts, Lauren leaves her hometown and her father's orthodox Christian religion behind and strikes out with two other survivors on a northbound journey in search of jobs and safety. Along the way she develops the religion she had begun to craft for herself as an alternative to her father's faith, a set of verses she calls Earthseed. The God of Earthseed is change:

> All that you touch
> You Change.
>
> All that you Change
> Changes you.
>
> The only lasting truth
> Is Change.
>
> God
> Is Change.[9]

God is change, and change is also God. Each of the Earthseed verses either directly or obliquely speaks to the nature of change, and the most important aspect of change is its ubiquity, its atmospheric, foundational, state-of-things, all-encompassing nature. Butler's theory of change can help us meet two central challenges in understanding postmodernism. I do not mean to say that Butler is overtly theorizing postmodernism in the Parable Series. I simply mean to draw parallels here, to consider her concept of change as a model for how we might conceptualize postmodernism in some way that is different from how scholars have conceptualized romanticism or realism or modernism.

The first of our central challenges is talking about postmodernism as an entity in the same way we have talked about other *isms* without reifying it as such. As Lauren develops her religion, she retains the language of "God" to talk about change. Various characters question this approach: "But it's not a god. It's not a person or an intelligence or even a thing. It's just ... I don't know an idea," says a young man named Travis (200). Her new religion changes traditional Christianity by reimagining God as an impersonal force rather than a personal being. When Travis points out that no one worships impersonal forces such as change or the second law of thermodynamics, Lauren responds, "I hope not [...] Earthseed deals with ongoing reality not with supernatural authority figures" (202). Most of Butler's characters do not struggle with Earthseed as a practice. They struggle with changing their minds about who or what God is. They struggle with "ongoing reality." Postmodernism deals with ongoing reality. It is concerned with the processual nature of material actors and the collectives they form. Postmodernism is a way of seeing this process. Because it is not an *ism* with a clear set of aesthetic criteria, the discourse of literary studies has struggled with its place in literary history. The clumsy nomenclature of "postmodernism" has certainly not helped.

The very term "postmodernism" reserves no positive attributes for itself. It merely describes a relation to an *ism*. As unfortunate as the term has proven to be, its absent presence is finally helpful, as it points us toward its fundamentally relational character. Now we must recalibrate what comes to mind when we say "postmodernism." If it is a way of representing ongoing reality, and not a static denominator of artistic or philosophical features, then how should we talk about it? Is it a practice, an aesthetic, a period? None of these denominations will do. Butler's characters struggle to conceptualize ongoing reality as God because they are accustomed to thinking of God as a static entity. So too, literary studies is used to thinking of postmodernism much like realism or modernism—that is, postmodernism has typically been conceptualized as a static entity, a known *ism*. But postmodernism cannot be reduced to any single feature, form, function, or even set of any of these. It is, as I have suggested, a space, an atmosphere.

A space is a void. It has no positive attributes. And yet it exists. This line of thought is very abstract, and so I would like to borrow the image of the house from Gaston Bachelard's *The Poetics of Space* to help make it more concrete. The house, for Bachelard, is a "felicitous space," meaning literally "the space we love."[10] We all have fond memories, Bachelard assumes, of houses in which we have lived. They are spaces of comfort, familiarity, and memory. As a phenomenologist, Bachelard has set himself the task of explaining the experience of the poetic image: "How can an image, at times very unusual, appear to be a concentration of the entire psyche?"[11] Or, how can I encounter an image in a poem and be wholly captured by that image when it has not come out of my own imagination? How can a poetic image be so universal that it appeals to a broad range of readers and yet does so by calling entirely distinctive experiences to their individual minds? The answer, Bachelard argues in part, becomes clearest when we examine images of spaces, like houses, that have strong ties to memory.[12] When a writer uses the image of a house, she may describe the house, or allow the house to stand in for some idea, but readers think of the houses in which they have lived and map their own experiences with a warmly lit house on a snowy evening, say, with the images utilized by the writer. Thus, the image of the house activates our memories and experiences by calling to mind spaces we have inhabited.

The house is a space of common experience—common, that is, to anyone who has lived in a house of some kind. Yet our individual experiences are uncommon. The image of the house registers universally, but this registering process in each individual reader is particular. The empty space of a house can be actively populated in different ways by different readers. The chair in the corner may be overstuffed in one reader's mind, wooden in another's. The space thus simultaneously creates the "concentration of the entire psyche," as Bachelard says, and represents an ongoing process of creation from experience. "Images are incapable of repose," he argues.[13] Images always quicken or enliven imaginations, and Bachelard's house is an image whose spatial dimensions make room for all the attendant images, ideas, and emotions that fire the imagination and hold the attention of the "entire psyche."

Postmodernism, in my estimation, is something like Bachelard's house. It is a space in which images of everyday life move about freely, creating the very concepts we often think we are bringing to the work of art. If postmodernism is anything, positively speaking, it is a recognition of the space actors require to swerve, connect, and enact. Postmodern fiction, then, is read much in the way Bachelard says we "read a house": "very quickly, at the very first word, at the first poetic overture, the reader who is 'reading a room' leaves off reading and starts to think of some place in his own past."[14] The familiar actors that populate the worlds of postmodern fiction move about in a space that leaves room for us to imagine such sites and spaces in our own experiences. All good literature does this to some extent, as is Bachelard's point, and my point is not that the fiction of the postwar era does this any better than that of any other era. My point is that postmodern fiction's preoccupation with the material domain foregrounds this poetics of space as necessary to the assembly of the social. Postmodernism, then, is a poetic space. Rather than talking about postmodernism by delimiting its presence with a set of criteria, I propose that we approach it as a space, and talk about it in terms of how it allows actors to circulate.

My resistance to talking about postmodernism as an *ism* leads to the second of our central challenges: conceiving of postmodernism as something other than a traditional, *ism*-driven literary period, given that "a strongly contrastive, periodized model of cultivation has shaped literary study even more deeply and enduringly than it shaped the discipline of history itself."[15] In *Why Literary Periods Mattered*, Ted Underwood argues that the significance of literary culture since the late eighteenth century has depended on the principle of "historical contrast" derived from the juxtaposition of clearly defined cultural moments:

> What matters more than boundary-drawing is the broader premise that literature's power to cultivate readers depends on vividly particularizing and differentiating vanished eras, contrasting them implicitly against the present as well as against each other. It's a premise bound up with broader assumptions about literature's power to mediate historical change and transmute it into community—or in other words, with a model of literary culture.[16]

Underwood shows quite convincingly how periodization has persisted in defense of the disciplinary autonomy of literary studies "because it allowed literary scholars to avoid reliance on other disciplines, and organize themselves instead around contrasted systems of purely critical norms."[17] The tendency of scholars from Jameson and Hutcheon on to locate postmodernism as the next *ism* in the dialectical series of *isms* that stretches back at least to romanticism should come as no surprise. If Underwood's analysis is correct, then the prevailing critical discourse of postmodernism has relied on the normative claims of periodization to contextualize postmodern fiction because the contrast that such claims produce has been the source of literature's significance and power for a hundred and fifty years. But my reconsideration of postmodernism suggests that it should be conceived in terms of process, not contrast. What would it mean to think of postmodernism in non-contrastive terms? How would we talk about such a non-*ism*?

First, I should point out that *isms* have not always dominated periodization. Take the history of literature in the United States as an example. Most anthologies and literary histories only begin to pick up the language of *isms* with romanticism and transcendentalism in the early to mid-nineteenth century. The literature produced before this period is typically presented in terms of indigeneity, exploration, first contact, settlement, colonization, enlightenment, revolution, and so on. Literary history and literature existed before *isms*, and I simply mean to say that it can exist after *isms* as well. Postmodernism is not an *ism*. Postmodernism describes literature after, or, to shed the language of temporal contrast altogether, beyond *isms*. As an alternative, I suggest that we think of postmodernism in general and postmodern fiction in particular as a literature of revelation, a literature that focuses on the present, the now, to reveal the processual nature of whatever it represents. Postmodernism is a kind of prophecy, not the kind that tells the future, but the kind that lays bare the truth of how the world works. It is the finger pointing not to a vast number of things, as Lethem says, but pointing in the face of the present. It is the aesthetic space required to represent the constant change that is the state of things. The question remains: How do we locate postmodernism on the continuum of literary history's past, present, and future if it does not embody some large historical phenomenon (i.e., colonization) or fit into the dialectic of *isms*?

If change is the only constant, then imagining past, present, and future does not have to be a zero-sum game. Butler enacts such an alternative historical paradigm with these Earthseed verses written by Lauren:

The ground beneath your feet moves,
Changes.
The galaxies move through space.

> The stars ignite,
>> burn,
>> age,
>> cool,
> Evolving.
> God is Change.
> God prevails. (207)

Whereas much speculative fiction distinguishes the future from the present and past by imagining some type of apocalyptic event, Butler's continuum is much more fluid. "The future of Butler's *Parable* novels is unique," Marlene D. Allen maintains, "because the situation is not caused by a catastrophic event like nuclear war, an invasion by alien beings, or hostile takeover by robots or cyborgs. Rather, the devastation of both the Earth itself and human social and economic structures occurs because of humanity's inactivity, its refusal to deal with many social, economic, and environmental issues that plague our contemporary world."[18] Or, we might say this devastation is the result of a refusal to change, adapt, and grow with these various challenges. The prototypical catastrophic event creates a clear separation between the past/present and the future. Operating under this synchronic vision of time, of course it makes sense to envision the recreation of the past as distinct from imagining the future. But for Butler, as for other speculative fiction writers of color who write in the tradition of the African diaspora (Samuel Delany, Tananarive Due, Nalo Hopkinson, and others) past, present, and future are more like stars that ignite, burn, age, and cool—evolving and yet remaining stars.

But how can we conceive literature and its place in the broader context of literary history both now, and moving forward, without the contrastive capital of *isms*? How can we focus on the process of the supernova without defaulting to the temporal markers it defies? To answer this question I would like to return to Barth's essay "Postmodernism Revisited" that helped set the tone for this study:

> Perhaps because I'm a novelist by trade, I am by temperament more Aristotelian than Platonist in my attitude toward reality: more

nominalist than realist, especially as regards human beings and the things they do and make. Fred and Shirley and Mike and Irma seem intuitively realer to me than does the category *human beings*; [. . .] and the writings of Gabriel García Marquez and Italo Calvino and Salman Rushdie and Thomas Pynchon—even the writings of John Barth—have ontological primacy, to my way of thinking over the category *Postmodern fiction*.[19]

Although he goes on to explore and, by turns, affirm and reject various definitions of postmodernism, Barth consistently privileges individual works and their qualities over broader categories. Leaving aside his claims to nominalism, Barth's impulse to emphasize the particular over the general can provide a methodological alternative to thinking of literature in large-scale categories, an alternative that does not demand we ignore particularity. Literature, like Butler's stars, may ignite, burn, age, and cool, but it remains literature. The label "postmodernism," when used to talk about fiction, should operate as a reminder that literature is not beholden to the *isms* we use to delimit it.

In the same way that Lethem's allegory falls apart when the literary critics can't kill the outlaw postmodernism, and the outlaw himself somehow refuses to die, and the righteous avenger's great victory turns out to be hollow, so too all our attempts to analogize, pin down, and detain literature fail. Literature cannot be contained by *isms*, and, far from being yet another failed attempt to nail literature down, postmodernism is the revelation, recognition, and admission of this impossibility. Literary *isms*, like any other categories, are constructed out of the material components they purport to name. So, when Barth calls our attention away from the category of "*Spanish Gothic*" and toward "the cathedrals at Seville and Barcelona and Santiago de Compostela,"[20] he is explicitly acknowledging that the category depends for its existence on the things it claims to represent. The things are primary; the category is secondary. Postmodernism is a rejection of the literary historical tendency to put the category first. Its great weakness is that it is, itself, typically presented as a category. My argument here is simply that if postmodern is a term that describes fiction that privileges the particular over the general, the everyday over the ready-made, it can only ever come after the work of art. And if that is so, then it cannot be plugged into the dialectic of literary *isms*. I am not necessarily arguing against the idea of postmodernism as a period, but against the idea of postmodernism as an *ism*.

If postmodernism does not somehow follow modernism as the next *ism*, then what are we to do with the decades of literary production between World War II and the turn of the millennium? Is there some gap between modernism and what some critics are now attempting to identify as yet another new *ism* supposedly following postmodernism? I would suggest, rather, that we consider the great promise of postmodernism to be putting an end to *isms*. I am not arguing for some dramatic death of *isms*; the canonical *isms*—romanticism, realism, naturalism, modernism—while problematic and still contested, are useful for talking about literary history between roughly the late eighteenth and the late twentieth centuries. I simply think that such a model is no longer as helpful as it once was. While we may say that the specific *isms* themselves are somehow dead, I do not think it is in any way helpful to insist that talking about those *isms* as *isms* is dead. Postmodern fiction's attunement to the material domain of everyday life, its attendant focus on the processual nature of that material realm, and its subjugation of all experience to material process offer the opportunity to move literary studies away from the categorical approach that has dominated for so long. Just as the fiction of Morrison, Lethem, Silko, Barth, and many others teaches us to think and talk about categories like race, nation, class, and language as products of material processes, so too does postmodernism push us away from broader historical and categorical ways of thinking toward the here and now.

In *The Origins of Postmodernity*, Perry Anderson tracks the geographical evolution of postmodernism, noting significantly that the concepts "postmodernism" and "modernism" were both "born in the distant periphery rather than at the center of the cultural system of the time: they come not from Europe or the United States, but from Hispanic America."[21] While I take issue with Anderson's notion of cultural centrality, I would call our attention to his choice of the spatial trope of "periphery" to describe the origins of postmodernism. It seems that from the very beginning postmodernism has been conceived in spatial terms. This observation comes full circle when Anderson traces the source of North American postmodernism to the poet Charles Olson, who, "writing to his fellow-poet Robert Creeley on return from Yucatan in the summer of 1951, started to speak of a 'post-modern world' that lay beyond the imperial age of Discoveries and the Industrial Revolution."[22] Note that Anderson uses the term "beyond," which could connote time or space. Either way, there seems to be, in Olson's mind, not merely a postmodern age or era, but a postmodern world, or space. Looking back at Olson's attempts to theorize a new poetics, it should come as no surprise that the earliest efforts to move literature beyond modernism come from a writer who set out to think about art in terms other than those that had dominated for a century and a half. In his manifesto "Projective Verse," Olson describes his idea of poetry as "projective," or "OPEN," arguing that the poet must first and foremost have a sense of poetry's most fundamental unit of composition, the syllable, and reasoning that "it is a matter, finally, of OBJECTS, what they are, what they are inside a poem, how they got there."[23] This from the same writer who begins his most famous prose work, *Call Me Ishmael*, with these lines: "I take SPACE to be the central fact to man born in America, from Folsom cave to now. I spell it large because it comes large here. Large, and without mercy. It is geography at bottom, a hell of wide land from the beginning. That made the first American story (Parkman's): exploration."[24] Both of Olson's references, Folsom and Parkman, mark moments in history, yes, but they also refer to spaces.

There has been a leeriness about postmodernism's spatial dimensions since Jameson's landmark essay on postmodernism as the cultural logic of late capitalism in 1984. The broader Marxist anxiety over the critical distance between material foundations and their cultural manifestations goes back further. In a 1973 essay, Raymond Williams explains this anxiety by pointing out that "any modern approach to a Marxist theory of culture must begin by considering the proposition of a determining base and a determined superstructure," but that difficulties arise when critics encounter what seems a necessarily "definite and fixed spatial relationship" between the two.[25] For Jameson, the "spatial logic" of postmodernism renders it ahistorical. The challenge is to develop a totalizing theory of postmodernism that will locate it within the historical scope of capitalism as a cultural dominant, "a conception which allows for the presence and coexistence of a range of very different, yet subordinate, features."[26] "The claim," as Adam Kelly summarizes, "is that identifying the cultural dominant, in this case postmodernism, through a process of Totalization will allow the emergence of 'a capacity to act and struggle which is neutralized by our spatial as well as our social confusions.'"[27] The objection Jameson anticipates is that such a totalizing logic will risk the "possible obliteration of heterogeneity." He is willing to take the risk, however, because he feels "that it was only in light of some conception of a dominant cultural logic or hegemonic norm that genuine difference could be measured and assessed." His ultimate fear is that we might fall into a view of history as "sheer heterogeneity, random difference, a coexistence of a host of distinct forces whose effectivity is undecidable."[28]

This study clearly resists Jameson's totalizing approach, but my concluding emphasis on postmodernism as space is not intended to oppose or refute him, much less to argue that we have arrived at the end of history. Rather, it should ease the fear that a spatial theory is somehow ahistorical. After all, Jameson's historical perspective does not somehow negate the spatial dimensions of postmodernism, so why should the reverse be true? Jameson refers to the postmodern as a "force field in which very different kinds of cultural impulses must make their way."[29] Postmodernism is spatial in this sentence; it is a "field." While he draws on Raymond Williams's theories of the residual and emergent to insist that the spatial logic of postmodernism ignores these historical processes, I would go back to Williams's reconciliation of feeling and thought as a model for relating time and space. Williams famously theorizes "structures of feeling" as historical models that do not position "feeling against thought, but thought as felt and feeling as thought."[30] Following suit, I would say: not space against time, but time as experienced in space, and space as experienced in time. This model is not ahistorical, but resolutely historical in that it mandates a view of time as a narrative whose limits are determined by the material conditions in which it is unfolds. Those material conditions can only be understood in spatial terms as a network of relations between actors. Understanding that stories proceed from things in *Ceremony* does not negate Betonie's insight that "the ceremonies have always been changing." Nor does the spatial trajectory of DeLillo's baseball somehow outstrip its historical trajectory as postwar Americana. Postmodernism's spatial logic is fundamentally historical. Far from representing the exhaustion or end of history or literature, postmodernism is a recognition of the breadth, and not just the length, of history.

A spatial approach also attempts to avoid the necessarily reductive treatment of literary texts as intermediaries that so often attends the totalizing readings of conventional periodization. Jameson's reading of E. L. Doctorow's *Ragtime*, while brilliant, is a case in point. What Linda Hutcheon sees as "an extended critique of American democratic ideals through presentation of class conflict rooted in capitalist property and moneyed power," Jameson can only read as a media analysis.[31] The drive to situate the novel in a larger totalizing historical and political logic is what creates such a limited reading. "Hutcheon is, of course, absolutely right," he argues, "and this is what the novel would have meant had it not been a postmodern artifact."[32] The concept of the postmodern acts as a crucible here, a rubric to which all literary production must be subject. There is no room for the dynamism that Williams, and Jameson himself, sees as integral to the material process of history. Jameson's characterization of the novel as an "artifact," or a determined object, can help us see more clearly how this conventional periodizing approach deprives the literary text of its agency as an actor, that is, deprives it of its thingliness. Its mediating capacity has been nullified. *Ragtime* is not an actor at all; it is an intermediary under Jameson's postmodernism. The dominant, categorical logic is no longer a dynamic material process but a determining force. Everyday actors, even literary texts, do not count in this view because they are subjected to the ethereal force of culture, or to the *ism* in postmodernism.

My rejection of the *ism* and privileging of space is consonant with the postmodern interest in everyday actors. After all, an *ism* is always a force conceived in abstraction. We look to industrialism or capitalism as vague and ethereal forces that shape the way events unfold and entities interact. But of course, industrialism and capitalism are both products of events and entities. The more one tries to use these so-called forces to explain other phenomena, the more mired one becomes in overlooking how such forces are themselves in process. Bachelard recognizes that even the most isolated poetic image has causes that cannot be fully accounted for, and so argues that nothing "general and co-ordinated [can] serve as a basis for a philosophy of poetry. The idea of principle or 'basis' in this case would be disastrous, for it would interfere with the essential psychic actuality, the essential novelty of the poem."[33] Much like Barth, Bachelard is suspicious of any general theory or force we might use to explain the more constituent elements of a work of art. And so, because postmodernism can be understood as an attempt to avoid confusing what should be explained with the explanation, it is the circulation of both human and nonhuman actors through space that makes fiction postmodern.

The world has always been in process, and postmodern fiction puts us in a position to see how the objects of everyday life are invested in the material construction of the social. The railroad calendars, baseballs, toy drums, glass bottles, target arrows, and rings that inhabit postmodern fiction do not exist as mere reminders or symbols in case we just so happen to pick up a book and find them there. We are just as much in case of the objects. Their presence in these texts draws our hands forward to turn pages, jogs our memories in relation to experiences with similar objects, and evokes the many stories contained by the Coke bottles and screwdrivers in our own lives. When we talk about postmodernism, what we are talking about is our desire to find in art itself a reprieve from the *isms* we have created to fix the unfixable, to help us process the processual. Or, as I imagine it, postmodernism is most beautifully rendered in the final demand of Morrison's mysterious narrator to "look, look. Look where your hands are. Now." The possibility that we might actually look and see is the promise of postmodernism.

NOTES

Introduction

1. See Josh Toth's *The Passing of Postmodernism* (Albany: State University of New York Press, 2010); Neil Brooks and Josh Toth's *The Mourning After: Attending the Wake of Postmodernism* (New York: Rodopi, 2007); Klaus Stierstorfer's *Beyond Postmodernism: Reassessments in Literature, Theory, and Culture* (New York: Walter de Gruyter, 2003); and Robert Rebein's *Hicks, Tribes and Dirty Realists: American Fiction after Postmodernism* (Lexington: University of Kentucky Press, 2001). Also see Andrew Hoberek's "After Postmodernism: Form and History in Contemporary American Fiction," a special issue of *Twentieth-Century Literature* 53, no. 3 (Fall 2007); Jason Gladstone and Daniel Worden's "Postmodernism, Then," a special issue of *Twentieth-Century Literature* 57, nos. 3–4 (Fall–Winter 2011).
2. For metamodernism, see Timotheus Vermeulen and Robin van den Akker, "Notes on Metamodernism," *Journal of Aesthetics & Culture* 2 (2010): 1–14; Mary Holland, *Succeeding Postmodernism* (New York: Bloomsbury, 2013); David James and Urmila Seshagiri, "Metamodernism: Narratives of Continuity and Revolution," *PMLA* 129, no. 1 (January 2014): 87–100. Christian Moraru details his theory of the cosmodern in *Cosmodernism: American Narrative, Globalization, and the New Cultural Imaginary* (Ann Arbor: University of Michigan Press, 2011). "Digimodernism" is a coinage of Alan Kirby and signifies a clean break with postmodernism in the aesthetic form of texts with complex technological relationships that cannot be limited by conventional connections between writers. See Kirby's *Digimodernism: How New Technologies Dismantle the Postmodern and Reconfigure Our Culture*

NOTES

(New York: Continuum, 2009). Jeffrey Nealon outlines the coterminous relation between culture and economy as the starting point for cultural theory in *Post-Postmodernism; Or, The Cultural Logic of Just-In-Time Capitalism* (Stanford, CA: Stanford University Press, 2012).

3. Hutcheon makes this pronouncement in the epilogue to the 2nd edition of her classic *The Politics of Postmodernism* (New York: Routledge, 2002), 166.

4. Toth begins *The Passing of Postmodernism* with this line from Hutcheon and an extended meditation on its significance (1–2). Jeremy Green, *Late Postmodernism: American Fiction at the Millennium* (New York: Palgrave MacMillan, 2005), 17.

5. From its earliest invocations in the discourse of literary criticism, critics—such as Irving Howe, Leslie Fiedler, and Susan Sontag—and academic scholars—such as Linda Hutcheon and Paul Maltby—have figured postmodernism as a fundamentally critical aesthetic designed to subvert dominant ways of thinking. Fiedler argues that the "post-Modernist" novel emerged as writers attempted to challenge the narratives of WASP masculinity in particular in "The New Mutants," *Partisan Review* 32, no. 4 (Fall 1965): 508–513. In "Mass Society and Post-Modern Fiction," one of the earliest essays addressing postmodernism, Howe argues that the new "post-modern" fiction "seems to lend itself irrevocably to the spirit of criticism" in *Partisan Review* 26, no. 3 (Summer 1959): 429. Looking back on the emergence of postmodern fiction in his influential work, Maltby observes that "in the 1960s a number of critics, notably Leslie Fiedler, Ihab Hassan, and Susan Sontag, welcomed postmodernism as a species of subversive writing" in *Dissident Postmodernists: Barthelme, Coover, Pynchon* (Philadelphia: University of Pennsylvania Press, 1991), 17. Hutcheon theorizes postmodernism as a "complicitously critical" mode, one that can't help but perpetuate the problems it sets out to parody, critique, and ironize in *The Politics of Postmodernism* (New York: Routledge, 2002), 34, 94–101. More recently, Mark McGurl has recharged the aesthetically subversive definition of literary postmodernism with the alternative formulation "technomodernism" in recognition of the role media technology has played in the experimental narratives that dominate postwar American literature in *The Program Era: Postwar Fiction and the Rise of Creative Writing* (Cambridge, MA: Harvard University Press, 2009), 37–46.

6. Madhu Dubey, *Signs and Cities: Black Literary Postmodernism* (Chicago: University of Chicago Press, 2003), 7.

7. Andrew Hoberek, *The Twilight of the Middle Class: Post-World War II American Fiction and White-Collar Work* (Princeton, NJ: Princeton University Press, 2005), 127.

8. Marianne DeKoven, *Utopia Limited: The Sixties and the Emergence of the Postmodern* (Durham, NC: Duke University Press, 2004), 9.

9. W. Lawrence Hogue, *Postmodern American Literature and Its Other* (Urbana: University of Illinois Press, 2009); Hogue, *Postmodernism, Traditional Cultural Forms, and African American Narratives* (Albany: State University of New York Press, 2013); Amy Hungerford, *Postmodern Belief: American Literature and Religion since 1960* (Princeton, NJ: Princeton University Press, 2010).
10. Adam Kelly, "Beginning with Postmodernism," *Twentieth-Century Literature* 57, no. 3–4 (Fall–Winter 2011): 392.
11. Toth, *The Passing of Postmodernism*, 2.
12. Mary Holland, *Succeeding Postmodernism: Language and Humanism in Contemporary American Literature* (New York: Bloomsbury, 2013), 17.
13. Michel Foucault, *The Order of Things* (New York: Vintage, 1994), 53.
14. Fredric Jameson, *Postmodernism, or, The Cultural Logic of Late Capitalism* (Durham, NC: Duke University Press, 1991), 4. Linda Hutcheon, *A Poetics of Postmodernism: History, Theory, Fiction* (New York: Routledge, 1988), 4.
15. Amy J. Elias, *Sublime Desire: History and Post-1960s Fiction* (Baltimore, MD: Johns Hopkins University Press, 2001), xx.
16. Daniel Grausam, *On Endings: American Postmodern Fiction and the Cold War* (Charlottesville: University of Virginia Press, 2011), 2.
17. Adam Kelly, *American Fiction in Transition: Observer-Hero Narrative, the 1990s, and Postmodernism* (London: Bloomsbury, 2013), 6.
18. McClure's study identifies a postsecular vein in US fiction of the late twentieth century, countering the prevailing sense established by the early postmodern critics that this body of literature has little to say about the transcendent beyond noting its impossibility. "Post secular narratives," McClure maintains, "affirm the urgent need for a turn toward the religious even as they reject (in most instances) the familiar dream of full return to an authoritative faith." Thus, he claims, "a body of contemporary North American fiction contributes vigorously to the more general cultural debate over the place of the religious in postmodern life and society and that it does so in ways that distinguish it sharply both from defenses of philosophical secularism and from the most salient forms of religious revival." *Partial Faiths: Postsecular Fiction in the Age of Pynchon and Morrison* (Athens: University of Georgia Press, 2007), 6, 7.
19. Hungerford, *Postmodern Belief*, xix.
20. McGurl, *The Program Era*, 32.
21. Dubey, *Signs and Cities*, 17.
22. Michael Bérubé, *Public Access: Literary Theory and American Cultural Politics* (New York: Verso, 1994), 122.
23. Brian McHale, *Postmodernist Fiction* (New York: Methuen, 1987), 5.
24. Irving Howe, "Mass Society and Post-Modernist Fiction," *Partisan Review* 26, no. 3 (Summer 1959): 426.

25. Ibid., 429.
26. John Barth, "The Literature of Replenishment," in *The Friday Book: Essays and Other Nonfiction* (Baltimore, MD: The Johns Hopkins University Press, 1997), 205.
27. Ihab Hassan, *The Dismemberment of Orpheus: Toward a Postmodern Literature*, 2nd ed. (Madison: University of Wisconsin Press, 1982), 12.
28. John Barth, "Postmodernism Revisited," *The Review of Contemporary Fiction* 8, no. 3 (Fall 1988): 16.
29. William Carlos Williams, *Paterson* (New York: New Directions, 1992), 6.
30. William Dean Howells, *Criticism and Fiction* (New York: Harper and Brothers, 1891), 73.
31. Bill Brown, *A Sense of Things: The Object Matter of American Literature* (Chicago: University of Chicago Press, 2003), 4.
32. Valdes is quoted in Howells, *Criticism and Fiction*, 72; my emphasis.
33. The first definition comes from a review of John Ruskin's *Modern Painters*, and relates specifically to the term "realism." Caroline Levine offers a brief and helpful analysis in her essay "Surprising Realism" in *A Companion to George Eliot*, ed. Amanda Anderson and Harry E. Shaw (Malden, MA: Wiley-Blackwell, 2013), 64. The second definition comes from the seventeenth chapter of Eliot's novel *Adam Bede* (Chicago: Belford, Clarke, 1888), 163.
34. Eliot, *Adam Bede*, 163.
35. Brown, *A Sense of Things*, 3.
36. Ibid.
37. John Frow, "Matter and Materialism: A Brief Pre-History of the Present," in *Material Powers: Cultural Studies, History and the Material Turn*, ed. Tony Bennett and Patrick Joyce (New York: Routledge, 2010), 26–27.
38. Working in direct conversation with Marx and Engels's *The German Ideology* and *A Contribution to the Critique of Political Economy*, Terry Eagleton articulates the thrust of Marxist materialism: "The social relations between men, in other words, are bound up with the way they produce their material life. Certain 'productive forces'—say, the organization of labour in the middle ages—involve the social relations of villain to lord we know as feudalism. At a later stage, the development of new modes of productive organization is based on a changed set of social relations—this time between the capitalist class who owns those means of production, and the proletarian class whose labour-power the capitalist buys for profit. Taken together, these 'forces' and 'relations' of production form what Marx calls 'the economic structure of society,' or what is more commonly known by Marxism as the 'base' or 'superstructure.'" Terry Eagleton, *Marxism and Literary Criticism* (Berkeley: University of California Press, 1976), 4–5. Thus, Marxist materialism is interested in the "social" relations whose literally material constitution remains unexamined. I turn our attention to the material composition of these "relations." The point here is to examine how the larger social phenomena that determine literary

interpretation in the Marxist tradition are themselves the products of more fundamentally material interactions between humans and nonhumans.
39. See, for instance, the only title to combine postmodernism and materialism, *Postmodern Materialism and the Future of Marxist Theory: Essays in the Althusserian Tradition*, in which editors Antonio Callari and David F. Ruccio offer a collection of essays that "find echoes in postmodernism" and offer a new Marxism that "retain[s] a focus on class, but [does so] on different grounds and in a different way. Its specific contributions would continue to be found in its analyses of the class aspects of social practices in capitalist (and other) social formations. It, however, would negotiate the relations between class and nonclass aspects of social processes in a quite different way, assigning a strategic, not tactical, function to the proposition that social beings and processes are multidimensional and multiplicitous" (3). Thus Callari and Ruccio's "postmodern materialism" continues to rely on the immaterial "social," rather than offering a material explanation for the social itself.
40. Clifford Geertz, "The Impact of the Concept of Culture on the Concept of Man," in *The Interpretation of Cultures: Selected Essays* (New York: Basic Books, 1973), 49.
41. Renato Rosaldo, *Culture and Truth* (Boston: Beacon Press, 1989), 34, 36.
42. Raymond Williams, *Marxism and Literature* (Oxford: Oxford University Press, 2009), 4.
43. Bill Brown, "Thing Theory," *Critical Inquiry* 28, no. 1 (Autumn 2001): 6.
44. Graham Harman, "The Well-Wrought Broken Hammer: Object-Oriented Literary Criticism," *New Literary History* 43, no. 2 (Spring 2012): 193.
45. Bruno Latour, *Reassembling the Social: An Introduction to Actor-Network-Theory* (New York: Oxford University Press, 2005), 5; my emphasis.
46. Ibid., 3–5.
47. Ibid., 13.
48. Ibid., 143.
49. Ian Bogost, *Alien Phenomenology, or What It's Like to Be a Thing* (Minneapolis: University of Minnesota Press, 2012), 6. I draw on Bogost frequently because this concise study cogently synthesizes the research of Harman, Meillassoux, Grant, and Brassier toward an object-oriented ontology. Bogost's introduction builds on this literature to construct a viable phenomenological alternative to the scientific naturalism and social relativism that dominate our current intellectual climate. For a helpful parsing of the similarities and differences between the Speculative Realists and the new materialists, see Steven Shaviro, *The Universe of Things: On Speculative Realism* (Minneapolis: University of Minnesota Press, 2014).
50. Graham Harman, *Guerrilla Metaphysics: Phenomenology and the Carpentry of Things* (Chicago: Open Court, 2005), 1.
51. Quentin Meillassoux, *After Finitude: An Essay on the Necessity of Contingency* (New York: Continuum, 2008), 5.

52. Bogost, *Alien Phenomenology*, 3–4.
53. Ibid., 8.
54. Graham Harman identifies "object-oriented ontology" as Bryant's coinage in his "Series Editor Preface" to Bryant's *Onto-Cartography: An Ontology of Machines and Media* (Edinburgh: Edinburgh University Press, 2014), ix.
55. Bogost, *Alien Phenomenology*, 7, 19.
56. Cary Wolfe, *What Is Posthumanism?* (Minneapolis: University of Minnesota Press, 2010), xxv. Bogost, *Alien Phenomenology*, 8.
57. In her persuasive and clearly written book *Vibrant Matter: A Political Ecology of Things*, political theorist Jane Bennett articulates her guiding question in this way: "How would political responses to public problems change were we to take seriously the vitality of (nonhuman) bodies? By 'vitality' I mean the capacity of things—edibles, commodities, storms, metals—not only to impede or block the will and designs of humans but also to act as quasi agents or forces with trajectories, propensities, or tendencies of their own" (viii). Like Latour, Bennett is less directly interested in the philosophical problem of correlationism than in the possibilities of how the agency of non-human actors might open up new possibilities for thinking about the world. Although this emphasis may sometimes leave new materialists open to the charge of correlationism, there is no pretense on the part of thinkers such as Latour and Bennett that their work is primarily concerned with anything other than human social networks. And it strikes me as significant to consider the effects of object-oriented philosophy and Speculative Realism on how humans think about the world. In other words, I don't see the new materialist focus on human networks or the social as guilty of correlationism in an obtuse way.
58. Shaviro, *The Universe of Things*, 11.
59. Harman, specifically, would object to being termed a "neomaterialist." He goes so far as to avow himself an "anti-materialist." https://doctorzamalek2.wordpress.com/2010/07/23/brief-srooo-tutorial/. But I do not equate materialism with atomism in the way Harman does in an essay like "Realism without Materialism," *SubStance* 40, no. 2 (Issue 136, 2011): 60.
60. Latour, *Reassembling the Social*, 8.
61. Alexander R. Galloway, "The Poverty of Philosophy: Realism and Post-Fordism," *Critical Inquiry* 39, no. 2 (Winter 2013): 366.
62. James A. Knapp and Jeffrey Pence, "Between Thing and Theory," *Poetics Today* 24, no. 4 (Winter 2003): 654.
63. Bertrand Russell, *The Problems of Philosophy* (New York: Dover, 1999). Russell opens his second chapter by asking, "is there a table which has a certain intrinsic nature, and continues to exist when I am not looking, or is the table merely a product of my imagination, a dream-table in a very prolonged dream? [. . .] For if we cannot be sure of the independent existence of objects,

we cannot be sure of the independent existence of other people's bodies" (9). Russell identifies a certain material equanimity between things and people with regard to their physical existence, and goes on to consider the ethical importance of sense-data in establishing the presence of physical objects as it relates to our ultimate responsibilities to one another. Martin Heiddegger, "The Thing," in *Poetry, Language, Thought*, trans. Albert Hofstadter (New York: Harper and Row, 1971), 165–86. Heidegger considers the famous question: "what is the thing in itself?" in his discrimination between a "thing" and an "object": "Plato, who conceives of the presence of what is present in terms of the outward appearance, had no more understanding of the nature of the thing than did Aristotle and all subsequent thinkers. Rather, Plato experienced (decisively, indeed, for the sequel) everything present as an object of making. Instead of 'object'—as that which stands before, over against, opposite us—we use the more precise expression 'what stands forth.' In the full nature of what stands forth, a twofold standing prevails. First, standing forth has the sense of stemming from somewhere, whether this be a process of self-making or of being made by another. Secondly, standing forth has the sense of the made thing's standing forth into the unconcealedness of what is already present. Nevertheless, no representation of what is present, in the sense of what stands forth and of what stands over against as an object, ever reaches to the thing *qua* thing. The jug's thingness resides in its being *qua* vessel" (168–69). For Heidegger, a thing is not its human-madeness nor its self-madeness, but the void that it holds, as the jug's thingness is defined by the space into which liquid is poured. The maker shapes the sides and bottom but cannot shape the actual void. Donald Winnicott, *Playing and Reality* (New York: Routledge, 1989). In this touchstone psychoanalytic work, Winnicott develops his theory of the transitional object, which most of us know as the security blanket. For Winnicott, this object aids in an infant's transition away from oral fixation on fingers and fists. "I have introduced the term 'transitional objects' and 'transitional phenomena,'" Winnicott writes, "for designation of the intermediate area of experience, between the thumb and the teddy bear, between the oral erotism and the true object-relationship, between primary creative activity and projection of what has already been introjected, between primary unawareness of indebtedness and the acknowledgment of indebtedness" (2).

64. Walter Abish, *How German Is It* (New York: New Directions, 1979), 19.
65. Heiddegger, *Poetry, Language, Thought*, 166–67.
66. Brown, "Thing Theory," 4.
67. Erich Auerbarch, *Mimesis: The Representation of Reality in Western Literature* (Princeton, NJ: Princeton University Press, 2003), 23.
68. Roland Barthes, "The Reality Effect," in *The Rustle of Language*, trans. Richard Howard (Berkeley: University of California Press, 1989), 146, 148.

NOTES

69. Brown, *A Sense of Things*, 3.
70. René Girard, *To Double Business Bound: Essays on Literature, Mimesis, and Anthropology* (Baltimore, MD: Johns Hopkins University Press, 1978), viii. Brown, *A Sense of Things*, 190n.
71. Girard, *To Double Business Bound*, 2–3.
72. McHale, *Postmodernist Fiction*, 28.
73. Rosaldo, *Culture and Truth*, 32.
74. Ibid., 92.
75. Williams, *Marxism and Literature*. See especially "Part I: Basic Concepts" in which Williams examines each of these concepts as processual rather than ready-made.
76. DeKoven, *Utopia Limited*, x.
77. Ibid., xi.
78. Rosaldo, *Culture and Truth*, 35.
79. Renato Rosald, "Foreword," in *Hybrid Cultures: Strategies for Entering and Leaving Modernity*, by Néstor García Canclini, trans. Christopher L. Chiappari and Silvia L. López (Minneapolis: University of Minnesota Press, 1995), xiv.
80. DeKoven, *Utopia Limited*, xv, 3.
81. Rosi Braidotti, *Metamorphoses: Towards a Materialist Theory of Becoming* (Malden, MA: Polity, 2002), 1.
82. Timothy Morton, *Realist Magic: Objects, Ontology, Causality* (Ann Arbor, MI: Open Humanities Press, 2013), 19–20.
83. Jameson, *Postmodernism, or, The Cultural Logic of Late Capitalism*, xiv–xv. Guy Debord, *The Society of the Spectacle*, trans. Ken Knabb (London: Rebel Press, 2006). Jean Baudrillard, *Simulation and Simulacra*, trans. Sheila Faria Glaser (Ann Arbor: University of Michigan Press, 1994).
84. Brown, *A Sense of Things*, 5–6, 19.
85. Ibid., 19. Brown's language here bears the marks of Jameson's claim that in the postmodern era "the producers of culture have nowhere to turn but to the past: the imitation of dead styles, speech through all the masks and voices stored up in the imaginary museum of a now global culture" (*Postmodernism* 17–18). Jameson's argument builds on Debord's, Baudrillard's, and Lyotard's claims regarding postmodernism as fundamentally cultural, meaning that "reality" or "the real" is not a matter of, well, matter, but of socioeconomic and cultural convention. My argument is that socioeconomic and cultural conventions are themselves material networks comprised of both human and nonhuman "actors," to borrow Latour's term.
86. As James A. Knapp and Jeffrey Pence, editors of "Between Thing and Theory," a special issue of *Poetics Today*, have argued, "In scholarly fields as diverse as our own specializations—early modern culture and film studies—a widespread trend has emerged consisting in the privileging of the historical record as corrective to the vagaries of interpretation and the allegedly unproductive

reflexivity that is often associated with the influence of French intellectual thought—especially that of Jacques Derrida, Jacques Lacan, and Michel Foucault but also of Jean-François Lyotard, Jean Baudrillard, Giles Deleuze and Félix Guattari—on the literary and cultural theory of the 1970s and 1980s" (642). Across the board, the work of theorists and philosophers most often identified with postmodernism has been understood as vague, ethereal, abstract, immaterial, in need of a more concrete corrective.
87. Hutcheon's argument is articulated most lucidly in *The Politics of Postmodernism* (34), although she also takes up this problem in her earlier and more definitional *A Poetics of Postmodernism*: "Postmodernism teaches that all cultural practices have an ideological subtext which determines the conditions of the very possibility of their production of meaning" (xii–xiii).
88. Susan Stewart, *On Longing: Narratives of the Miniature, the Gigantic, the Souvenir, the Collection* (Durham, NC: Duke University Press, 1993).
89. Lori Merish, *Sentimental Materialism: Gender, Commodity Culture, and Nineteenth-Century American Literature* (Durham, NC: Duke University Press, 2000), 2, 90.
90. Barbara Johnson, *Persons and Things* (Cambridge, MA: Harvard University Press, 2008), 28.
91. Samuel Cohen, *After the End of History: American Fiction in the 1990s* (Iowa City: University of Iowa Press, 2009), 4.
92. Barth, "Postmodernism Revisited," 17.
93. McGurl, *The Program Era*, 28.
94. Ibid., 32.
95. Foucault, *The Order of Things*, 53.
96. Rita Felski, "Suspicious Minds," *Poetics Today* 32, no. 2 (Summer 2011): 217.
97. Bruno Latour, "Why Has Critique Run Out of Steam? From Matters of Fact to Matters of Concern," *Critical Inquiry* 30, no. 2 (Winter 2004): 241.
98. Ibid., 246.

Chapter 1

1. Amy J. Elias, *Sublime Desire: History and Post-1960s Fiction* (Baltimore, MD: Johns Hopkins University Press, 2001), xxvi.
2. W. Lawrence Hogue, "Postmodernism, Traditional Cultural Forms, and the African American Narrative: Major's *Reflex*, Morrison's *Jazz*, and Reed's *Mumbo Jumbo*," *Novel* 35, no. 2–3 (Spring–Summer 2002): 171–72.
3. Wendy Steiner, "Rethinking Postmodernism," in *The Cambridge History of American Literature Volume 7: Prose Writing, 1940–1990*, ed. Sacvan Bercovitch (New York: Cambridge University Press, 1999), 431–32.
4. Amy Hungerford, "On the Period Formerly Known as Contemporary," *American Literary History* 20, no. 1–2 (Spring–Summer 2008): 411.

NOTES

5. Steiner, 442.
6. Steiner maintains that "critics who equate postmodernism with technical experiment—for example, Jerome Klinkowitz—unselfconsciously produce a strikingly gender- and race-restricted canon: John Barth, John Hawkes, Gilbert Sorrentino, Thomas Pynchon, William Gass, Donald Barthleme, Jerzk Kosinski, Ronald Sukenick, Raymond Federman, Richard Coover, and Kurt Vonnegut" (431). She goes on to argue, in light of the gap between experimental postmodernism and the "broad heterogeneity of the postmodern period as a whole" (432), that the experimental brand of postmodernism is wrapped up in "linguistic imperialism" and should thus be considered more in line with high modernism and its tradition than in relation to the postmodern project of political subversion and rewriting of what she calls the "radical traditionalism" (441).
7. Jeremy Green, *Late Postmodernism: American Fiction at the Millennium* (New York: Palgrave MacMillan, 2005), 28.
8. Timothy Parrish, *From the Civil War to the Apocalypse: Postmodern History and American Fiction* (Amherst: University of Massachusetts Press, 2008), 4–5.
9. Ibid., 5.
10. Mark McGurl, *The Program Era: Postwar Fiction and the Rise of Creative Writing*, 58. McGurl argues that "high cultural pluralism enacts a layering of positively marked differences: in the modernist tradition, it understands its self-consciously crafted and/or intellectually substantial products as importantly distinct from mass culture or genre fiction [. . .] The high cultural pluralist writer is additionally called upon to speak from the point of view of one or another hyphenated population, synthesizing the particularity of the ethnic—or analogously marked—voice with the elevated idiom of literary modernism" (57). Roth is the ultimate case study, McGurl insists, because "he can seem to figure either as a culturally conservative white male writer," or "as a conspicuously 'ethnic' writer ('The Jew You Can't Permit in the Parlor') who introduces cultural difference into that system" (56). Thus, McGurl's insightful reinterpretation of the institutional circumstances of postmodernism in the form of high cultural pluralism provides an alternative way of accounting for the clear tension between white male writers and women writers and writers of color, but without actually addressing its causes or effects.
11. W. Lawrence Hogue, *Postmodern American Literature and Its Other* (Urbana: University of Illinois Press, 2009), v.
12. bell hooks, "Postmodern Blackness," in *Postmodern American Fiction: A Norton Anthology*, ed. Paula Geyh, Fred G. Leebron, and Andrew Levy (New York: Norton, 1998), 629.
13. Craig Womack, "Theorizing American Indian Experience," in *Reasoning Together: The Native Critics Collective*, ed. Craig S. Womack, Daniel Heath

Justice, and Christopher B. Teuton (Norman: University of Oklahoma Press, 2008), 353.

14. Paula Gunn Allen, *The Sacred Hoop: Recovering the Feminine in American Indian Traditions* (Boston: Beacon Press, 1992), 119; Rick Mott, "Ceremony Earth: Digitizing Silko's Novel for Students of the Twenty-First Century," *Studies in American Indian Literatures* 23, no. 2 (Summer 2011): 25–26; Chadwick Allen, *Blood Narrative: Indigenous Identity in American Indian and Maori Literary and Activist Texts* (Durham, NC: Duke University Press, 2002), 172.

15. Sara L. Spurgeon, *Exploding the Western: Myths of Empire on the Postmodern Frontier* (College Station: Texas A & M University Press, 2005), 76. See especially chapter 4, "Decolonizing Imperialism: Captivity Myths and the Postmodern World in Leslie Marmon Silko's *Ceremony*." Also see Lou Freitas Caton's chapter on Silko in *Reading American Novels and Multicultural Aesthetics: Romancing the Postmodern Novel* (New York: Palgrave MacMillan, 2008); Elvira Pulitano, *Toward a Native American Critical Theory* (Lincoln: University of Nebraska Press, 2003). Pulitano's claim has produced perhaps the most reverberations along these lines, as all three contributions to the collection *American Indian Literary Nationalism* are, in part, responses to Pulitano's claims (see the "Preface" to *American Indian Literary Nationalism*, xx).

16. Steiner, 428.

17. Gerald Vizenor, *Manifest Manners: Postindian Warriors of Survivance* (Hanover, NH: Wesleyan University Press, 1994), 67.

18. Ibid., 6.

19. Gerald Vizenor, "A Postmodern Introduction," in *Narrative Chance: Postmodern Discourse on Native American Indian Literatures*, ed. Gerald Vizenor (Norman: University of Oklahoma Press, 1993), 4.

20. Paula M. L. Moya defines the type of essentialism that postmodernism seeks to avoid as "the notion that individuals or groups have an immutable and discoverable 'essence'—a basic, unvariable, and presocial nature. As a theoretical concept, essentialism expresses itself through the tendency to see one social category (class, gender, race, sexuality, etc.) as determinate in the last instance for the cultural identity of the individual or group in question" (7). Craig Womack points out a gap in Moya's and the broader "postpositivist realist" reaction to postmodernism's endless fictions by arguing that this reaction is "a version of postmodernism that describes much the same theoretical commitment as the old version, without any real theoretical difference but with a new theoretical jargon constituting its main distinctive feature" ("Theorizing," 355). The postpositive realist position is one that sees the value of postmodernism's move away from foundationalism but is also leery of its inability to, as Womack expresses it, "make normative truth claims"

("Theorizing," 353). Womack argues that while the impulse of postpositive realists is promising, they "might be described as 'having their cake and eating it too.' They want to retain the theoretical sophistication of postmodernism in terms of looking at how history and culture give rise to ideas that are always mediated by human knowledge [...] while also insisting that truth claims can be judged *relatively* true or false..." ("Theorizing" 355).

21. Kimberly Blaeser, *Gerald Vizenor: Writing in the Oral Tradition* (Norman: University of Oklahoma Press, 1996), 73.
22. Craig Womack, "A Single Decade: Book-Length Native Literary Criticism between 1986 and 1997," in *Reasoning Together: The Native Critics Collective*, ed. Craig S. Womack, Daniel Heath Justice, and Christopher B. Teuton (Norman: University of Oklahoma Press, 2008), 65.
23. Jace Weaver, "Splitting the Earth: First Utterances and Pluralist Separatism," in *American Indian Literary Nationalism* (Albuquerque: University of New Mexico Press, 2006), 20.
24. Ibid., 28.
25. Paula M. L. Moya, "Introduction: Reclaiming Identity," in *Reclaiming Identity: Realist Theory and the Predicament of Postmodernism*, ed. Paula M. L. Moya and Michael Haimes-Garcia (Berkeley: University of California Press, 2000), 6.
26. Satya P. Mohanty, *Literary Theory and the Claims of History: Postmodernism, Objectivity, Multicultural Politics* (Ithaca, NY: Cornell University Press, 1997), 30.
27. Latour, *Reassembling the Social*, 90.
28. In his contribution to *American Indian Literary Nationalism*, Womack makes the claim that "[c]harges of essentialism have become far too easy in critical debates these days. [...] it is ironic that accusations of essentialism have often become a substitute for historical work and philosophical scrutiny, instead simply labeling people with an abstraction, one might even say with an essentialism" (102). Womack's observation highlights the worst dimensions of theoretical discourse, namely, those in which critics argue for or against an idea for fear of being labeled or tagged.
29. Womack, "Theorizing American Indian Experience," 354.
30. Robert Dale Parker, *The Invention of Native American Literature* (Ithaca, NY: Cornell University Press, 2003), 5.
31. Weaver explains this phrase by arguing that "American Indian Literary Nationalism espouses a kind of separatism, but it *is* a pluralist separatism. In this it mirrors the pluralistic aspects of the broader Native community. Though it is popular to refer to Native America, it is perhaps more correct to refer to Native *Americas*, in the plural" (46).
32. David Herman, *Story Logic: Problems and Possibilities of Narrative* (Lincoln: University of Nebraska Press, 2002). In his theory of narrative as a means of structuring experience, Herman conceptualizes "storyworlds" as "mental models

of who did what to and with whom, when, where, why, and in what fashion in the world to which recipients relocate—or make a deictic shift—as they work to comprehend a narrative" (5). Calling on the work of Algirdas Julien Greimas in a later chapter, Herman goes on to point out that "actants are what enable language users to [. . .] build a manifested universe of meaning from the materials provided by the immanent universe of meaning" (121).

33. Ibid., 65.
34. Bruno Latour, *Politics of Nature*, trans. Catherine Porter (Cambridge, MA: Harvard University Press, 2004), 237.
35. Latour, *Reassembling the Social*, 71.
36. Womack, "A Single Decade: Book-Length Native Literary Criticism between 1986 and 1997," 65.
37. Womack, "Theorizing American Indian Experience," 370.
38. Linda Hogan, *Power* (New York: Norton, 1998), 79.
39. Leslie Marmon Silko, "America's Iron Curtain: The Border Patrol State," *The Nation* 259, no. 12 (October 17, 1994): 414.
40. Leslie Marmon Silko, *Ceremony* (New York: Viking, 1977), 67.
41. Bill Brown, *A Sense of Things: The Object Matter of American Literature*, 18.
42. Allen, *The Sacred Hoop: Recovering the Feminine in American Indian Traditions*, 118.
43. Latour's distinction between the sociology of the social and the sociology of associations is helpful here, as it further clarifies the distinction both Allen and I see between the different characters in *Ceremony*: "In most situations, we use 'social' to mean that which has already been assembled and acts as a whole, without being too picky on the precise nature of what has been gathered, bundled, and packaged together. When we say that 'something is social' or 'has a social dimension,' we mobilize one set of features that, so to speak, march in step together, even though it might be composed of radically different types of entities. This unproblematic use of the word is fine as long as we don't confuse the sentence 'Is social what goes together?' with one that says, 'social designates a particular kind of stuff.' With the former we simply mean that we are dealing with a routine state of affairs whose binding together is the crucial aspect, while the second designates a sort of substance whose main feature lies in its differences with other types of materials. We imply that some assemblages are built out of social stuff instead of physical, biological, or economical blocks" (*Reassembling the Social* 43).
44. Like Tayo, Betonie himself comes from a family in which social categories are not static, but fluid, as he has a Navajo grandfather, Mexican grandmother, and lives on the outskirts of a Navajo reservation overlooking the white town of Gallup, where he is ostracized by most everyone.
45. Bill Brown, "Thing Theory," *Critical Inquiry* 28, no. 1 (Autumn 2001): 7.
46. Susan L. Dunston, "Physics and Metaphysics: Lessons from Leslie Marmon Silko's *Ceremony*," *Arizona Quarterly* 66, no. 4 (Winter 2010): 140.

NOTES

47. See Louis Owens, *Other Destinies: Understanding the American Indian Novel* (Norman: University of Oklahoma Press, 1992). Owens argues that the central lesson of *Ceremony* is "that through the dynamism, adaptability, and syncretism inherent in Native American cultures, both individuals and the cultures within which individuals find significance and identity are able to survive, grow, and evade the deadly traps of stasis and sterility" (167). Chadwick Allen's *Blood Narrative*, referenced earlier, includes a chapter titled "Blood/Land/Memory: Narrating Indigenous Identity in the American Indian Renaissance," in which he emphasizes the "changing cultural and historical contexts" that Tayo must interpret in the novel in order to experience healing (172). Allen goes on to draw parallels between Tayo's experiences and the literary aesthetic of writers such as Silko and James Welch, among others, whose "representations of pictographic traditions serve as metonyms for indigenous memory in the contemporary written text. They evoke the continuity of that memory across generations and the endurance of indigenous historical memory despite cultural change" (172).
48. See most famously Toni Morrison, *Playing in the Dark* (New York: Vintage, 1992).
49. Allen, *The Sacred Hoop*, 119.
50. Caton, 102.
51. Ibid., 108.
52. Womack, "Theorizing American Indian Experience," 377.
53. Weaver, "Splitting the Earth: First Utterances and Pluralist Separatism," 38.
54. Andreas Huyssen, *After the Great Divide: Modernism, Mass Culture, Postmodernism* (Bloomington: Indiana University Press, 1986), 198.
55. Richard Delgado and Jean Stefancic, *Critical Race Theory: An Introduction* (New York: New York University Press, 2012), 9.

Chapter 2

1. Alan Sokal, "A Physicist Experiments with Cultural Studies," *Lingua Franca* (May–June 1996): 63.
2. Andrew Ross, "Introduction," in "Science Wars," ed. Andrew Ross, special issue, *Social Text* 46–47 (Spring–Summer 1996): 10–11.
3. Ibid., 5.
4. Sokal, "A Physicist Experiments," 62.
5. Ibid., 63.
6. Ibid., 64.
7. Bruce Robbins and Andrew Ross, "Mystery Science Theater," *Lingua Franca* (July–August 1996): 57.
8. Bogost, *Alien Phenomenology*, 13. Levi R. Bryant, *The Democracy of Objects* (Ann Arbor, MI: Open Humanities Press, 2011), 17. I've adopted Bogost's

term, "scientific naturalism," for what Bryant calls the "pro-science crowd," and Bryant's term, "social constructivists," for what Bogost calls "social relativism." I chose "constructivism" over "relativism" because of what I perceive as the unnecessarily and overly negative connotations of the term "constructivism" in critical discourse, connotations that I set out to modify in this book.
9. Bogost, *Alien Phenomenology*, 14. For more on correlationism, see the review of the literature on neomaterialism in the Introduction, as well as Quentin Meillassoux, *After Finitude: An Essay on the Necessity of Contingency* (New York: Continuum, 2008), 1–27.
10. Bryant, *The Democracy of Objects*, 14.
11. Jakobson quoted in Brian McHale, *Postmodernist Fiction* (New York: Routledge, 1989), 6.
12. Ibid., 7.
13. Ibid., 39.
14. Bogost, *Alien Phenomenology*, 11.
15. Bryant, *The Democracy of Objects*, 25.
16. Jonathan Safran Foer, *Everything Is Illuminated* (New York: Harper/Perennial, 2003), 147.
17. Ibid., 192.
18. Ibid., 193–93.
19. Brown, "Thing Theory," 7.
20. Billy Taylor, "What Is Jazz? Four Lectures," recorded February 14, 1995, *John F. Kennedy Center for the Performing Arts*, accessed March 27, 2012, http://town.hall.org/radio/Kennedy/Taylor/bt_11.html.
21. Marcel Cornis-Pope, *Narrative Innovation and Cultural Rewriting in the Cold War and After* (New York: Palgrave, 2001), 235.
22. Toni Morrison, "Toni Morrison, The Art of Fiction No. 134," *The Paris Review* 128 (Fall 1993): 109.
23. Toni Morrison, *Jazz* (New York: Alfred A. Knopf, 1992), 3.
24. Morrison, "Toni Morrison, The Art of Fiction No. 134," 110.
25. Shirley Ann Stave, "*Jazz* and *Paradise*: Pivotal Moments in Black History," in *The Cambridge Companion to Toni Morrison*, ed. Justine Tally (New York: Cambridge University Press, 2007), 65; Marcel Cornis-Pope, *Narrative Innovation and Cultural Rewriting in the Cold War and After*, 264; Eusebio Rodrigues, "Experiencing Jazz," *MFS: Modern Fiction Studies* 39, no. 3–4 (Fall–Winter 1993): 749; Paula Eckard, "The Interplay of Music, Language, and Narrative in Toni Morrison's *Jazz*," *CLA Journal* 28, no. 1 (September 1994): 13–14; Caroline Rody, "Impossible Voices: Ethnic Postmodern Narration in Toni Morrison's *Jazz* and Karen Tei Yamashita's *Through the Arc of the Rain Forest*," *Contemporary Literature* 41, no. 1 (Winter 2000): 624.
26. Angels Carabi and Toni Morrison, "Interview: Toni Morrison on *Jazz*," *Belles Lettres* 10, no. 2 (Spring 1995): 42.

27. Jürgen E Grandt, "Kinds of Blue: Toni Morrison, Hans Janowitz, and the Jazz Aesthetic," *African American Review* 38, no. 2 (Summer 2004): 305; Andrew Sheiber, "Jazz and the Future Blues: Toni Morrison's Urban Folk Zone," *Modern Fiction Studies* 52, no. 2 (Summer 2006): 471–72; Caroline Brown, "Golden Gray and the Talking Book: Identity as a Site of Artful Construction in Toni Morrison's *Jazz*," *African American Review* 36, no. 4 (Winter 2002): 632.
28. Nancy J. Peterson, "Say Make Me, Remake Me: Toni Morrison and the Reconstruction of African-American History," in *Toni Morrison: Critical and Theoretical Approaches*, ed. Nancy J. Peterson (Baltimore, MD: Johns Hopkins University Press, 1997), 212.
29. Ibid., 214.
30. Morrison, "Toni Morrison, The Art of Fiction No. 134," 110.
31. Charles Johnson, *Being and Race: Black Writing since 1970* (Bloomington: Indiana University Press, 1988), 26.
32. Toni Morrison, "The Site of Memory," in *Writing and Remembering*, ed. William Zinsser (Boston: Houghton Mifflin, 1987), 103.
33. David R. Roediger, *Towards the Abolition of Whiteness: Essays on Race, Politics, and Working Class History* (New York: Verso, 1994), 181.
34. Ian Haney López, *White by Law: The Legal Construction of Race* (New York: New York University Press, 2006), 73, 74.
35. Morrison, *Playing in the Dark*, 8, 47.
36. Heidegger, "The Thing," 169.
37. Henry Louis Gates, Jr., *The Signifying Monkey: A Theory of African-American Literary Criticism* (New York: Oxford University Press, 1988). Gates traces the trope of the talking book in the African American literary tradition back to "five black texts published in English by 1815" that demonstrate the significance of "recording an authentic black voice in the text of Western letters" as an answer to the rising significance of writing as an indicator of humanness (130). Gates characterizes the trope of the talking book as "the ur-trope of the Anglo-African tradition" (131), and insists that "the trope of the Talking Book is not a trope of the presence of voice at all, but of its absence" (167). Thus, as we consider the significance of Morrison's talking book speaking in the 1920s and being written by Morrison herself in the late 1980s and early 1990s, we should consider the novel itself as an absent space.
38. In her essay "Signifyin(g) on Reparation in Toni Morrison's *Jazz*," Marjorie Pryse argues that by making the book itself the narrator of *Jazz*, Morrison creates a relationship between text and reader that renders their positions interchangeable, but preserves the distance between them. Pryse relies here on the psychoanalytic theory of transference offered by Melanie Klein: "While agreeing with Sigmund Freud that transferences 'are new editions or facsimiles of the impulses and phantasies which are aroused and made conscious

during the progress of the analysis,' Melanie Klein maintains, unlike Freud, that transference 'originates in the same processes which in the earliest stages determine object-relations'" (583–84). This transferential relationship between text and reader is important to Pryse because it enables *Jazz* to explore the region between the two "to create the possibility that a talking book may engage in a psychodynamic relationship with a reader" (584).

39. Latour, *Reassembling the Social*, 83.
40. Jonathan Lethem, *The Fortress of Solitude* (New York: Vintage, 2003), 136.
41. Jonathan Lethem, "Jonathan Lethem, The Art of Fiction, No. 177," *The Paris Review* 45, no. 166 (Summer 2003): 241.
42. Jonathan Lethem and Sarah Anne Johnson, "Interview with Jonathan Lethem," in *Conversations with Jonathan Lethem*, ed. Jaime Clark (Jackson: University of Mississippi Press, 2011), 95–96.
43. Lev Grossman, "The Bard of Brooklyn," *Time* 162, no. 11 (2003): 77; Jason Picone, "Always Staying Home," *American Book Review* 25, no. 3 (March–April 2004): 27; A. O. Scott, "When Dylan Met Mingus," *New York Times Book Review*, September 21, 2003, 7; Peter Bradshaw, "Flight of Fancy," *New Statesman*, January 19, 2004, 51–52; Michiko Kakutani, "White Kid, In a Black World," *New York Times*, September 16, 2003.
44. Marc Singer, "Embodiments of the Real: The Counterlinguistic Turn in the Comic-Book Novel," *Critique: Studies in Contemporary Fiction* 49, no. 3 (Spring 2008): 276.
45. Matt Godbey, "Gentrification, Authenticity and White Middle-Class Identity in Jonathan Lethem's *The Fortress of Solitude*," *Arizona Quarterly* 64, no. 1 (Spring 2008): 146.
46. David Coughlan, "Jonathan Lethem's *The Fortress of Solitude* and *Omega: The Unknown*, a Comic Book Series," *College Literature* 38, no. 3 (Summer 2011): 206, 207.
47. Singer, "Embodiments of the Real," 277.
48. Coughlan, "Jonathan Lethem's *The Fortress of Solitude* and *Omega: The Unknown*," 200.
49. As reviewer A. O. Scott suggests, in the latter half of the novel Dylan comes across as a "moody, thwarted 30-something in 1999, an obsessive, pedantic music critic who seems to love the fact that he has a black girlfriend more than he loves the girlfriend herself" (7).
50. Godbey, "Gentrification, Authenticity and White Middle-Class Identity," 140.

Chapter 3

1. Richard Rorty, ed., *The Linguistic Turn* (Chicago: University of Chicago Press, 1967), 3.

NOTES

2. Jean-François Lyotard, *The Postmodern Condition: A Report on Knowledge*, trans. Geoff Bennington and Brian Massumi (Minneapolis: University of Minnesota Press, 1984), xxiv.
3. David Harvey, *The Condition of Postmodernity* (Cambridge, MA: Blackwell, 1990), 49.
4. Geoffrey Galt Harpham, *Language Alone: The Critical Fetish of Modernity* (New York: Routledge, 2002), 13.
5. Latour, *Reassembling the Social*, 39.
6. Ibid., 153, 155.
7. Andreas Huyssen, "Mapping the Postmodern," *New German Critique* 33 (Autumn 1984): 5–52. Huyssen acknowledges an overlap between poststructuralism and postwar literature but questions "the way in which this impact is automatically evaluated in the United States as postmodern and thus sucked into the orbit of the kind of critical discourse that emphasizes radical rupture and discontinuity" (37). Marianne DeKoven, *Utopia Limited: The Sixties and the Emergence of the Postmodern*, 52. DeKoven sees "poststructuralism not as postmodern but rather as the epitome of modernist thought and language," although it certainly plays "a key role in initiating postmodernism [...] by theorizing its multiplicities and indeterminacies, and by critiquing the governing hierarchical dualisms of modernity" (52).
8. In his chapter on the transition from post-Marxism to postmodernism, Harpham goes out of his way to note that the work of the most well-known thinkers who have influenced the dominant ideas about language in the twentieth century "pivots on the work of Saussure, for whom language was a social construction. They generally ignore the work of Chomsky, which discounts the role of society and awakens the slumbering, or anesthetized giant of biologically determined human nature" (119). See also E. F. K. Koerner, *Toward a History of American Linguistics* (New York: Routledge, 2002). Koerner points out that, in the middle years of his career, Chomsky "criticizes [Saussure] for taking language to be a social product, necessitating a fictitious idealized speech community and preventing it from capturing 'the sociopolitical and normative-teleological aspects' of E[xternal]-language" (145–46). But, it should be noted, Koerner goes on to critique Chomsky for failing to attempt any such endeavor and for, what is in his mind, an oversimplification of Saussure.
9. Noam Chomsky, "Knowledge of Language: Its Elements and Origins," *Philosophical Transactions of the Royal Society of London. Series B, Biological Sciences* 295, no. 1077 (October 1981): 9.
10. Williams, *Marxism and Literature*, 43. Williams notes that while Chomskyan linguistics allows for the possibility of flux and change in ways that structuralist linguistics does not, it also "stresses deep structures of language formation which are certainly incompatible with ordinary social and historical

accounts of the origin and development of language. An emphasis on deep constitutive structures, at an evolutionary rather than a historical level, can of course be reconciled with the view of language as a constitutive human faculty: exerting pressures and setting limits, in determinate ways, to human development itself. But while it is retained as an exclusively evolutionary process, it moves, necessarily, towards reified accounts of 'systemic evolution': development by constituted systems and structures [. . .] rather than by actual human beings in a continuing social practice."

11. Roy Harris and Talbot J. Taylor, *Landmarks in Linguistic Thought I: The Western Tradition from Socrates to Saussure*, 2nd ed. (New York: Routledge, 1997), xvii.
12. Meillassoux, *After Finitude*, 7.
13. Bogost, *Alien Phenomenology*, 40.
14. Ibid.
15. John Barth, *Lost in the Funhouse* (1968; repr. New York: Anchor, 1988), xi.
16. Ibid., xi–xii.
17. John Barth, *The Friday Book: Essays and Other Nonfiction* (Baltimore, MD: The Johns Hopkins University Press, 1997), 79.
18. Charles Harris, *Passionate Virtuosity: The Fiction of John Barth* (Urbana: University of Illinois Press, 1983), ix.
19. Charles Altieri, "Ovid and the New Mythologists." *Novel* 7, no. 1 (Fall 1973): 32; see also Carol Kyle, "The Unity of Anatomy: The Structure of Barth's *Lost in the Funhouse*," *Critique* 13, no. 3 (1972): 31–43.
20. Christopher Morris, "Barth and Lacan: The World of the Moebius Strip," *Critique* 17, no. 1 (1975): 70.
21. Jerome Klinkowitz, *Literary Disruptions: The Making of a Post-Contemporary American Fiction* (Urbana: University of Illinois Press, 1975), 14.
22. Raymond Federman, *Critifiction: Postmodern Essays* (Albany: State University of New York Press, 1993), 13.
23. Deborah Woolley, "Empty 'Text,' Fecund Voice: Self-Reflexivity in Barth's *Lost in the Funhouse*," *Contemporary Literature* 26, no. 4 (1985): 460.
24. Ibid., 460, 463, 465.
25. Max Schulz, *The Muses of John Barth: Tradition and Metafiction from* Lost in the Funhouse *to* The Tidewater Tales (Baltimore, MD: The Johns Hopkins University Press, 1990), 10.
26. See Roland Barthes, "Introduction to the Structural Analysis of Narratives," in *A Barthes Reader*, ed. and intro. Susan Sontag (New York: Hill and Wang, 1982), 251–295. Barthes suggests that a narrative is made up of the representation of at least two events; see also Brian Richardson, *Unlikely Stories: Causality and the Nature of Modern Narrative* (Newark: University of Delaware Press, 1997). Richardson argues that these events must even be related causally.

NOTES

27. Schulz, *The Muses of John Barth*, 6.
28. Harpham, *Language Alone*, 28.
29. Woolley, "Empty 'Text,' Fecund Voice," 476.
30. William J. Krier, "*Lost in the Funhouse*: 'A Continuing, Strange Love Letter,'" *boundary 2* 5, no. 1 (Fall 1976): 114.
31. Morris, "Barth and Lacan," 73.
32. Woolley, "Empty 'Text,' Fecund Voice," 472.
33. Harris, *Passionate Virtuosity*, 115.
34. John Barth, *The Friday Book*, 79.
35. James Rother, "Reading and Riding the Post-Scientific Wave: The Shorter Fiction of David Foster Wallace," *Review of Contemporary Fiction* 13, no. 2 (Summer 1993): 218.
36. David Foster Wallace, *Girl with Curious Hair* (New York: Norton, 1989), 235.
37. For a discussion of the division between first- and second-generation postmodernism, see the introduction to Chapter 1 in this study.
38. Paul Giles, "Sentimental Posthumanism: David Foster Wallace," *Twentieth-Century Literature* 53, no. 3 (Fall 2007): 331.
39. Toon Staes, "'Only Artists Can Transfigure': Kafka's Artists and the Possibility of Redemption in the Novellas of David Foster Wallace," *Orbis Litterarum* 65, no. 6 (2010): 468.
40. Marshall Boswell, *Understanding David Foster Wallace* (Columbia: University of South Carolina Press, 2003), 104.
41. Ibid., 112.
42. Adam Kelly, "David Foster Wallace and the New Sincerity in American Fiction," in *Consider David Foster Wallace: Critical Essays*, ed. David Hering (Los Angeles: Sideshow Media Group Press, 2010), 133. Kelly's introduction provides both popular and scholarly context for situating Wallace among a cohort of culture producers that has been labeled representative of a "new sincerity."
43. Ibid.
44. Latour, *Reassembling the Social*, 143.
45. Ibid., 35.
46. See Woolley's "Empty 'Text,' Fecund Voice: Self-Reflexivity in Barth's *Lost in the Funhouse*" (471); Morris's "Barth and Lacan: The World of the Moebius Strip" (73); Kyle's "The Unity of Anatomy: The Structure of Barth's *Lost in the Funhouse*" (40).
47. I am following the direction of Jonathan Culler in "Story and Discourse in the Analysis of Narrative" from *The Pursuit of Signs: Semiotics, Literature, Deconstruction*, in which he problematizes the conventional narratological distinction between story and discourse by suggesting that there is only discourse. However, I am doing so under the rubric of my own argument that complicates our understanding of discourse in poststructural terms.
48. Brown, "Thing Theory," 3.

NOTES

49. David Foster Wallace, *Infinite Jest* (Boston: Back Bay 1996), 556.
50. Latour, *Reassembling the Social*, 85.
51. James K. A. Smith, *Jacques Derrida: Live Theory* (New York: Continuum, 2005), 44.
52. Rita Felski, *Doing Time: Feminist Theory and Postmodern Culture* (New York: New York University Press, 2000), 6.

Chapter 4

1. Ihab Hassan, *The Dismemberment of Orpheus: Toward a Postmodern Literature*, 2nd ed. (Madison: University of Wisconsin Press, 1982), 266.
2. Leslie Fiedler, "The New Mutants," *Partisan Review* 32, no. 4 (Fall 1965): 511.
3. Ibid.
4. Fredric Jameson, "Notes on Globalization as a Philosophical Issue," in *The Cultures of Globalization*, ed. Fredric Jameson and Masao Miyoshi (Durham, NC: Duke University Press, 1998), 56.
5. Terry Eagleton, *The Illusions of Postmodernism* (Malden, MA: Blackwell, 1996), 121.
6. K. Anthony Appiah, "Is the Post- in Postmodernism the Post- in Postcolonial?" *Critical Inquiry* 17, no. 2 (Winter 1991): 336–57; Lyotard, *The Postmodern Condition*, xxiv.
7. Appiah, "Is the Post- in Postmodernism the Post- in Postcolonial?" 354.
8. Ibid., 344.
9. Terry Eagleton, *After Theory* (New York: Basic Books, 2003), 46.
10. Huyssen, "Mapping the Postmodern," 50.
11. Jean-Luc Nancy, *The Inoperative Community* (Minneapolis: University of Minnesota Press, 1991), 3–4.
12. Ibid., 20. While this distinction between society and community can be traced back to Plato's *Laws* and *Republic* and perhaps further, Ferdinand Tönnies's influential work *Gemeinschaft und Gesellschaft* (*Community and Society*) is the touchstone for the modern discussion.
13. Frank O. Copley, introduction to *On the Nature of Things*, by Lucretius (New York: Norton, 1977), xii. Lucretius explains that collisions between atoms occur due to unaccountable movements, or what he calls the "swerve" of atoms toward each other in space: "And if they did not swerve, they all would fall / downward like raindrops through the boundless void; / no clashes would occur, no blows befall / the atoms; nature would never have made a thing." Lucretius, *On the Nature of Things*, trans. Frank O. Copley (New York: Norton, 1977), 34. Without the inclination of atoms toward one another, for Lucretius, there would be no world as we know it, let alone the vast and complex networks of subjects and objects that we understand as making and remaking various social groups.

NOTES

14. Stephen Greenblatt, *The Swerve: How the World Became Modern* (New York: Norton, 2011), 5, 7.
15. See Christopher Fynsk's helpful "Foreword" to *The Inoperative Community*, xii–xiii.
16. Latour, *Reassembling the Social*, 34.
17. Rey Chow, "The Interruption of Referentiality: Poststructuralism and the Conundrum of Critical Multiculturalism," *South Atlantic Quarterly* 101, no. 1 (Winter 2002): 171.
18. Sue J. Kim, *Critiquing Postmodernism in Contemporary Discourses of Race* (New York: Palgrave Macmillan, 2009), 22.
19. Appiah, "Is the Post- in Postmodernism the Post- in Postcolonial?" 341, 346.
20. Nancy, *The Inoperative Community*, 19.
21. Latour, *Reassembling the Social*, 36.
22. John N. Duvall, "Baseball as Aesthetic Ideology: Cold War History, Race, and DeLillo's 'Pafko at the Wall,'" *Modern Fiction Studies* 41, no. 2 (Summer 1995): 286.
23. As I explain in the Introduction, for Latour, under the sociology of the social, society or the social order is a "domain of reality" distinct from "other domains such as economics, geography, biology, psychology, law, science, and politics" (*Reassembling* 3). This approach views the social as substance, phenomenon, source that can be used to illuminate other phenomena, rather than as the phenomenon that needs to be explained.
24. Gerald Howard, "The American Strangeness: An Interview with Don DeLillo," in *Conversations with Don DeLillo*, ed. Thomas DePietro (Jackson: University of Mississippi Press, 2005), 123.
25. Ibid., 124.
26. Don DeLillo, *Underworld* (New York: Scribner, 1997), 12.
27. Nancy, *The Inoperative Community*, xxxix.
28. This "demythologizing" is the subject of Duvall's essay, "Baseball as Aesthetic Ideology: Cold War History, Race, and DeLillo's 'Pafko at the Wall'" referenced earlier. Also see Donald J. Greiner, "John Updike, Don DeLillo, and the Sustaining Power of Myth," in *Underwords: Perspectives on Don DeLillo's Underworld*, ed. Joseph Dewey, Steven G. Kellman, and Irving Malin (Newark: University of Delaware Press, 2002), 103–13. But, as I discuss in the Introduction, this "spirit of criticism" (Howe 429), has been cast as characteristic of postmodern fiction on the whole (see Hutcheon's *The Politics of Postmodernism*; Maltby's *Dissident Postmodernists*; and Felski's "Suspicious Minds"). Not all critics read DeLillo's retelling of the 1951 pennant game as an exposure of myth, as John Duvall does, or as an interruption of myth, as I do. Donald J. Greiner, for example, argues that "[t]he point is not that myth fosters forgetfulness but that myth offers renewal" (108). Greiner calls on DeLillo's essay "The Power of History" to suggest that in *Underworld* DeLillo

uses "Thomson's home run as a feat of strength and skill that both mythologizes a moment in history and forges unity among the living" (109).
29. Nancy, *The Inoperative Community*, 47, 52.
30. John N. Duvall, *Don DeLillo's Underwold: A Reader's Guide* (New York: Continuum, 2002), 25.
31. Lucretius, *On the Nature of Things*, 34.
32. Kathleen Fitzpatrick, "The Unmaking of History: Baseball, Cold War, and Underworld," in *Underwords: Perspectives on Don DeLillo's Underworld*, ed. Joseph Dewey, Steven G. Kellman, and Irving Malin (Newark: University of Delaware Press, 2002), 150.
33. Manuel Lopez Michelone and Marcelo Perez Medel, "Understanding Photomosaics," *Dr. Dobb's Journal* 26, no. 11 (Nov. 2001): 58.
34. Don DeLillo, "The Power of History," *New York Times Book Review* (Sept. 7, 1997): 5.
35. Latour, *Reassembling the Social*, 5, 8.
36. Don DeLillo, "In the Ruins of the Future," *Harper's* (Dec. 2001): 35.
37. Ibid.
38. Brian McHale, *Constructing Postmodernism* (New York: Routledge, 1992), 1–3.
39. Catherine Romagnolo, "Initiating Dialogue: Narrative Beginnings in Multicultural Narratives" in *Analyzing World Fiction: New Horizons in Narrative Theory*, ed. Frederick Luis Aldama (Austin: University of Texas Press, 2011), 183–98. Romagnolo argues that "texts such as Zora Neale Hurston's *Their Eyes Were Watching God*, Toni Morrison's *Beloved* and Julia Alvarez's *How the García Girls Lost Their Accents*, to name just a few, highlight the interwoven signification of conceptual and formal beginnings" (184). Romagnolo's goal in investigating narrative beginnings is especially important in a novel like Alvarez's where the chronological beginning can be found at the novel's end, and the beginning of the novel is, as she argues, "discursive." That is, the beginning of Alvarez's novel is not the beginning of the story, but only a beginning at the level of narrative discourse.
40. Jacqueline Stefanko, "New Ways of Telling: Latinas' Narratives of Exile and Return," *Frontiers: A Journal of Women Studies* 17, no. 2 (1996): 50.
41. Maribel Ortiz-Márquez, "From Third World Politics to First World Practices: Contemporary Latina Writers in the United States," in *Interventions: Feminist Dialogues on Third World Women's Literature and Film*, ed. Bishnupriya Ghosh and Brinda Bose (New York: Garland Publishing, 1997), 236.
42. Julie Barak, "'Turning and Turning in the Widening Gyre': A Second Coming into Language in Julia Alvarez's *How the García Girls Lost Their Accents*," *MELUS* 23, no. 1 (Spring 1998): 159.

NOTES

43. Ricardo Castells, "The Silence of Exile in *How the García Girls Lost Their Accents*," *Bilingual Review/La Revista Bilingüe* 26, no. 1 (January 2002): 34. See also Joan M. Hoffman, "'She Wants to Be Called Yolanda Now': Identity, Language, and the Third Sister in *How the García Girls Lost Their Accents*," *Bilingual Review/La Revista Bilingüe* 23, no. 1 (January–April 1998): 21–22; Juan Pablo Rivera, "Language Allergy: Seduction and Second Languages in *How the García Girls Lost The Accents*," *Rupkatha* 2, no. 2 (2012): 123–35; Manuela Matas Llorente, "And Why Did the García Girls Lose Their Accents? Language, Identity and the Immigrant Experience in Julia Alvarez's *How the García Girls Lost The Accents*," *Revista de Estudios Norteamericanos* 8 (2001): 69–75.
44. Recall from Chapter 1 Sara Spurgeon's *Exploding the Western: Myths of Empire on the Postmodern Frontier* and Lou Caton's *Reading American Novels and Multicultural Aesthetics: Romancing the Postmodern Novel*, both of which discuss Tayo's identity in terms of the clash and hybridization of Native and non-Native cultures.
45. William Luis, "A Search for Identity in Julia Alvarez's *How the García Girls Lost Their Accents*," *Callaloo* 23, no. 3 (Summer 2000): 839–49. Luis argues that "Yolanda is caught between two worlds, the Hispanic and the North American ones" (846).
46. Sarika Chandra, "Re-Producing a Nationalist Literature in the Age of Globalization: Reading (Im)migration in Julia Alvarez's *How the García Girls Lost Their Accents*," *American Quarterly* 60, no. 3 (September 2008): 832.
47. Katarzyna Marciniak, *Alienhood: Citizenship, Exile, and the Logic of Difference* (Minneapolis: University of Minnesota Press, 2006), 59.
48. Chandra, "Re-Producing a Nationalist Literature in the Age of Globalization," 848.
49. Here we should bear in mind Latour's most elemental argument in *Reassembling the Social*, namely that "the social is not some glue that could fix everything including what other glues cannot fix; it is *what* is glued together by many other types of connectors" (5). And as he later observes about the use of the term "social forces": "When I begin to ask naïve questions about what is really meant by social explanation, I am told not to take the existence of social forces 'literally,' since no reasonable sociologists ever claimed that they could really *substitute* society for the object it explains" (103).
50. Julia Alvarez, *How the García Girls Lost Their Accents* (New York: Plume, 1992), 9.
51. Nancy, *The Inoperative Community*, 31.
52. Latour, *Reassembling the Social*, 34–35.
53. Barth, *The Friday Book*, 72. Ihab Hassan recognizes this self-consciousness in his first edition of *The Dismemberment of Orpheus: Toward a Postmodern Literature* in 1971. A host of postmodern fiction writers seems readily identifiable: "In recent American fiction, its votaries include Joseph Heller,

Thomas Pynchon, James Purdy, J. P. Donleavy, Terry Southern, Thomas Berger, Donald Barthelme, Ishmael Reed, Richard Brautigan, and Raymond Federman, among others" (254).

54. Roland Barthes, "From Work to Text," in *Image—Music—Text*, trans. Stephen Heath (New York: Hill and Wang, 1977), 162.

Afterism

1. McHale, *Constructing Postmodernism*, 1.
2. Ibid., 2.
3. Jonathan Lethem, "Postmodernism as Liberty Valance: Notes on a Ritual Killing," in *The Ecstasy of Influence* (New York: Vintage, 2012), 83.
4. McHale, *Postmodernist Fiction*, 5.
5. Lyotard, 81, 79.
6. Ibid., 81.
7. Gao Xingjian, *The Case for Literature* (New Haven, CT: Yale University Press, 2007), 25–26.
8. Ibid., 26, 67.
9. Octavia Butler, *The Parable of the Sower* (New York: Four Walls Eight Windows, 1993), 3.
10. Gaston Bachelard, *The Poetics of Space*, trans. Maria Jolas, Foreword Etienne Gilson (New York: The Orion Press, 1964), xxxi.
11. Ibid., xiv.
12. The connection between memory and space is an ancient one, initially explored in the Western tradition by the Sophists and popularized by the *Ad C. Herennium*, classically (although no longer) attributed to Cicero. For a popular account of this history, see Joshua Foer, *Moonwalking with Einstein: The Art and Science of Remembering Everything* (New York: Penguin, 2011). Foer opens with the famous account of the memory palace, the memory invention of a fifth-century Greek poet named Simonides. For an academic account of this history, see Paolo Rossi and Stephen Clucas, *Logic and the Art of Memory: The Quest for a Universal Language* (Chicago: University of Chicago Press, 2000). Rossi and Clucas also begin with Simonides, Cicero, and the *Ad C. Herennium*.
13. Bachelard, *The Poetics of Space*, 36.
14. Ibid., 14.
15. Ted Underwood, *Why Literary Periods Mattered: Historical Contrast and the Prestige of English Studies* (Palo Alto, CA: Stanford University Press, 2013), 5.
16. Ibid., 3.
17. Ibid., 132–33.
18. Marlene D. Allen, "Octavia Butler's Parable Novels and the 'Boomerang' of African American History," *Callaloo* 32, no. 4 (Fall 2009): 1355.

19. John Barth, "Postmodernism Revisited," 16.
20. Ibid.
21. Perry Anderson, *The Origins of Postmodernity* (New York: Verso, 1998), 3.
22. Ibid., 7.
23. Charles Olson, "Projective Verse" in *Collected Prose: Charles Olson*, ed. Donald Allen and Benjamin Friedlander (Berkeley: University of California Press, 1997), 239, 241, 243.
24. Charles Olson, *Call Me Ishmael*, in *Collected Prose: Charles Olson*, ed. Donald Allen and Benjamin Friedlander (Berkeley: University of California Press, 1997), 17.
25. Raymond Williams, "Base and Superstructure in Marxist Cultural Theory," *New Left Review* 82 (November–December 1973): 3.
26. Jameson, *Postmodernism*, 4.
27. Kelly, *American Fiction in Transition*, 25.
28. Jameson, *Postmodernism*, 5, 6.
29. Ibid., 6.
30. Williams, *Marxism and Literature*, 132.
31. Linda Hutcheon, *A Poetics of Postmodernism*, 61.
32. Jameson, *Postmodernism*, 22.
33. Bachelard, *The Poetics of Space*, xi.

BIBLIOGRAPHY

Abish, Walter. *How German Is It.* New York: New Directions, 1979.
Allen, Chadwick. *Blood Narrative: Indigenous Identity in American Indian and Maori Literary and Activist Texts.* Durham, NC: Duke University Press, 2002.
Allen, Marlene D. "Octavia Butler's Parable Novels and the 'Boomerang' of African American History." *Callaloo* 32, no. 4 (Fall 2009): 1353–65.
Allen, Paula Gunn. 1986. *The Sacred Hoop: Recovering the Feminine in American Indian Traditions.* Boston: Beacon Press, 1992.
Altieri, Charles. "Ovid and the New Mythologists." *Novel* 7, no. 1 (Fall 1973): 31–40.
Alvarez, Julia. *How the García Girls Lost Their Accents.* New York: Plume, 1992.
Anderson, Perry. *The Origins of Postmodernity.* New York: Verso, 1998.
Appiah, Kwame Anthony. "Is the Post- in Postmodernism the Post- in Postcolonial?" *Critical Inquiry* 17, no. 2 (Winter 1991): 336–57.
Auerbach, Erich. *Mimesis: The Representation of Reality in Western Literature.* 1953. Princeton, NJ: Princeton University Press, 2003.
Bachelard, Gaston. *The Poetics of Space.* Translated by Maria Jolas. New York: The Orion Press, 1964.
Barak, Julie. "'Turning and Turning in the Widening Gyre': A Second Coming into Language in Julia Alvarez's *How the García Girls Lost Their Accents.*" *MELUS* 23, no. 1 (Spring 1998): 159–76.
Barth, John. *The Friday Book: Essays and Other Nonfiction.* Baltimore, MD: Johns Hopkins University Press, 1997.
———. *Lost in the Funhouse: Fiction for Print, Tape, Live Voice.* New York: Doubleday, 1968.

———. "Postmodernism Revisited." *The Review of Contemporary Fiction* 8, no. 3 (Fall 1988): 16–24.

Barthes, Roland. *A Barthes Reader*. Edited and introduced by Susan Sontag. New York: Hill and Wang, 1982.

———. *Image—Music—Text*. Translated by Stephen Heath. New York: Hill and Wang, 1977.

———. "The Reality Effect." In *The Rustle of Language*. Translated by Richard Howard. Berkeley: University of California Press, 1989.

Baudrillard, Jean. *The Consumer Society: Myths and Structures*. Translated by Chris Turner. Los Angeles: Sage Publications, 1998.

———. *Simulation and Simulacra*. Translated by Sheila Faria Glaser. Ann Arbor: University of Michigan Press, 1994.

———. *The System of Objects*. Translated by James Benedict. New York: Verso, 2005.

Bennett, Jane. *Vibrant Matter: A Political Ecology of Things*. Durham, NC: Duke University Press, 2010.

Bernstein, Richard J. *Beyond Objectivism and Relativism: Science, Hermeneutics, and Praxis*. Philadelphia: University of Pennsylvania Press, 1983.

———. *The Restructuring of Social and Political Theory*. Philadelphia: University of Pennsylvania Press, 1978.

Bérubé, Michael. *Public Access: Literary Theory and American Cultural Politics*. New York: Verso, 1994.

Blaeser, Kimberly. *Gerald Vizenor: Writing in the Oral Tradition*. Norman: University of Oklahoma Press, 1996.

Bogost, Ian. *Alien Phenomenology, or What It's Like to Be a Thing*. Minneapolis: University of Minnesota Press, 2012.

Boswell, Marshall. *Understanding David Foster Wallace*. Columbia: University of South Carolina Press, 2003.

Bradshaw, Peter. "Flight of Fancy." *New Statesman*, January 19, 2004.

Braidotti, Rosi. *Metamorphoses: Towards a Materialist Theory of Becoming*. Malden, MA: Polity, 2002.

Brooks, Neil, and Josh Toth, eds. *The Mourning After: Attending the Wake of Postmodernism*. New York: Rodopi, 2007.

Brown, Bill. "The Dark Wood of Postmodernity (Space, Faith, Allegory)." *PMLA* 120, no. 3 (May 2005): 734–50.

———. *A Sense of Things: The Object Matter of American Literature*. Chicago: University of Chicago Press, 2003.

———. "Thing Theory." *Critical Inquiry* 28, no. 1 (Autumn 2001): 1–22.

Brown, Caroline. "Golden Gray and the Talking Book: Identity as a Site of Artful Construction in Toni Morrison's *Jazz*." *African American Review* 36, no. 4 (Winter 2002): 629–42.

Bryant, Levi R. *The Democracy of Objects*. Ann Arbor, MI: Open Humanities Press, 2011.

———. *Onto-Cartography: An Ontology of Machines and Media*. Edinburgh: Edinburgh University Press, 2014.

Butler, Octavia. *The Parable of the Sower*. New York: Four Walls Eight Windows, 1993.

Callari, Antonio, and David F. Ruccio, eds. *Postmodern Materialism and the Future of Marxist Theory: Essays in the Althusserian Tradition*. London: Wesleyan University Press, 1996.

Carabi, Angels, and Toni Morrison. "Interview: Toni Morrison on *Jazz*." *Belles Lettres* 10, no. 2 (Spring 1995): 40–3.

Castells, Ricardo. "The Silence of Exile in *How the García Girls Lost Their Accents*." *Bilingual Review/La Revista Bilingüe* 26, no. 1 (January 2002): 34–42.

Caton, Lou Freitas. *Reading American Novels and Multicultural Aesthetics: Romancing the Postmodern Novel*. New York: Palgrave MacMillan, 2008.

Chandra, Sarika. "Re-Producing a Nationalist Literature in the Age of Globalization: Reading (Im)migration in Julia Alvarez's *How the García Girls Lost Their Accents*." *American Quarterly* 60, no. 3 (2008): 829–50.

Chomsky, Noam. "Knowledge of Language: Its Elements and Origins." *Philosophical Transactions of the Royal Society of London, Series B. Biological Sciences* 295, no. 1077 (October 1981): 223–34.

Chow, Rey. "The Interruption of Referentiality: Poststructuralism and the Conundrum of Critical Multiculturalism." *South Atlantic Quarterly* 101, no. 1 (Winter 2002): 171–86.

Cohen, Samuel. *After the End of History: American Fiction in the 1990s*. Iowa City: University of Iowa Press, 2009.

Cornis-Pope, Marcel. *Narrative Innovation and Cultural Rewriting in the Cold War and After*. New York: Palgrave, 2001.

Coughlan, David. "Jonathan Lethem's *The Fortress of Solitude* and *Omega: The Unknown*, a Comic Book Series." *College Literature* 38, no. 3 (Summer 2011): 194–218.

Culler, Jonathan. *The Pursuit of Signs: Semiotics, Literature, Deconstruction*. Ithaca, NY: Cornell University Press, 1981.

Debord, Guy. *The Society of the Spectacle*. Translated by Ken Knabb. London: Rebel Press, 2006.

DeKoven, Marianne. *Utopia Limited: The Sixties and the Emergence of the Postmodern*. Durham, NC: Duke University Press, 2004.

Delgado, Richard, and Jean Stefancic. *Critical Race Theory: An Introduction*. 2nd ed. New York: New York University Press, 2012.

DeLillo, Don. "Don DeLillo, The Art of Fiction No. 135." *The Paris Review* 128 (Fall 1993): 274–306.

———. "In the Ruins of the Future." *Harper's* (December 2001): 33–40.

———. *Libra*. New York: Viking, 1988.

———. *Mao II*. New York: Viking, 1991.

———. *Underworld*. New York: Scribner, 1997.

———. *White Noise*. New York: Penguin, 1985.
Dubey, Madhu. *Signs and Cities: Black Literary Postmodernism*. Chicago: University of Chicago Press, 2003.
Dunston, Susan L. "Physics and Metaphysics: Lessons from Leslie Marmon Silko's *Ceremony*." *Arizona Quarterly* 66, no. 4 (Winter 2010): 135–62.
Duvall, John N. "Baseball as Aesthetic Ideology: Cold War History, Race, and DeLillo's 'Pafko at the Wall.'" *Modern Fiction Studies* 41, no. 2 (1995): 285–313.
———. *Don DeLillo's Underworld: A Reader's Guide*. New York: Continuum, 2002.
Eagleton, Terry. *After Theory*. New York: Basic Books, 2003.
———. "Capitalism, Modernism and Postmodernism." *New Left Review* 152 (July–August 1985): 60–73.
———. *The Illusions of Postmodernism*. Malden, MA: Blackwell, 1996.
———. *Marxism and Literary Criticism*. New York: Routledge, 2002.
Eckard, Paula. "The Interplay of Music, Language, and Narrative in Toni Morrison's *Jazz*." *CLA Journal* 28, no. 1 (September 1994): 11–19.
Elias, Amy J. *Sublime Desire: History and Post-1960s Fiction*. Baltimore, MD: Johns Hopkins University Press, 2001.
Eliot, George. *Adam Bede*. Chicago: Belford, Clarke, 1888.
Eternal Sunshine of the Spotless Mind. Dir. Michel Gondry. Screenplay by Charlie Kaufman and Michel Gondry. Focus Features, 2004.
Federman, Raymond. *Critifiction: Postmodern Essays*. Albany: State University of New York Press, 1993.
Felski, Rita. *Doing Time: Feminist Theory and Postmodern Culture*. New York: New York University Press, 2000.
———. "Suspicious Minds." *Poetics Today* 32, no. 2 (Summer 2011): 215–34.
Fiedler, Leslie. "The New Mutants." *Partisan Review* 32, no. 4 (Fall 1965): 505–25.
Fitzpatrick, Kathleen. "The Unmaking of History: Baseball, Cold War, and *Underworld*." In *Underwords: Perspectives on Don DeLillo's Underworld*, edited by Joseph Dewey, Steven G. Kellman, and Irving Malin, 144–60. Newark: University of Delaware Press, 2002.
Foer, Jonathan Safran. *Everything Is Illuminated*. New York: Harper/Perennial, 2002.
———. *Extremely Loud and Incredibly Close*. Boston: Houghton Mifflin, 2005.
Foer, Joshua. *Moonwalking with Einstein: The Art and Science of Remembering Everything*. New York: Penguin, 2011.
Forrest Gump. Dir. Robert Zemeckis. Screenplay by Eric Roth. Paramount Pictures, 1994. Film.
Foucault, Michel. *The Order of Things*. 1966. New York: Vintage, 1994.
———. *Power/Knowledge: Selected Interviews and Other Writings, 1972–1977*. New York: Vintage, 1980.
Frow, John. "Matter and Materialism: A Brief Pre-History of the Present." In *Material Powers: Cultural Studies, History and the Material Turn*, edited by Tony Bennett and Patrick Joyce, 25–37. New York: Routledge, 2010.

BIBLIOGRAPHY

Galloway, Alexander R. "The Poverty of Philosophy: Realism and Post-Fordism." *Critical Inquiry* 39, no. 2 (Winter 2013): 347–66.

Gates, Henry Louis, Jr. *The Signifying Monkey: A Theory of African-American Literary Criticism*. New York: Oxford University Press, 1988.

Geertz, Clifford. *The Interpretation of Cultures: Selected Essays*. New York: Basic Books, 1973.

Giles, Paul. "Sentimental Posthumanism: David Foster Wallace." *Twentieth-Century Literature* 53, no. 3 (Fall 2007): 327–43.

Girard, René. *To Double Business Bound: Essays on Literature, Mimesis, and Anthropology*. Baltimore, MD: Johns Hopkins University Press, 1978.

Gladstone, Jason, and Daniel Worden, eds. "Postmodernism, Then." Special issue, *Twentieth-Century Literature* 57, no. 3–4 (Fall–Winter 2011).

Godbey, Matt. "Gentrification, Authenticity and White Middle-Class Identity in Jonathan Lethem's *The Fortress of Solitude*." *Arizona Quarterly* 64, no. 1 (Spring 2008): 131–51.

Grandt, Jürgen E. "Kinds of Blue: Toni Morrison, Hans Janowitz, and the Jazz Aesthetic." *African American Review* 38, no. 2 (2004): 303–22.

Grausam, Daniel. *On Endings: American Postmodern Fiction and the Cold War*. Charlottesville: University of Virginia Press, 2011.

Green, Jeremy. *Late Postmodernism: American Fiction at the Millennium*. New York: Palgrave MacMillan, 2005.

Greenblatt, Stephen. *The Swerve: How the World Became Modern*. New York: Norton, 2011.

Greiner, Donald J. "Don DeLillo, John Updike, and the Sustaining Power of Myth." In *Underwords: Perspectives on Don DeLillo's Underworld*, edited by Joseph Dewey, Steven G. Kellman, and Irving Malin, 103–13. Newark: University of Delaware Press, 2002.

Grossman, Lev. "The Bard of Brooklyn." *Time*, September 7, 2003.

Haney López, Ian. *White by Law: The Legal Construction of Race*. New York: New York University Press, 2006.

Harman, Graham. *Guerilla Metaphysics: Phenomenology and the Carpentry of Things*. Chicago: Open Court, 2005.

———. "Realism without Materialism." *SubStance* 40, no. 2 (Issue 125, 2011): 52–72.

———. "The Well-Wrought Broken Hammer." *New Literary History* 43, no. 2 (Spring 2012): 183–203.

Harpham, Geoffrey Galt. *Language Alone: The Critical Fetish of Modernity*. New York: Routledge, 2002.

Harris, Charles. *Passionate Virtuosity: The Fiction of John Barth*. Urbana: University of Illinois Press, 1983.

Harris, Roy, and Talbot J. Taylor. *Landmarks in Linguistic Thought I: The Western Tradition from Socrates to Saussure*. 2nd ed. New York: Routledge, 1997.

Harvey, David. *The Condition of Postmodernity*. Cambridge, MA: Blackwell, 1990.

Hassan, Ihab. *The Dismemberment of Orpheus: Toward a Postmodern Literature.* 2nd ed. Madison: University of Wisconsin Press, 1982.

———. *The Literature of Silence: Henry Miller and Samuel Beckett.* New York: Alfred A. Knopf, 1967.

Heidegger, Martin. "The Thing." In *Poetry, Language, Thought.* Translated by Albert Hofstadter. 165–86. New York: Harper and Row, 1971.

Herman, David. *Story Logic: Problems and Possibilities of Narrative.* Lincoln: University of Nebraska Press, 2002.

Hoberek, Andrew, ed. "After Postmodernism: Form and History in Contemporary American Fiction." Special issue, *Twentieth-Century Literature* 53, no. 3 (Fall 2007).

———. *The Twilight of the Middle Class: Post-World War II American Fiction and White-Collar Work.* Princeton, NJ: Princeton University Press, 2005.

Hoffman, Joan M. "She Wants to Be Called Yolanda Now: Identity, Language, and the Third Sister in *How the García Girls Lost Their Accents.*" *Bilingual Review/La Revista Bilingüe* 23, no. 1 (January–April 1998): 21–7.

Hogan, Linda. *Power.* New York: Norton, 1998.

Hogue, W. Lawrence. *Postmodern American Literature and Its Other.* Urbana: University of Illinois Press, 2009.

———. "Postmodernism, Traditional Cultural Forms, and the African American Narrative: Major's *Reflex*, Morrison's *Jazz*, and Reed's *Mumbo Jumbo.*" *Novel* 35, no. 2–3 (Spring–Summer 2002): 169–192.

Holland, Mary K. *Succeeding Postmodernism: Language and Humanism in Contemporary American Literature.* New York: Bloomsbury, 2013.

hooks, bell. "Postmodern Blackness." In *Postmodern American Fiction: A Norton Anthology*, edited by Paula Geyh, Fred G. Leebron, and Andrew Levy, 624–31. New York: Norton, 1998.

Howard, Gerald. "The American Strangeness: An Interview with Don DeLillo." In *Conversations with Don DeLillo*, edited by Thomas DePietro, 119–30. Jackson: University of Mississippi Press, 2005.

Howe, Irving. "Mass Society and Post-Modern Fiction." *Partisan Review* 26, no. 3 (Summer 1959): 420–36.

Howells, William Dean. *Criticism and Fiction.* New York: Harper and Brothers, 1891.

Hungerford, Amy. "On the Period Formerly Known as Contemporary." *American Literary History* 20, no. 1–2 (Spring–Summer 2008): 410–19.

———. *Postmodern Belief: American Literature and Religion since 1960.* Princeton, NJ: Princeton University Press, 2010.

Hutcheon, Linda. "Gone Forever, But Here to Stay: The Legacy of the Postmodern." In *Postmodernism, What Moment?* edited by Pelagia Goulimari, 16–18. Manchester, UK: Manchester University Press, 2007.

———. *A Poetics of Postmodernism.* New York: Routledge, 1988.

———. *The Politics of Postmodernism.* New York: Routledge, 1989.

———. *The Politics of Postmodernism*. 2nd ed. New York: Routledge, 2002.
Huyssen, Andreas. *After the Great Divide: Modernism, Mass Culture, Postmodernism*. Bloomington: Indiana University Press, 1986.
———. "Mapping the Postmodern." *New German Critique* 33 (Autumn 1984): 5–52.
Jameson, Fredric. "Notes on Globalization as a Philosophical Issue." In *The Cultures of Globalization*, edited by Fredric Jameson and Masao Miyoshi, 54–77. Durham, NC: Duke University Press, 1998.
———. "Postmodernism, Or, The Cultural Logic of Late Capitalism." *New Left Review* 146 (July–August): 59–92.
———. *Postmodernism, Or, The Cultural Logic of Late Capitalism*. Durham, NC: Duke University Press, 1991.
Johnson, Barbara. *Persons and Things*. Cambridge, MA: Harvard University Press, 2008.
Johnson, Charles. *Being and Race: Black Writing since 1970*. Bloomington: Indiana University Press, 1988.
Kakutani, Michiko. "Books of the Times: White Kid, In a Black World." *New York Times*, September 16, 2003.
Kelly, Adam. *American Fiction in Transition: Observer-Hero Narrative, the 1990s, and Postmodernism*. London: Bloomsbury, 2013.
———. "Beginning with Postmodernism." In "Postmodernism, Then." Special issue, *Twentieth-Century Literature* 57 no. 3–4 (Fall–Winter 2011): 391–422.
———. "David Foster Wallace and the New Sincerity in American Fiction." In *Consider David Foster Wallace: Critical Essays*, edited by David Hering, 131–46. Los Angeles: Sideshow Media Group Press, 2010.
Kim, Sue J. *Critiquing Postmodernism in Contemporary Discourses of Race*. New York: Palgrave MacMillan, 2009.
Kirby, Alan. *Digimodernism: How New Technologies Dismantle the Postmodern and Reconfigure Our Culture*. New York: Continuum, 2009.
Klinkowitz, Jerome. *Literary Disruptions: The Making of a Post-Contemporary American Fiction*. Urbana: University of Illinois Press, 1975.
Knapp, James A., and Jeffrey Pence. "Between Thing and Theory." In "Between Thing and Theory, or, The Reflexive Turn, Part I," edited by James A. Knapp and Jeffrey Pence. Special issue, *Poetics Today* 24, no. 4 (Winter 2003): 641–71.
Koerner, E. F. K. *Toward a History of American Linguistics* New York: Routledge, 2002.
Krier, William J. "*Lost in the Funhouse*: 'A Continuing, Strange Love Letter.'" *boundary 2* 5, no. 1 (Fall 1976): 103–16.
Kyle, Carol A. "The Unity of Anatomy: The Structure of Barth's *Lost in the Funhouse*." *Critique* 13, no. 3 (1972): 31–43.
Lacan, Jacques. *The Four Fundamental Concepts of Psycho-Analysis*. New York: Norton, 1998.

Larson, Charles. *American Indian Fiction*. Albuquerque: University of New Mexico Press, 1978.

Latour, Bruno. *Politics of Nature*. Translated by Catherine Porter. Cambridge, MA: Harvard University Press, 2004.

———. *Reassembling the Social: An Introduction to Actor-Network-Theory*. New York: Oxford University Press, 2005.

———. "Why Has Critique Run Out of Steam? From Matters of Fact to Matters of Concern." *Critical Inquiry* 30, no. 2 (Winter 2004): 225–58.

Lethem, Jonathan. *The Fortress of Solitude*. New York: Vintage, 2003.

———. "Jonathan Lethem, The Art of Fiction, No. 177." *The Paris Review* 166 (Summer 2003): 218–51.

———. "Postmodernism as Liberty Valance: Notes on a Ritual Killing." In *The Ecstasy of Influence*. New York: Vintage, 2012.

Lethem, Jonathan, et al. *Omega: The Unknown*. New York: Marvel Comics, 2008.

Lethem, Jonathan, and Jaime Clarke. *Conversations with Jonathan Lethem*. Jackson: University of Mississippi Press, 2011.

Levine, Caroline. "Surprising Realism." In *A Companion to George Eliot*, edited by Amanda Anderson and Harry E. Shaw, 62–75. Malden, MA: Wiley-Blackwell, 2013.

Llorente, Manuela Mata. "And Why Did the García Girls Lose Their Accents? Language, Identity and the Immigrant Experience in Julia Alvarez's *How the García Girls Lost Their Accents*." *Revista de Estudios Norteamericanos* 8 (2001): 69–75.

Lucretius. *On the Nature of Things*. Translated by Frank Copley. New York: Norton, 1977.

Luis, William. "A Search for Identity in Julia Alvarez's *How the García Girls Lost Their Accents*." *Callaloo* 23, no. 3 (Summer 2000): 839–49.

Lyotard, Jean-François. *The Postmodern Condition: A Report on Knowledge*. Translated by Geoff Bennington and Brian Massumi. Minneapolis: University of Minnesota Press, 1984.

Maltby, Paul. *Dissident Postmodernists: Barthelme, Coover, Pynchon*. Philadelphia: University of Pennsylvania Press, 1991.

Marciniak, Katarzyna. *Alienhood: Citizenship, Exile, and the Logic of Difference*. Minneapolis: University of Minnesota Press, 2006.

McCaffery, Larry. "Literary Disruptions: Fiction in a 'Post-Contemporary' Age." *Boundary* 5 (1976): 137–51.

McClure, John. *Partial Faiths: Postsecular Fiction in the Age of Pynchon and Morrison*. Athens: University of Georgia Press, 2007.

McGurl, Mark. *The Program Era: Postwar Fiction and the Rise of Creative Writing*. Cambridge, MA: Harvard University Press, 2009.

McHale, Brian. *Constructing Postmodernism*. New York: Routledge, 1992.

———. "Postmodernism, or The Anxiety of Master Narratives." *Diacritics* 22, no. 1 (Spring 1992): 17–33.

———. *Postmodernist Fiction*. New York: Methuen, 1987.

Meillassoux, Quentin. *After Finitude: An Essay on the Necessity of Contingency*. New York: Continuum, 2008.

Merish, Lori. *Sentimental Materialism: Gender, Commodity Culture, and Nineteenth-Century American Literature*. Durham, NC: Duke University Press, 2000.

Michelone, Manuel Lopez, and Medel, Marcelo Perez. "Understanding Photomosaics." *Dr. Dobb's Journal* 26, no. 11 (November 2001): 58–62.

Mohanty, Satya P. *Literary Theory and the Claims of History: Postmodernism, Objectivity, Multicultural Politics*. Ithaca, NY: Cornell University Press, 1997.

Moraru, Christian. *Cosmodernism: American Narrative, Globalization, and the New Cultural Imaginary*. Ann Arbor: University of Michigan Press, 2010.

Morris, Christopher D. "Barth and Lacan: The World of the Moebius Strip." *Critique* 17, no. 1 (1975): 69–77.

Morrison, Toni. *Beloved*. 1987. New York: Signet, 1991.

———. *Jazz*. New York: Alfred A. Knopf, 1992.

———. *Paradise*. New York: Alfred A. Knopf, 1997.

———. *Playing in the Dark*. New York: Vintage, 1992.

———. "The Site of Memory." In *Writing and Remembering*, edited by William Zinsser, 101–24. Boston: Houghton Mifflin, 1987.

———. "Toni Morrison, The Art of Fiction No. 134." *The Paris Review* 128 (Fall 1993): 82–125.

Morton, Timothy. *Realist Magic: Objects, Ontology, Causality*. Ann Arbor, MI: Open Humanities Press, 2013.

Mott, Rick. "Ceremony Earth: Digitizing Silko's Novel for Students of the Twenty-first Century." *Studies in American Indian Literatures* 23, no. 2 (Summer 2011): 25–47.

Moya, Paula M. L. "Introduction: Reclaiming Identity." In *Reclaiming Identity: Realist Theory and the Predicament of Postmodernism*, edited by Paula M. L. Moya and Michael Haimes-Garcia, 1–26. Berkeley: University of California Press, 2000.

Nancy, Jean-Luc. *The Inoperative Community*. Minneapolis: University of Minnesota Press, 1991.

Nealon, Jeffrey. *Post-Postmodernism; Or, The Cultural Logic of Just-In-Time Capitalism*. Stanford, CA: Stanford University Press, 2012.

Olson, Charles. *Collected Prose: Charles Olson*, edited by Donald Allen and Benjamin Friedlander. Berkeley: University of California Press, 1997.

Ortiz-Márquez, Maribel. "From Third World Politics to First World Practices: Contemporary Latina Writers in the United States." In *Interventions: Feminist Dialogues on Third World Women's Literature and Film*, edited by Bishnupriya Ghosh and Brinda Bose, 227–44. New York: Garland Publishing, 1997.

Owens, Louis. *Other Destinies: Understanding the American Indian Novel*. Norman: University of Oklahoma Press, 1992.

Parker, Robert Dale. *The Invention of Native American Literature*. Ithaca, NY: Cornell University Press, 2003.

Parrish, Timothy. *From the Civil War to the Apocalypse: Postmodern History and American Fiction*. Amherst: University of Massachusetts Press, 2008.

Pérez Castillo, Susan. "Postmodernism, Native American Literature and the Real: The Silko-Erdrich Controversy." *Massachusetts Review* 32, no. 2 (Summer 1991): 285–94.

Peterson, Nancy J. "Say Make Me, Remake Me: Toni Morrison and the Reconstruction of African-American History." In *Toni Morrison: Critical and Theoretical Approaches*, edited by Nancy J. Peterson, 201–21. Baltimore, MD: Johns Hopkins University Press, 1997.

Picone, Jason. "Always Staying Home." *American Book Review* 25, no. 3 (March–April 2004): 27, 29.

Pryse, Marjorie. "Signifyin(g) on Reparation in Toni Morrison's *Jazz*." *American Literature* 80, no. 3 (September 2008): 583–609.

Pulitano, Elvira. *Toward a Native American Critical Theory*. Linconln: University of Nebraska Press, 2003.

Rebein, Robert. *Hicks, Tribes, and Dirty Realists: American Fiction after Postmodernism*. Lexington: University of Kentucky Press, 2001.

Richardson, Brian. *Unlikely Stories: Causality and the Nature of Modern Narrative*. Newark: University of Delaware Press, 1997.

Ricoeur, Paul. *Freud and Philosophy*. New Haven, CT: Yale University Press, 1970.

Rivera, Juan Pablo. "Language Allergy: Seduction and Second Languages in *How the García Girls Lost Their Accents*." *Rupkatha* 2, no. 2 (2012): 123–35.

Robbins, Bruce, and Andrew Ross. "Mystery Science Theater." *Lingua Franca* (July–August 1996): 54–65.

Rodrigues, Eusebio. "Experiencing Jazz." *MFS: Modern Fiction Studies* 39, no. 3–4 (Fall–Winter 1993): 733–54.

Rody, Caroline. "Impossible Voices: Ethnic Postmodern Narration in Toni Morrison's *Jazz* and Karen Tei Yamashita's *Through the Arc of the Rain Forest*." *Contemporary Literature* 41, no. 1 (Winter 2000): 618–41.

Roediger, David R. *Towards the Abolition of Whiteness: Essays on Race, Politics, and Working Class History*. New York: Verso, 1994.

Romagnolo, Catherine. "Initiating Dialogue: Narrative Beginnings in Multicultural Narratives." In *Analyzing World Fiction: New Horizons in Narrative Theory*, edited by Frederick Luis Aldama, 183–98. Austin: University of Texas Press, 2011.

Rorty, Richard, editor. *The Linguistic Turn*. Chicago: University of Chicago Press, 1967.

Rosaldo, Renato. *Culture and Truth: The Remaking of Social Analysis*. Boston: Beacon Press, 1989.

———. "Foreword." In *Hybrid Cultures: Strategies for Entering and Leaving Modernity*. Néstor García Canclini. Translated by Christopher L. Chiappari and Silvia L. López, xi–xvii. Minneapolis: University of Minnesota Press, 1995.

Ross, Andrew. "Introduction." In "Science Wars," edited by Andrew Ross. Special issue, *Social Text* 46–47 (Spring–Summer 1996): 1–13.

Rossi, Paolo, and Stephen Clucas. *Logic and the Art of Memory: The Quest for a Universal Language*. Chicago: University of Chicago Press, 2000.

Rother, James. "Reading and Riding the Post-Scientific Wave: The Shorter Fiction of David Foster Wallace." *Review of Contemporary Fiction* 13, no. 2 (Summer 1993): 216–34.

Russell, Bertrand. *The Problems of Philosophy*. 1912. New York: Dover, 1999.

Scheiber, Andrew Joseph. "Jazz and the Future Blues: Toni Morrison's Urban Folk Zone." *Modern Fiction Studies* 52, no. 2 (Summer 2006): 470–94.

Schulz, Max F. *The Muses of John Barth: Tradition and Metafiction from* Lost in the Funhouse *to* The Tidewater Tales. Baltimore, MD: Johns Hopkins University Press, 1990.

Scott, A. O. "When Dylan Met Mingus." *New York Times Book Review*, September 21, 2003.

Sedgwick, Eve Kosofsky. "Paranoid Reading and Reparative Reading: or, You're So Paranoid, You Probably Think This Introduction Is about You." In *Novel Gazing*, edited by Eve Kosofsky Sedgwick, 1–37. Durham, NC: Duke University Press, 1997.

Shaviro, Steven. *The Universe of Things: On Speculative Realism*. Minneapolis: University of Minnesota Press, 2014.

Silko, Leslie Marmon. "America's Iron Curtain: The Border Patrol State." *Nation* 259, no. 12 (October 17, 1994): 412–16.

———. *Ceremony*. 1977. New York: Penguin, 1986.

Singer, Marc. "Embodiments of the Real: The Counterlinguistic Turn in the Comic-Book Novel." *Critique: Studies in Contemporary Fiction* 49, no. 3 (Spring 2008): 273–89.

Smith, James K. A. *Jacques Derrida: Live Theory*. New York: Continuum, 2005.

Sokal, Alan. "A Physicist Experiments with Cultural Studies." *Lingua Franca* (May–June 1996): 62–4.

Sontag, Susan. *Against Interpretation and Other Essays*. New York: Doubleday, 1986.

Spurgeon, Sara L. *Exploding the Western: Myths of Empire on the Postmodern Frontier*. College Station: Texas A & M University Press, 2005.

Staes, Toon. "'Only Artists Can Transfigure': Kafka's Artists and the Possibility of Redemption in the Novellas of David Foster Wallace." *Orbis Litterarum* 65, no. 6 (2010): 459–80.

Stave, Shirley Ann. "*Jazz* and *Paradise*: Pivotal Moments in Black History." In *The Cambridge Companion to Toni Morrison*, edited by Justine Tally, 59–74. New York: Cambridge University Press, 2007.

Stefanko, Jacqueline. "New Ways of Telling: Latinas' Narratives of Exile and Return." *Frontiers: A Journal of Women Studies* 17, no. 2 (1996): 50–69.

Steiner, Wendy. "Rethinking Postmodernism." In *The Cambridge History of American Literature, Volume 7: Prose Writing, 1940–1990*, edited by Sacvan Bercovitch, 425–50. New York: Cambridge University Press, 1999.

Stewart, Susan. *On Longing: Narratives of the Miniature, the Gigantic, the Souvenir, the Collection.* 1984. Durham, NC: Duke University Press, 1993.

Stierstorfer, Klaus, ed. *Beyond Postmodernism: Reassessments in Literature, Theory, and Culture.* New York: Walter de Gruyter, 2003.

Taylor, Billy. "What Is Jazz? Four Lectures." Recorded February 14, 1995. *John F. Kennedy Center for the Performing Arts.* Accessed March 27, 2012. http://town.hall.org/radio/Kennedy/Taylor/bt_11.html.

Tönnies, Charles. *Community and Society (Gemeinschaft und Gesellschaft)*, edited and translated by Charles P. Loomis. East Lansing: Michigan State University Press, 1957.

Toth, Josh. *The Passing of Postmodernism: A Spectroanalysis of the Contemporary.* Albany: State University of New York Press, 2010.

Underwood, Ted. *Why Literary Periods Mattered: Historical Contrast and the Prestige of English Studies.* Palo Alto, CA: Stanford University Press, 2013.

Vizenor, Gerald. *Manifest Manners: Postindian Warriors of Survivance.* Hanover, NH: Wesleyan University Press, 1994.

———. "A Postmodern Introduction." In *Narrative Chance: Postmodern Discourse on Native American Indian Literatures*, edited by Gerald Vizenor, 3–16. Norman: University of Oklahoma Press, 1993.

Wallace, David Foster. *Girl with Curious Hair.* New York: Norton, 1989.

———. *Infinite Jest.* Boston: Little, Brown, 1996.

Weaver, Jace. "Splitting the Earth: First Utterances and Pluralist Separatism." In *American Indian Literary Nationalism*, 1–89. Albuquerque: University of New Mexico Press, 2006.

Weaver, Jace, Craig S. Womack, and Robert Warrior. *American Indian Literary Nationalism.* Albuquerque: University of New Mexico Press, 2006.

Williams, Raymond. "Base and Superstructure in Marxist Cultural Theory." *New Left Review* 82 (November–December 1973): 3–16.

———. 1977. *Marxism and Literature.* Oxford: Oxford University Press, 2009.

Williams, William Carlos. *Paterson.* 1963. New York: New Directions, 1992.

Winnicott, Donald. *Playing and Reality.* 1971. New York: Routledge, 1989.

Wittgenstein, Ludwig. *Philosophical Investigations.* 3rd ed. Translated by G. E. M. Anscombe. New York: MacMillan, 1958.

Wolfe, Cary. *What Is Posthumanism?* Minneapolis: University of Minnesota Press, 2010.

Womack, Craig S. "The Integrity of American Indian Claims, Or, How I Learned to Stop Worrying and Love My Hybridity." In *American Indian Literary Nationalism*, 91–177. Albuquerque: University of New Mexico Press, 2006.

———. "A Single Decade: Book-Length Native Literary Criticism between 1986 and 1997." In *Reasoning Together: The Native Critics Collective*, edited by Craig S. Womack, Daniel Heath Justice, and Christopher B. Teuton, 3–104. Norman: University of Oklahoma Press, 2008.

———. "Theorizing American Indian Experience." In *Reasoning Together: The Native Critics Collective*, edited by Craig S. Womack, Daniel Heath Justice, and Christopher B. Teuton, 353–410. Norman: University of Oklahoma Press, 2008.

Woolley, Deborah A. "Empty 'Text,' Fecund Voice: Self-Reflexivity in Barth's *Lost in the Funhouse*." *Contemporary Literature* 26, no. 4 (1985): 460–81.

Xingjian, Gao. *The Case for Literature*. Translated by Mabel Lee. New Haven, CT: Yale University Press, 2007.

INDEX

Abish, Walter 18
Acker, Kathy 23
Actor-Network-Theory 3, 13–14, 16, 28
Allen, Chadwick 40, 200 n. 47
Allen, Paula Gunn 40, 49, 56
Altieri, Charles 111
Alvarez, Julia 34, 139, 141, 143, 159–69
Anderson, Perry 182–3
Appadurai, Arjun 13
Appiah, K. Anthony 137–6
Aristotle 8–9, 193 n. 63
atomism 17, 192 n. 59
Auerbach, Erich 19–20
Austin, J. L. 107

Bachelard, Gaston 176–8, 186
Barth, John 33, 105, 110–21, 166
　"The Literature of Exhaustion" 7
　"The Literature of Replenishment" 7
　Lost in the Funhouse 33, 110–21, 124–5
　"Postmodernism Revisited" 8, 27, 180–1
Barthes, Roland 20, 168
Baudrillard, Jean 17, 194 n. 85
Bennett, Jane 16, 192 n. 57
Bernstein, Richard 12
Blaeser, Kimberly 42, 47, 63
Bogost, Ian 15–16, 66–7, 69, 109, 133, 159, 191 n. 49, 200 n. 8

Boswell, Marshall 122–3, 127
Braidotti, Rosi 25
Brassier, Ray 15
Brown, Bill 9–11, 13, 19, 25–6, 48, 53, 73
Bryant, Levi 16, 66–7, 69, 159, 201 n. 8
Butler, Octavia 174–6, 179–80

Caton, Lou Freitas 56–7, 197 n. 15, 210 n. 44
Chandra, Sarika 161, 162
Chomsky, Noam 107–8, 204 nn. 8, 10
clinamen 34, 139, 140
Cohen, Samuel 27
correlationism 15, 67, 109
cosmodernism 1, 187 n. 2
Culler, Jonathan 206 n. 47
Cultural Materialism 13

Davis, Miles 74–5
Debord, Guy 195 n. 85
DeKoven, Marianne 2, 23–4, 107, 172, 204 n. 7
DeLillo, Don 34, 143–58, 167–8
Derrida, Jacques 15, 104, 129, 135, 195 n. 86
digimodernism 1, 27, 187 n. 2
Doctorow, E. L. 185
Dubey, Madhu 1, 2, 5
Duvall, John 144, 147

227

INDEX

Eagleton, Terry 137–8, 140, 190 n. 38
Elias, Amy J. 4, 31, 36, 62
Eliot, George 10
Eliot, T. S. 24
Eternal Sunshine of the Spotless Mind 103

Federman, Raymond 112, 196 n. 6, 211 n. 53
Felski, Rita 29, 135
Fiedler, Leslie 34, 43, 137, 188 n. 5
flat ontology 11, 15, 32, 69, 74
Foer, Jonathan Safran 32, 70–4
Ford, John 171
Foucault, Michel 3, 29, 112
Frow, John 18

Galloway, Alexander R. 18
García Canclini, Néstor 24
Gates, Henry Louis, Jr. 85, 202 n. 37
Geertz, Clifford 12, 22
Girard, René 20–1
Gondry, Michel 103
Grant, Iain Hamilton 15
Grausam, Daniel 4
Great American Ballpark 21
Green, Jeremy 1, 31, 37–8, 62
Greenblatt, Stephen 139

Haney López, Ian 82
Harman, Graham 13, 15–17, 159, 191 n. 49, 192 n. 59
Harpham, Geoffrey Galt 104, 107, 116, 204 n. 8
Harris, Charles 111, 119
Hassan, Ihab 7–8, 17, 137, 210 n. 53
Heidegger, Martin 18, 19, 82–3, 165, 193 n. 63
Herman, David 45, 198 n. 32
Hoberek, Andrew 1–2, 187 n. 1
Hogan, Linda 46
Hogue, W. Lawrence 2, 31, 36, 38, 62
Holland, Mary 2
hooks, bell 39, 141
Howe, Irving 6–7, 29, 166, 188 n. 5
Howells, William Dean 9, 10
Hungerford, Amy 2, 4–5, 31, 37
Hutcheon, Linda 1, 3–4, 17, 43, 178, 185, 188 n. 5, 195 n. 87
Huyssen, Andreas 17, 62–3, 107, 138, 172, 204 n. 7

in medias res 61, 135, 167
inclination 34, 140, 158, 207 n. 13
intermediaries 33, 116, 130, 131, 135, 185

Jameson, Fredric 3, 17, 137, 183–5, 194 n. 85
jazz 74–5
Johnson, Barbara 26–7
Johnson, Charles 79–80

Kant, Immanuel 15, 108
Kaufman, Charlie 103
Kelly, Adam 2, 124, 184, 206 n. 42
Kiaer, Christina 13
Kirby, Alan 187 n. 2
Klinkowitz, Jerome 37, 112, 196 n. 6

Latour, Bruno 13–14, 29–30, 33, 43, 45, 86, 106, 126–7, 129, 140, 142, 145, 199 n. 43, 208 n. 23, 210 n. 49
Lethem, Jonathan 32, 87–102, 170–1, 179
linguistic turn 104
lists 109
Lucretius 139, 145, 149, 207 n. 13
Lyotard, Jean-François 17, 104, 138, 172

Maltby, Paul 188 n. 5, 208 n. 28
Marciniak, Katarzyna 161–2
Marx, Karl 11, 190 n. 38
materialism 11–12
 cultural 12, 13
 definitions of 11
 historical 12
 postmodern 8, 105, 191 n. 39
McClure, John 4, 189 n. 18
McGurl, Mark 4–5, 28, 38, 62, 188 n. 5, 196 n. 10
McHale, Brian 6, 21, 32, 41, 67–8, 159, 170, 172
mediators 33, 107, 135, 159
Meillassoux, Quentin 15–16, 108–9, 133, 191 n. 49, 201 n. 9
Merish, Lori 26
metamodernism 1, 27, 187 n. 2
Mohanty, Satya P. 43
Moraru, Christian 187 n. 2
Morris, Christopher 112, 118

228

INDEX

Morrison, Toni 32, 74–86
Morton, Timothy 15, 25
Moya, Paula M. L. 42, 197 n. 20

Nagel, Sidney 13
Nancy, Jean-Luc 34, 139–43, 145–58
Nealon, Jeffrey 188 n. 2
New Historicism 13
new materialism 16, 192 n. 57
nominalism 108
nonhuman actors 14–18, 22, 29, 45–7, 55–6, 58, 60, 68–70, 73–5, 100, 108, 119–21, 131, 140–1, 159, 174, 186. *See also* objects; things

object-oriented ontology 16, 108, 191 n. 49, 192 n. 54
object-oriented philosophy 3, 11, 15–16, 69, 192 n. 57
objects 9, 14, 15, 18–19, 21, 45–6, 135
  agency of 18–19, 32, 46, 48, 58, 68, 72–3, 83, 98, 105, 113, 151, 185, 192 n. 57
  and language 126
  in literature 20
  and postmodernism 25–6, 33
  and subjects 11, 48, 53, 69, 73, 80
  See also nonhuman actors; things
Olson, Charles 7, 183
ontological dominant 67–8
otherness 34, 137–43, 145, 168
Owens, Louis 200 n. 47

Parker, Robert Dale 44
Parrish, Timothy 31, 38
periodization 35, 173–86
Peterson, Nancy J. 76–7
Plato 8–9, 115, 127, 180, 193 n. 63, 207 n. 12
posthumanism 3, 16
postmodernism
  death of 1–2, 30
  definitions of 3–4
  and language 104–5
  and ontology 67–9
  as a period 170–86
  phases of 30–1, 36–9, 41, 62–3
  and social construction 38–9

postpositivist realism 197 n. 20
post-postmodernism 1, 27
postsecularism 4–5, 189 n. 18
poststructuralism 42, 102, 104–5, 107, 115, 124, 141, 204 n. 7
processual 17, 22, 23, 27, 56, 61, 63, 64, 82, 110, 164, 168, 176, 179, 182, 186, 194 n. 75
Pulitano, Elvira 197 n. 15
Pynchon, Thomas 23, 37, 145

Reed, Ishmael 23, 37, 211 n. 53
Richardson, Brian 205 n. 26
Robbins, Bruce 66–7
Roediger, David 81
Romagnolo, Catherine 161, 209 n. 39
Rosaldo, Renato 12, 22, 24
Ross, Andrew 65–7
Roth, Philip 37, 38, 196 n. 10
Russell, Bertrand 18, 192 n. 63

Saussure, Ferdinand de 107–8, 113, 116, 204 n. 8
Schulz, Max 112, 113
scientific naturalism 66–7, 201 n. 8
Shaviro, Steven 16, 191 n. 49
Silko, Leslie Marmon 31, 40–64
Smith, James K. A. 135
social construction 5, 30–1, 38–9, 65
  vs. essentialism 38–9, 43, 53, 61
  and Native writing 41–5
  of whiteness 47, 48, 54, 60, 81–2, 97
Sokal, Alan 65–7
Sontag, Susan 43, 166, 188 n. 5
Speculative Realism 15, 108
Spurgeon, Sara L. 56, 197 n. 15, 210 n. 44
Steiner, Wendy 31, 36–8, 62, 196 n. 6
Stewart, Susan 13, 26

talking book 202 n. 37
Taussig, Michael 13
Taylor, Billy 74
The Man Who Shot Liberty Valance 171
thing theory 3, 13, 26, 53, 73
things 9–13, 15–17, 48–9, 69, 86, 159, 181
  definitions of 18–19
  and humans 70–4

229

INDEX

things (*Cont.*)
  human vs. natural 45–6
  and language 20–1, 104–5, 108–9, 110–21, 123, 126, 129, 134
  vs. objects 18–19, 82–3, 97, 151
  stories in 51–3, 58
  thingliness of 18, 93, 98, 185
  in US literature 26–7
  See also nonhuman actors; objects
Thomas, Nicholas 13
Toth, Josh 1, 2

Underwood, Ted 178

van den Akker, Robin 187 n.2
Vermeulen, Timotheus 187 n. 2
Vizenor, Gerald 41–2

Wallace, David Foster 33, 105, 121–36
Weaver, Jace 42, 45, 47, 61, 63, 198 n. 31
Weber, Max 138
whiteness 48, 54, 59–60, 80–2, 85, 92, 99, 151
Williams, Raymond 12, 22, 108, 183–4, 204 n. 10
Williams, William Carlos 9
Winnicott, Donald 18, 193 n. 63
Wittgenstein, Ludwig 107
Wolfe, Cary 16
Womack, Craig 31, 39, 42, 44–6, 53, 58, 63, 197 n. 20, 198 n. 28
Woolley, Deborah 112, 113, 118
worknets 14, 17, 126, 135, 140, 143, 168

Xingjian, Gao 173–2

CPSIA information can be obtained
at www.ICGtesting.com
Printed in the USA
FFHW020755020519
52205635-57569FF